The South Carolina Review

THE SPECTRAL SOUTH

Edited by Sarah Juliet Lauro and
Kimberly Manganelli

The South Carolina Review, Volume 47, No. 2, Spring 2015
is published by Clemson University.
©2015 Clemson University.

ISBN: 978-1-942954-92-7

EDITOR: Wayne Chapman

FICTION EDITOR: Keith Morris

POETRY EDITOR: Jillian Weise

BOOK REVIEW EDITOR: Cameron Bushnell

CONTRIBUTING EDITORS:
John Morgenstern, Sterling Eisminger, Catherine Paul, and Rhondda Thomas

ADVISORY BOARD:
Susanna Ashton, Ray Barfield, Nic Brown, Cameron Bushnell, Jonathan Field, Michael LeMahieu, Kimberly Manganelli, Dominic Mastroianni, Brian McGrath, Angela Naimou, Aga Skrodzka-Bates, and John Warner

BUSINESS MANAGER: Emily C. Clarke

ACCOUNTING FISCAL ANALYST: Beverly Pressley

EDITORIAL ASSISTANTS:
Charis Chapman, Teneshia Head, and Karen Stewart

COVER: Julia Legare Burial Plot, Edisto Island, SC—courtesy of Alrinthea F. Carter

CONTENTS

Doris Somerville Calhoun (1929-2014)

We honor the passing of a good friend of this journal. Doris Calhoun, wife of our late editor-emeritus Richard J. Calhoun, was co-founder of a reading series in the English Department and provided a small subsidy to *The South Carolina Review* for a few years after his death. In remembrance of Dick's remarkable life and work, Doris permitted us to publish one of his representative essays, "A Study of the New Criticism" (*SCR* 37.1 [fall 2004]: 17-24), preceded by tributes by many of his colleagues and followed, aptly, by a poem called "Ghost Ranch" by Louisiana poet Catharine Savage Brosman. Doris gave Dick the last word, however, by allowing us to trawl through the memory notebook assembled on the occasion of their simultaneous retirements, in 1994 (from CU Libraries and English, respectively), and to publish his humorous riposte to their send off. They remained very generous donors to the arts at Clemson, with funding to support music, visual art, library acquisitions, and literary programs in the College of Liberal Arts and then Architecture, Arts and Humanities. Later on, with Doris's relocation to northern Virginia, the Richard J. Calhoun Distinguished Readers series morphed into the one or more "*SCR* Presents" panels that have attached themselves to the annual Clemson Literary Festival since 2007.

In the interim, a number of distinguished American poets and fiction writers have been able to visit Clemson over the years, some of them virtually in the manner of Dick's method of snagging them off of the Amtrak line on their way to somewhere else. Perhaps the first to note is Galway Kinnell because he also died recently and, in 1994, had been brought to Clemson by a fluke of soft money in the English Department and introduced in honor of Dick's retirement. Albert Goldbarth and Paget Powell followed Kinnell. But in the next six and a half years, Dick and Doris Calhoun funded the series, blessing us with the likes of Fred Chappell, Clyde Edgerton, Virgil Suarez, Jill McCorkle, Laurence Lieberman, Richard Michelson, and Doris Betts.

Doris Somerville Calhoun's passing is an occasion to express our gratitude for her patronage, unwavering good will, and friendship. Without the Calhouns, there might not have been a *South Carolina Review*, a literary enterprise capable of developing themed numbers such as the present one, with our 50th anniversary only two years away. —WKC

I N T R O D U C T I O N

Listening to the Past:
New Orleans and the Creolization of History

by Sarah Juliet Lauro and Kimberly S. Manganelli

W e were two grown women attempting to contact the dead through a clock radio. Maybe we had been on one too many ghost tours on this research trip to New Orleans, or maybe it was the influence of the chamber maids we had overheard whispering about strange occurrences in our wing of the Prince Conti hotel, and then, when we asked them directly, the admission that our room sat upon what had once been the slaves' quarters. But when our bedside radio began mysteriously turning on by itself and intermittently chirruping at us—and this after items began uncannily disappearing and reappearing in different places in the room—we decided to see if we could detect in the blasts of sound that came, unbidden, from the open channel of the AM radio, a pattern in the static, an intent to communicate in the emissions that did seem, at times, as if they were trying (alas, unintelligibly) to answer our questions.[1]

We had come to New Orleans to research two historical figures that had lately been resurrected for popular culture in the FX television series *American Horror Story*'s third season, "Coven": the terrible Madame Delphine Lalaurie, a notorious slave owner whose grotesque torturing of her human property had been detected when a fire brigade discovered mutilated bodies in the attic rooms of her lavish mansion at 1140 Royal Street, which is now touted as the most haunted building in Crescent City, and Voodoo Queen Marie Laveau, a benevolent force in the African American community of the time, a hairdresser whose occult practices have earned her a reputation as a shrewd business woman and a fearsome force to be reckoned with.

Both women are represented among the life-sized tableaux of historic New Orleans scenes that comprise the Musée Conti Wax Museum, which includes figures as diverse as Napoleon Bonaparte and Jelly Roll Morton. Immortalized in her attic, a beautiful white woman in fancy satin and lace gown represents Mme. Lalaurie, who presumably, if we read this moment in the light of the local legendry, has come upstairs during one of her parties to check on or even further torture her prisoners. She is accompanied by a well-dressed black footman, who may represent Bastien, her real life chauffeur, who is often cast in the narratives as a kind of traitor to his race: her only well-treated slave who may have even helped her escape the angry mob after her gruesome secret was discovered.[2] In the vignette at the wax museum, Mme. Lalaurie fittingly holds a candlestick in one hand and a bull whip behind her back, representing the face that she showed to haute Creole society as a beautiful socialite, and the dark truth she kept hidden from view in the attic of her home. There are three other black bodies within the tableau's mis-en-scène: a shirtless, emaciated man chained to the wall, a woman sitting in the foreground in tattered dress, her hand apparently chained to her throat. Her face wears an expression of terror or agony, with her eyes rolling back into her head. A young girl in the background casts a look over her shoulder at the Madame and her footman, who appears to be making a motion toward her. This, the smallest figure, may represent an 8-year-old slave girl that the historical record shows Madame Lalaurie chased off of the upper floors of her house.

In the waxworks's depiction of Marie Laveau, a light-skinned black woman wearing her trademark "tignon" or headscarf stands in the doorway of her house.[3] A carriage has pulled up with a black woman inside who wears a curious expression, casting a suspicious glance at Laveau's house, as a white woman stands in the doorway as if engaging in a transaction with the Voodoo priestess, perhaps even having her palm read. Somewhat uncannily, the white client seems as if she might have been created from the same wax model as Madame Lalaurie, as both figures are pale, slender women with long dark hair, but this woman's visage is obscured, her hair and a white veil hanging over her face. The description beneath this tableau reads, in part: "Was Marie an evil woman, or was she good? Accounts differ. But all agree she was feared by white and Negro Orleanians alike for the occult power it was alleged she possessed...Part Indian, part Negro, part white, Marie Laveau was the last great American witch!"[4] (Musee Conti display)

Perhaps this language supports the inclusion of Marie Laveau in Ryan Murphy and Brad Falchuk's *American Horror Story* series about a coven of witches in New Orleans. In the series, both Laveau and Lalaurie are immortals who tangle with a present-day coven of witches searching for their next leader, called the "Supreme." But, of course, both Laveau and Lalaurie *are* alive and well in New Orleans today: they live in gift shops that capitalize upon Laveau's occult powers by selling charms or "gris-gris," and they accompany every ghost tour that crisscrosses the quarter from Esplanade to Canal street raising goosebumps or merely eyebrows for a cost. Rather like Haitian zombies, these women have been raised from the dead to labor for the profit of others. In New Orleans, ghosts are conjured daily in such narratives, and history—as seen in the still lifes in the wax museum, or in the variety of tales we examined at the Williams Research Center and heard standing across from 1140 Royal Street—is creolized.

It's not surprising that these women should have been brought together in the television series. In fact, one of the more obscure legends that draws these two powerful women together is a bizarre story in which Laveau asked Lalaurie to serve as the godmother of a so-called "devil baby."[5] According to this story, "a deformed or insane child, rumored to be the spawn of a mortal woman and a demon...was found by voodoo queen Marie Laveau and given to Delphine and Louis Lalaurie to raise" (Love and Shannon 36). Victoria Cosner Love and Lorelei Shannon postulate that, if there's any truth to the legend, the child was probably a Harlequin baby born with a "rare birth defect" that results in the "extreme thickening of the keratin layer in the baby's skin," which produces "diamond-shaped scales on the baby's body" (99-100). As far-fetched as this particular tale is, it bespeaks Lalaurie's and Laveau's reign over the imaginations of their contemporaries and those of the millions of visitors who make their pilgrimage to the voodoo shops, haunted homes, and cemeteries in the French Quarter each year. This and other legends surrounding these women place them above their husbands, above the law, above science, and even above God.

During their lifetimes, they were both respected and feared within their communities, in control of money at a time when this was rare, and had husbands who were either completely erased from their narratives or rendered little more than footnotes in the popular ghost stories told throughout the French Quarter each night. Delphine Lalaurie, for example, was worth $66,389.58 (approximately $1.5 million in today's currency) when she married her third and final husband, Dr. Louis Lalaurie in 1828 (Long *Madame* 63-64). Defying the nineteenth-century laws of coverture, she added a note to her marriage contract, which "stipulated that she would retain her title to her 'paraphernal goods,' meaning all of the property that she brought into the marriage" (Long *Madame* 64). Laveau did not have the fortune that Lalaurie had amassed during her first two marriages. In fact, her "domestic partner" Captain Christophe Glapion, who was descended from French aristocrats, left her in debt when he died in 1855 (Long *A New Orleans* 51, 84).[6] However, despite these debts, Laveau still had sufficient funds to pay security bonds ranging from $200 to $500 for several free women of color who had been arrested for "'grossly insulting, abusing, and threatening'" white women, an act which violated the city's Black Code (Long *A New Orleans* 84).

In the television series, Lalaurie and Laveau are engaged in a battle that stretches across the centuries. When the fictional Lalaurie, played by Kathy Bates, turns Laveau's lover Bastien, who must be named after the madame's faithful manservant, into a human minotaur, grafting onto his shoulders the head of a bull, the Voodoo Queen (played by Angela Bassett) raises an angry mob that storms her house and after giving her a draught of poison to make her immortal, buries her beneath the paved courtyard of her mansion. In the present day, their conflict continues after the Supreme witch of the Coven (played by Jessica Lange) frees Lalaurie to make her an unpaid servant in the witches' household. Laveau, herself made immortal by a pact she has with Papa Legba (the intermediary between humanity and the loas, the pantheon of Vodun gods), continues to exact her revenge, including even raising an army of zombies—Lalaurie's grotesquely decayed daughters among them—to storm the witches' Garden District den.

We have some qualms about the series's treatment of these historical figures, including the fact that the horrible Lalaurie is nearly offered a kind of absolution: her character is treated at times with comical pathos (in one memorable scene, the racist pitifully weeps when she realizes that Barack Obama is president of the nation) and at others, she seems capable of growth, in her reluctant friendship with the African American witch Queenie (Gabourey Sidibe). Further, at the series's end, both Laveau and Lalaurie are placed on equal footing when Papa Legba sends them to hell where they must interminably reenact a scene of their own torture. But the fictional representation of these figures also disrupts the historical account in ways that are productive to our thinking about these women and the affect they produce today as figures of the living dead in New Orleans.

The show itself creolizes history, weaving certain strands of truth together and taking poetic license in others. But this is to be expected given the archives from which the creators of the series drew inspiration for their depictions of Lalaurie and Laveau. Over time the mixture of voices and genres that have retold the stories of Lalaurie and Laveau have transformed the narratives of these women into something new. In this creolized archive, newspaper articles mingle with fiction, legal documents mix with travel narratives, and the voices of British and European narrators blend with those of Americans to form ghost stories that, repeated like a spell, conjure the sadistic socialite and voodoo queen in the French Quarter night after night. Depending on the genre, narrator, and time period, the story of what happened in the house on 1140 Royal Street changes and shifts as some details are highlighted and others are obscured in each retelling.

For example, Harriet Martineau's version of the Lalaurie tale published in her *Retrospect of Western Travel* (1838) indicts not only Lalaurie but also the French creole community in New Orleans who protected the earlier crimes that were harbingers of the horrors that lay inside her attic. Martineau, a British travel writer, arrived in New Orleans in 1836, two years after Lalaurie fled the mob that came to destroy her and her home. Although Martineau characterized the wives of planters as the "chief slave of the harem" (*Society* 2:81), with the story of Delphine Lalaurie she encountered an entirely different kind of wife and slaveholder. In her retelling, Lalaurie is insane, possessed with the kind of madness that only a slaveholding country could create and foster, but in another version, Lalaurie's tortures are not senseless, but aim to extract the truth from her slaves about her mother's murder during a slave uprising (The States-Item).

In Martineau's account, Lalaurie's French creole identity is also a key detail in her story. Describing the "mutual jealousy between the French and American creoles in Louisiana," Martineau asserts that the French creole community concealed their neighbor's infractions of the Black Code, which decreed that owners would be fined an amount between $200 and $500 if their slaves were "'mutilated, beaten, or ill-treated'" (Long *Madame* 72-73). As evidence of the unwillingness of the "gallant French creoles" to investigate the rumors surrounding Lalaurie, Martineau shares that one of her American friends, an "eminent lawyer," attempted to remind Lalaurie of the Black Code: "My friend, being of the American party, did not appear in the matter himself, but sent a young French creole, who was studying with him. The young man returned full of indignation against all who could suspect this amiable woman of doing anything wrong. He was confident that she could not harm a fly, or give pain to any human being." Soon after this visit a neighbor watched a young slave girl fall to her death from the roof after Madame Lalaurie chased her "from story to story," a cowhide whip in her hand.[7] Lalaurie was charged with "illegal cruelty" and fined $300 (*Retrospect* 1:265, 264). The nine slaves who were confiscated by the state were eventually purchased by a family member and returned to her. As Martineau's narrative reveals, slave owners could be convicted, fined, and have their "property" taken away, but the punishment was ultimately inconsequential as the cruelty of slaveholders like Lalaurie continued.

Although Martineau condemns Delphine's crimes, her narrative completely exonerates Louis Lalaurie whom she tells her readers was "many years younger than his lady, and had nothing to do with the management of her property, so that he has been in no degree mixed up with her affairs and disgraces" (*Retrospect* 1:264). Fredrika Bremer, a Swedish writer and feminist activist, who traveled to the United States in 1849-1850, offers a similar description of Dr. Lalaurie in her retelling: "Madame Lallorue's [sic] husband, a Frenchman, still resides in New Orleans, and is said to be a man of good character. He must at that time have lived separate from his wife" (2:245). Some ghost tours, however, portray Dr. Lalaurie as a mad scientist who was conducting medical experiments in his attic. Evoking images of Dr. Frankenstein or Dr. Moreau, these stories often depict Madame Lalaurie as a co-conspirator in her husband's "wantonly cruel" experiments (Wells 23). On *American Horror Story*, the attic of horrors is clearly Delphine's domain, but her husband looks on with a mixture of admiration and gleeful anticipation as she constructs her newest creature, a Minotaur. In the historical archive, the details of the "experiments" vary greatly from one source to another. An article in the afternoon edition of the April

10 *Courier* reported that one man had been found with "'a large hole in his head, his body from head to foot was covered with scars and filled with worms!!'" (Long *Madame* 91). The day after the fire, the April 11,1834 issue of *The Bee* reported that "seven slaves more or less horribly mutilated, were seen suspended by the neck, their limbs apparently stretched and torn from one extremity to the other." Since then, most writers and tour guides have taken up *The Bee's* suggestion that since language is "too wordless and inadequate to give a proper cognition of the horror which a scene like this must have inspired," "we shall not attempt it, but leave it rather to the reader's imagination to picture what it was."

Over the years, the catalog of horrors in the Lalauries' attic has grown to include the flaying of live bodies, the breaking and resetting of bones at opposite angles, as well as other grotesqueries, including a crude sex change operation (Love and Shannon 15). On *American Horror Story*, Kathy Bates's Lalaurie strides through the attic holding a nosegay of white blossoms as she pauses to greet each of her caged "pets," including a man whose eyes and lips are sewn shut and a woman who has maggots crawling over the muscle tissue of her flayed face ("Bitchcraft"). After describing the atrocities discovered in the Lalauries' attic, one of our tour guides suggested that these horrific tortures were perhaps Madame Lalaurie's attempt to find a cure for one of her daughters who had an unnamed incurable ailment. Long explains that this particular version of the legend might arise from letters Dr. Lalaurie and his father exchanged about his attempts to perfect a treatment that would allow him to straighten the spine of his wife's daughter, Pauline Blanque.[8] *American Horror Story*, however, ascribes to Delphine Lalaurie a "wantonness" that calls to mind H. G. Wells's description of Dr. Moreau (74).[9] When one man asks in a broken voice why she's treating them in this way, she simply smiles at him and replies, "Because I can" ("Bitchcraft").

On *American Horror Story*, vanity is one of the underlying motives for Lalaurie's merciless cruelty. Although the television series portrays her as a matronly woman whose beauty has long since faded (if it was ever there at all), in the historical record, Lalaurie's allure is repeatedly emphasized. As Martineau reports, "the lady was so graceful and accomplished, so charming in her manners and so hospitable, that no one ventured openly to question her perfect goodness" (*Retrospect* 1:264). In fact, the death of the young slave girl Lalaurie chased to the roof of her house can be linked to her vanity since the child's crime was snagging a tangle while combing her mistress's hair. Other stories recount her lavish parties and her costume changes at such events, which some theorize were staged to cover the sounds of human screams coming from her attic. According to these stories, she had to change dresses while playing hostess because her clothes became covered in blood when she would disappear during her soirees to menace her prisoners.

In the first episode of "Coven," we discover that she keeps her skin looking young by applying a poultice to her face made of human pancreas extracted from live victims ("Bitchcraft"). After watching Lalaurie entertain the bon ton of New Orleans, viewers are transported to her boudoir where she performs her toilette. The smiles and pink-cheeked laughter that accompanied her clever repartee have dropped away from Lalaurie's face, which fills the whole screen as she stares straight into the camera. With an expression of dead calm mingled with a hint of repulsion, we watch as Lalaurie methodically paints her face with the poultice. "When the blood dries, my skin's supposed to be tight as a drum," she remarks when her husband enters ("Bitchcraft"). "Just look at this wattle," she says in disgust as she brushes the bloody mixture under her chin, her gaze never leaving the mirror. Later in the episode when she commands her oldest daughter, Borquita, to extract the organ from a new victim, we learn that her vanity is tied to a deeper anxiety that her husband will leave her for a "fresh-faced" free woman of color. When Borquita pleads with her mother not to send her to the attic to retrieve a new pancreas, Lalaurie replies in a pained voice, "You think I want to do this? You can blame your father and his 'fresh-faced' whore unless you'd like to split your inheritance with an endless parade of colored bastards" ("Bitchcraft").

Lalaurie's anxiety that she would be displaced by a quadroon or octoroon mistress was shared by many white Creoles in New Orleans. Because anti-miscegenation laws prohibited interracial marriage, the institution of *plaçage* gained power as a social custom that sanctioned unions between free women of color, who were referred to as *placées*, and wealthy white men, who were referred to as their "protectors." Mixed-race mothers served as chaperones at Quadroon Balls where they hoped to find eligible suitors with whom they could "place" their daughters. By the 1830s, in fact, Quadroon Balls had become a regular part of New Orleans's tourist industry since most wealthy male visitors to the city accompanied their hosts to the Washington or Orleans ballrooms to converse and dance with beautiful women who were "almost white." *Plaçage* threatened the institution of marriage in New Orleans by distracting eligible bachelors from white women on the marriage market and by inviting married men to set up a second household for their mixed-race mistresses. And as *American Horror Story*'s Madame Lalaurie is all too aware, this custom also had the potential to jeopardize the inheritance of property since many "protectors" included their *placées* and any children born from their unions in their wills.[10] In Bremer's retelling of Lalaurie's story, the author speculates that the socialite "tormented her victims" because "the behavior of her brother to his mistresses of the colored race excited her hatred toward them" (2:244). Here, "behavior" might be read as the desire or perhaps even the preference Lalaurie's brother exhibited toward his mixed-race mistresses. Bremer's assertion is corrected and recontextualized in Long's biography of Lalaurie in which we learn that her brother, Louis Macarty, cohabited with a white woman. Lalaurie's father, uncle, and cousins, however, all had concubinages with free women of color. "In almost every case," Long notes, "the Macarty men acknowledged the offspring of these liaisons by allowing their names to be included in the baptismal record or signing the register, by going before a notary to claim paternity, or by remembering their concubines and children in their wills" (19).[11]

The history of concubinage and miscegenation in the historical Lalaurie's family offers an avenue for understanding the representations of interracial desire as grotesque on *American Horror Story*. As in some of retellings of the Lalaurie legend, the television series connects the body of Delphine's daughter, Pauline, to the torturous experiments occurring in the attic. But rather than trying to straighten her spine, her mother and stepfather punish Bastien, the victim of Pauline's "deviant" desire. During the dinner party held earlier that evening, Pauline gives the following response to her mother's criticism that, unlike her accomplished sisters, her "major talent has yet to reveal itself": "Perhaps my talent is in the boudoir, mother dear" ("Bitchcraft"). Gazing past several of the marriageable gentlemen her mother invited into their home, Pauline gives the house servant Bastien a challenging look. Upon learning that Pauline seduced Bastien during the party, Lalaurie slaps and beats her daughter as she screams between clinched teeth, "Stupid slut. I invite all the eligible bachelors just to meet you and you spread your filthy legs for the house-man? You might as well rut with the family dog" ("Bitchcraft"). Here, the series reveals the double standards of interracial desire in the nineteenth century. Whereas the *plaçages* between white men and free women of color were romanticized, interracial desire between white women and black men was akin to bestiality. Ignoring Bastien's pleas, Lalaurie declares that she will tell everyone that he took Pauline "by force like the savage he is." She then orders her husband to take him to the attic where she transforms Bastien into a Minotaur, telling him, "You wanna rut like a beast, then we're going to treat you like one" ("Bitchcraft").

The mixture of awe and pleasure in Lalaurie's expression as she looks upon her new creation suggests that her own sexual desires inspire the punishment she chooses for Bas-tien. While both inspecting and admiring Bastien's mutilated body, she tells her husband, "My great literacy began with Greek mythology. I used to sit on Daddy's lap and he would read me those stories full of their vengeful gods and wondrous, miraculous creatures. But the Minotaur was *always* my favorite. Half man, half bull. And now, I have one of my very own" ("Bitchcraft"). As someone well-versed in mythology, Lalaurie would know that the Minotaur was a creature born out of vengeance and lust. Poseidon punished Minos, the King of Crete, for not following his order to sacrifice the beautiful white bull he sent him. Poseidon asks Aphrodite to curse Minos's wife with desire for the animal. The Queen was so enraptured by the creature that she asked Daedalus to build a wooden cow that she could climb inside in order to mate with the bull; the Minotaur was born from this union. Instead of transforming herself as the Queen of Crete did in order to satisfy her desires for the bull, Lalaurie sublimates her desires for Bastien by transforming him into a creature she can freely desire. Indeed, Martineau's version of Lalaurie's story underscores the intimacy between Delphine and her "sleek coachman," who was named Bastien in subsequent retellings of the legend. Describing his appearance as "sleek and comfortable," Martineau says that Lalaurie "pampered this obsequious negro," who served as her spy in order to "preserve her life from the vengeance of her household" (*Retrospect* 1:265). This act of vengeance came on an April morning in 1834 when a fire broke out in her kitchen.

The full scope of Lalaurie's psychopathy revealed itself when a slave chained to the kitchen stove purposefully set the house on fire, sacrificing herself to raise the alarm. In *American Horror Story*'s translation of this event, the agency of that nameless kitchen slave is given over to Marie Laveau, who preys upon Lalaurie's vanity and her anxieties about *plaçage*, convincing the socialite to drink a love potion that will ensure her husband's fidel-ity. The Laveau of legend embodied all of Lalaurie's anxieties about the power of *placeés* within the *plaçage* system. According to local lore, Laveau was the daughter of a former slave and a wealthy white planter, Charles Laveaux, who gave her a dowry of a house in Faubourg Marigny when she married in 1819. In such stories, Laveau was born into *pla-çage* but rejected the future of a *placeé* by marrying instead, Jacques Paris, a free man of color and carpenter. The historical Laveau, however, was not born into *plaçage*; her father, Charles Laveaux, was a wealthy free man of color.[12] After her husband disappeared in the early 1820s, Laveau, who was thereafter referred to as "the widow Paris," formed a *plaçage* with Christophe Glapion, a soldier in the Louisiana militia who was descended from French aristocracy. But the word "*plaçage*" is almost never used to describe their union and

Laveau is never referred to as Glapion's *placeé*; instead, authors refer to Laveau and Glapions's "domestic relationship" or "domestic partnership." Laveau seems to have transcended the *plaçage* system. Indeed, during this time period, her status as a widow would have given her both sexual and financial autonomy. She was not a *placeé* in need of a "protector" who would supply her with a home and money. Laveau was a businesswoman who, according to legend, received a cottage on St. Anne Street as a gift for a voodoo spell that prevented a young man from being convicted of a crime (Long, *Voudou* 60). *American Horror Story*'s portrayal of Laveau maintains her autonomy; she belongs to no man. Even though Bastien is her lover, as Bastien tries to explain to Lalaurie before the bull's head is grafted onto his, he "belongs" to Laveau.

In *American Horror Story*, Marie Laveau is a figure of vengeance. She leads a mob of mostly black men and women carrying torches to storm Lalaurie's mansion in a scene that evokes images of a slave rebellion. Before commanding the mob to bury Lalaurie, who has been cursed with immortality by means of the potion Laveau gave her, the voodoo priestess directs the socialite to look up at the second-floor gallery of the house. The sight of her husband and daughters hanging by their necks brings Lalaurie to her knees. But even as she cries and asks in a forsaken voice of both Laveau and of God: "Oh, God! What have you done? Oh dear God, what have you done," Lalaurie shows no awareness that her own crimes have brought her to this moment ("Boy Parts").

Laveau will continue to reap this vengeful crop: she later raises these corpses to serve in her zombie army ("Fearful Pranks Ensue"). *American Horror Story*, in turn, brings Delphine Lalaurie and Marie Laveau back from the dead, inviting a new generation of viewers to become acquainted with their legends. But perhaps more importantly, the series conjures the specters of slavery, miscegenation, and racial violence (from the bullwhip to the noose) that continue to haunt our present day. Our intention with this edited collection was to summon to one place different voices that speak about the legacy of slavery and other traumas that specifically haunt the Southern United States. In this special issue of the *South Carolina Review*, we have drawn together various creative pieces in keeping with this theme, and a photo essay by Alrinthea Carter showcasing modern day ruins, hauntingly lit in sepia tones and chiaroscuro. The critical essays incorporated herein conjure various definitions of "The Spectral South." Among them are three essays on the flourishing ghost tourism industry, each with a unique perspective and employing different methodologies: Tiya Miles's "Ghost Bones in the Basement" highlights the author's own experiences touring a haunted location—the Sorrell Weed house in Savannah, Georgia — that has a racially charged narrative; her attention to this locale underscores the importance of sensitivity to the treatment of deceased slaves in ghost tours more broadly. In "A City Built Upon its Dead," Glenn Gentry and Derek Aldermann present some of their ethnographic research on the larger ghost tourism industry and the history of the rise of its popularity in Savannah in which the Sorrell Weed house Miles profiles is but one stop on a grid that covers the country's "most haunted city." Ben D'Harlingue's contribution, "On the Plantation with Ghosts," provides even more context, expanding our perspective outward from Savannah, to many different haunted plantation sites across the South, while keeping with many of the same concerns expressed by Miles about the way that power structures are upheld in narratives of haunting. Leaving aside the tourism industry, Brent Cline delves into the rich ghost mythology of Appalachia in his treatment of the folklore of the coal mines, "Buried Bodies, Buried Treasure," presenting narratives that preserve in spectral tales anecdotes about this dangerous industry, which have their own tales to tell about exploited laborers and lives that are deemed expendable. Other contributions look specifically to literary texts and screen media. Maxine Montgomery's "Bearing Witness to Forgotten Wounds" engages with one of American literature's most spectral authors, Toni Morrison, who gave us *Beloved*, what we would have to consider as a foundational text in any definition of the Spectral South. Here, Montgomery investigates Morrison's most recent novel *Home* (2012) for the way it "interweaves a focus on the spectral image with memories of a southern home and the raced trauma that continues to haunt [the characters] even after the novel's close." Sarah Hirsch's "Specters of Slavery and the Corporeal Materiality of Resurrection" continues the discussion of spectral wounds by examining the trope of the "phantom limb" in George Washington Cable's and Octavia Butler's representations of black revolutionaries. In tracing Cable's representation of Bras-Coupé in *The Grandissimes* (1880) back to the Haitian revolutionary François Makandal, Hirsch explores the significance of Butler's heroine, Dana, in *Kindred* (1979) losing her arm as she time-travels from a plantation in antebellum Maryland to her home in 1970s Los Angeles. Cameron E. Williams's "Confronting the 'Ghosts' of Southern Masculinity" carries our investigation of the Spectral South into the realm of musical theater with this examination of Stephen King and John Mellencamp's "musical horror story," *Ghost Brothers of Darkland County* (2013). Williams explores the ways in which the Civil Rights movement and the presidential campaigns of 2008 and 2012 haunt the setting and staging of the musical, "invok[ing] many of the South's deeply entrenched mythologies" of white masculinity. In "I Want to Do Bad Things with You," Lisa Woolfork carries the discussion of race and masculinity into the post-racial South in her examination of HBO's *True Blood* (2008-2014). Her reading of Bill Compton illuminates the ways in which the series's vampires "provide an allegorical connection to black bodies, black cultural mythologies and the social history of black struggles for civil rights in a southern context."

This collection of essays represents a first foray in our individual attempts as scholars to honor this category we call the Spectral South. It was never our attempt to conjure new narratives about historical events here, but, as in our experiments with the clock radio at the Prince Conti hotel, we wanted to tune in to just the right frequency, to let other voices come through, to listen to what others have to say, to see proof that the past is present, and to hear confirmation that the dead do speak.

Notes

1.   Sarah Juliet Lauro was perhaps influenced by years of watching ghost hunting reality TV shows and research she had previously done on the Spiritualist movement and Marcello Bacci, who claimed to have built a series of vacuum tubes that could contact the other side. See Lauro, SJ and Catherine Paul. "'Make Me Believe!': Ghost hunting technology and the postmodern fantastic" in *Horror Studies* 4.2, p. 221-239, 2013.

2.   See, for example, George Washington Cable's *Strange True Stories of Louisiana*.

3.   In 1786, the Spanish governor Esteban Miró decreed in his *Bando De Buen Gobierno* (Proclamation of Good Government) that free women of color were not to "'wear feathers, nor curls in their hair, combing same flat or covering it with a tignon,' the head wrap worn by slaves." As Carolyn Morrow Long observes, the purpose of this law was to punish the free women of color who "arrayed themselves in beautiful gowns, bonnets, jewels, and elaborate hairstyles" that they paid for through *plaçage* or concubinage with wealthy white men. But, perhaps more importantly, it was the governor's attempt to "distinguish women of color

from white women" since the clothing, homes, and even the skin color of the free women of color could easily erase both racial and socio-economic distinctions (Long *A New Orleans* 20).

4.   Martha Ward clarifies her ancestry as West African, Native American, and Latin European.

5.   Although both Lalaurie and Laveau were living in the French Quarter in the 1830s, there's no historical record of them actually meeting.

6.   Carolyn Morrow Long's recent biographies provide detailed background information on the husbands of Delphine Lalaurie and Marie Laveau. Delphine's first husband, Ramon López y Ángulo, was a Spanish diplomat who was responsible for reopening the slave trade in 1800 even though the Cabildo, the colonial government in Louisiana, had banned the importation of slaves in 1796 in response to fears of slave revolt raised by the Haitian Revolution (Long *Madame* 30). Two years after López y Ángulo was killed in a shipwreck in 1805, Delphine married the politician and slave trader, Jean Paul Blanque. Even though the US government had outlawed the importation of slaves, Blanque "circumvented the 1804 law by procuring captives by way of Charleston instead of engaging in the more dangerous activity of smuggling them directly from Africa." According to Long, by the time Blanque died in 1815, "367 enslaved persons had passed through his hands" (Long *Madame* 43, 44). Before Marie Laveau's relationship with Glapion, she was married to Jacques Paris, a carpenter and free man of color from Saint Domingue, who is believed to have immigrated to New Orleans to escape the Haitian Revolution. Long reports that Paris mysteriously disappeared a few years after marrying Laveau in 1819 (Long *A New Orleans* 47, 49-50).

7.   Although the girl is unnamed in Martineau's narrative, in the ghost stories inspired by this incident the girl has been named Lia (see Jeanne Delavigne's 1946 story "The Haunted House of the Rue Royale" in *Ghost Stories of Old New Orleans*) and Nina (see "The Legend" in Love and Shannon's *Mad Madame Lalaurie*). During one of our tours, our guide referred to the slave girl as Nina.

8.   For more on "orthopraxy," see Long, *Madame Lalaurie* pp 58-62.

9.   Describing Dr. Moreau's hybrid creatures, Edward Prendick, the narrator of *The Island of Dr. Moreau* remarks, "their mock-human existence, begun in agony, was one long internal struggle, one long dread of Moreau—and for what? It was the wantonness of it that stirred me" (74).

10.   For more about the custom of *plaçage* and Quadroon Balls, see CH 2 of Kimberly Manganelli's *Transatlantic Spectacles of Race: The Tragic Mulatta and the Tragic Muse*.

11.   Following the death of her uncle, Eugène Macarty, in 1845, Lalaurie's relatives contested his will, which left his mistress, Eulalie Mandeville, a house and $12,000; the court ruled in Mandeville's favor (Manganelli 54).

12.   Many of the details in stories that circulated about Laveau were taken from interviews conducted in the late 1930s with elderly New Orleanians as part of the Louisiana Writers' Project. See, Long's *A New Orleans Voudou Priestess*.

Special thanks to Clemson University's Department of English for the Faculty Research Completion and Support Award that funded our trip to New Orleans, Chloe Whitaker for her assistance in transcribing materials from the Williams Research Center, and Teneshia Head and Karen Stewart, who along with Chloe, helped to prepare this issue for print.

Sources

American Horror Story: Coven. Creator Ryan Murphy. FX, 2013–14.

American Horror Story: Inside the Coven (Featurettes) Creator Ryan Murphy. FX, 2013-14.

"Ask A. Labas—History of the Warrington House," *New Orleans States-Item*, May 6, 1975. Vieux Carré Survey, 1140 Royal Street, Historic Williams Center, New Orleans. Print.

"Authentic Particulars," *New Orleans Bee*, April 12, 1834. Microfilm.

Bremer, Fredrika. *Homes of the New World: Impressions of America*. Vol. 2. New York: Negro Universities Press, 1968. Print.

Cable, George Washington. *Strange True Stories of Louisiana*. Freeport, NY: Books for Libraries Press, 1970. Print.

Castellanos, Henry C. *New Orleans As It Was: Episodes of Louisiana Life*. 2nd Ed. New Orleans: L. Graham Co., Ltd., 1905. Print.

Cemetery/Voodoo History Tour. (Historic Tours). New Orleans, LA.

"The conflagration at the house…," *New Orleans Bee*, April 11, 1834. Microfilm.

"Death of Marie Laveau," *Times-Picayune*, June 17, 1881. Microfilm.

DeLavigne, Jeanne. *Ghost Stories of Old New Orleans*. Baton Rouge: Louisiana State University Press, 2014. Print.

Fandrich, Ina Johanna. *The Mysterious Voodoo Queen, Marie Laveaux: A Study of Powerful Female Leadership in Nineteenth-century New Orleans*. New York: Routledge, 2004. Print.

"Flagitious Fiction: Cable's Romance about Marie Laveau and the Voudous," *Daily Picayune*, April 11, 1886. Microfilm.

French Quarter Ghost Tour (Haunted History Tours). French Quarter. New Orleans, LA. July 29, 2014.

French Quarter History Tour (Historic Tours). New Orleans, LA.

Frost, Meigs, "Was Madame Lalaurie of Haunted House Victim of Foul Plot?" *New Orleans Times-Picayune*, February 4, 1934. Microfilm.

Ghost Haunts and Voodoo Tour (Magic Tours). French Quarter. New Orleans, LA. July 30, 2014.

Haunted French Quarter Walk (Historic Tours). New Orleans, LA.

Lauro, Sarah Juliet, and Catherine Paul. "'Make Me Believe!': Ghost hunting technology and the postmodern fantastic," *Horror Studies* 4.2 (2013): 221-239.

Long, Carolyn Morrow. *Madame Lalaurie: Mistress of the Haunted House*. Tampa: University of Florida Press, 2012. Print.

———. *A New Orleans Voodoo Priestess: The legend and reality of Marie Laveau*. Tampa: University of Florida Press, 2006. Print.

Love, Victoria Cosner., and Lorelei Shannon. *Mad Madame Lalaurie: New Orleans' Most Famous Murderess Revealed*. Charleston, SC: History, 2011. Print.

"Making a Night of It: A Search for the Vous Dous Queen," *New Orleans Times,* June 26, 1872. Microfilm.

Manganelli, Kimberly Snyder. *Transatlantic Spectacles of Race: The Tragic Mulatta and the Tragic Muse*. New Brunswick, NJ: Rutgers University Press, 2012.

"Marie Lavaux—Death of the Queen of the Voudous Just Before St. John's Eve," *Democrat*, June 17, 1881. Microfilm.

Martineau, Harriet. *Retrospect of Western Travel*. Vol. 1. London: Saunders and Otley, 1838. Print.

Musée Conti Wax Museum, self-guided tour. New Orleans, LA. December 19, 2014.

"New Owner to Restore Haunted House," *Times-Picayune*, August 9, 1964. Vieux Carré Survey, 1140 Royal Street, Historic Williams Center, New Orleans. Print.

Pitts, Stella. "New Paint, Old Stories Stir Interest in 'Haunted House," *Times-Picayune*, August 11, 1974. Vieux Carré Survey, 1140 Royal Street, Historic Williams Center, New Orleans. Print.

"A Sainted Woman," *Democrat* June 18, 1881. Microfilm.

Ward, Martha. *Voodoo Queen: The Spirited Lives of Marie Laveau.* Jackson: University of Mississippi, 2004. Print.

Wells, H. G. *The Island of Dr. Moreau*. New York: Dover Publications, 1996. Print.

WPA Louisiana Writers' Project. *Guide to New Orleans*. Boston: Houghton-Mifflin, 1938. Print.

"Virgin of the Voudous," *Daily Delta*, August 10, 1850. Microfilm.

Bearing Witness to Forgotten Wounds:
Toni Morrison's *Home* and the Spectral Presence

by Maxine Montgomery

What returns to haunt the victim, these stories tell us, is not only the reality of
the violent event but also the reality of the way that its violence has not yet been
fully known.
—Cathy Caruth, *Unclaimed Experience*

That scar that's left to bear witness. We got to keep it as visible as our blood.
—Gayl Jones, *Corregidora*

At the end of Toni Morrison's *Home*, twenty-four year-old Korean War veteran
Frank "Smart" Money and his younger sister Cee journey to an abandoned southern field in order to re-inter an elderly man's bones. The gesture on the part of the
brother-sister duo is much more than just an act of kindness; it is a ritual performance
rife with folkloric significance as the two pay tribute to a past that refuses to release its
stranglehold on the present. In the fictional world that Morrison constructs, nothing ever
dies, and ancestral spirits emanating from an Africanist cultural belief system serve a vital
role in refiguring that which is no longer visible. Because of the novel's close engagement
with the mnemonic dimensions of a lost past, the burial occurring at the novel's ambiguous conclusion points to the role of ghosts as enabling entities that allow traumatized
individuals to mediate the psychologically fragmenting effects of anterior events.

Tales of haunting in the black novel mirror the collective experiences of a people
once denied access to the means of recording history, a marginalized group of individuals
whose history is often ignored or misrepresented within written, "official" descriptions
of anterior events. Ghostly apparitions function as a sign of a buried past that interrupts
the present, frequently without warning, forcing the reader to question fixed ideological
assumptions. Kathleen Brogan coins the term "cultural haunting" in describing contemporary ethnic narratives of ghostly intrusions (1998). Elements such as haunted houses,
dark passageways, hidden family secrets, scenes of violence, death, and dying, and elaborate burial rituals conjured within the pages of fiction by American multi-ethnic writers
carry a meaning extending beyond the private function critics ascribe to similar concerns
in canonical texts by Nathaniel Hawthorne, Edgar Allen Poe, and others. She goes on
to point out regarding black texts that "The figure of the ghost itself emerges from the
cultural history of that group: one of the key elements of African religious thought to
survive in syncretic forms of new-world religious practice and in slave folklore is the belief
in ancestor spirits" (2).

For Marisa Parham, haunting and ghostliness offer important ways of thinking about
the complex relationship between memory, art, and representation in African-American
Literature. "Haunting is not compelling because it resonates with the supernatural," she
astutely points out, "but rather because it is appropriate to a sense of what it means to

live in between things—in between cultures, in between times, in between spaces—to live with various kinds of doubled consciousness" (2009, 3). Relying upon the scholarly work of Cathy Caruth and other trauma theorists, Laurie Vickroy offers an experiential approach to memory and history as she directs attention to the ways that contemporary authors utilize fiction in an effort to "fill in gaps left by official histories, pointing to unhealed wounds that linger in or on the body, in sexuality, intrusive memory, and emotional relations" (2002, 169).

Both Brogan and Vickroy offer insightful analyses of Toni Morrison's *Beloved* which serves as an Ur-text in terms of its engagement with ghostliness and haunting in a New World setting. My purpose here is not to belabor their observations on the Pulitzer Prize-winning novel whose dedication to "Sixty Million and More" announces Morrison's re-inscription of the stories of subjects rendered nameless, faceless, and invisible in written accounts of the transatlantic slave trade. Rather, my aim is to offer a reading of the author's most recent novel *Home* concerning the influence of the spectral presence on Morrison's narrative and rhetorical choices.[1] The novel recounts the first-hand experiences of an alcoholic, amnesiac black Korean War veteran who returns to America only to face ongoing racial conflict. Much of narrative action involves an episodic account of Money's life over the course of a few days as he journeys from a veteran's hospital in Portland, Oregon back to the South in order to save the life of his sister Cee. Ghosts from long-ago haunt Money at every turn, reminding him of the troubled past he seeks to escape. Morrison's comments regarding the ancestor in the black narrative shed light on the role that ghostly apparitions play in refiguring what is no longer able to be seen, in making present or visible that which is absent. For her, the ancestors "are not just parents, they are sort of timeless people whose relationships to the characters are benevolent, instructive, and protective, and they provide a certain kind of wisdom" (1984, 343). Whereas the mysterious ghost-child Beloved serves as a singular embodiment of slavery and the Middle Passage, the fictional landscape in Morrison's latest text is strewn with a host of spectral figures—each one bearing the physical and psychic injury of a traumatic history involving not only slavery and continuing racial violence, but also the crisis and upheaval associated with war.

Memories of the carnage taking place on the Korean battlefield co-exist alongside recollections of trauma associated with raced violence in America. Yet Morrison is careful to point out the ways in which the suffering blacks' experience differs from the pain stemming from war. Money's assertion that "Lotus, Georgia is the worst place in the world, worse than any battlefield" directs attention to the communal plight of African-Americans.[2] Ghostly apparitions therefore emanate out of a shared history traceable to the South and ancient beliefs about the interconnection between sacred and secular, past and present, the world of the living and dead. Money, the novel's tormented veteran, is emblematic of the malaise afflicting a host of postwar subjects who exist in a nether world with established fixed bounds. As one of the walking wounded, he is a figure whose plight directs attention to vexed issues of identity and culture present in mid twentieth-century America.

Narrative action occurs during the 1950s—an in-between moment whose transitional nature mirrors a shift in cultural attitudes toward a range of issues, including race, gender, class, and the trauma associated with armed combat. The novel's concern with matters of national identity and belonging in a postmodern world brings to mind W. E.

B. DuBois' theory of psychological dualism or double consciousness, itself a philosophical meditation on the intermediacy or 'in-between-ness' associated with cultured difference in a society polarized along racial lines (1903, 45). Money is a mediating figure who must define himself both within and against a world sharply divided into fixed ideological camps, and the novel's preoccupation with masculinity is part of the anxiety of identity in a society bent on defining individuals as the 'other.' One is reminded of the work of post-colonial theorists such as Homi Bhabha and others whose scholarly enterprises shed light on the role of cultural production in charting an alternate, third space not bound by tra-ditional conceptions of time, place, or self (1994; Gilroy 1993). "The borderline work of culture," Bhabha asserts, "renews the past, refiguring it as a contingent 'in-between' space, that innovates and interrupts the performance of the present" (7). Bhabha cites *Beloved* as an example of a text whose haunting recapitulation of slavery destabilizes temporality in creating a radically altered portrait of the present. For him, "The recesses of the domestic space become sites for history's most intricate invasions" (8).

Offering a critical perspective on the task of writing trauma with respect to historical events, Dominick La Capra draws upon the work of Roland Barthes and Hayden White in examining the role of the middle voice as " 'the in-between' voice of undecidability and the unavailability or radical ambivalence of clear-cut positions" (2001, 20). It is this voice that engages in a *Derridian* play of difference prompting a resistance to binary opposites such as black and white, masculine and feminine, past and present.

It is the undecipherability of intermediacy in re-inscribing the spectral presence that is of paramount importance in an appraisal of Morrison's most recent novel. The text seizes upon notions of 'in-between-ness' in refiguring both historical loss and the persis-tent longing for recovery. Caruth argues that trauma is a symptom of history, because "the traumatized person…carries an impossible history within them, or they become them-selves the symptom of a history that they cannot entirely possess" (1991, 5). Useful to the present discussion are Caruth's observations elsewhere regarding the referential nature of traumatic occurrences, the manner in which painful events, by virtue of their incompre-hensibility, return to haunt the survivor at a later time (1996, 7).

As if to indicate the intermittency associated with Money's painful experiences be-fore, during, and after the war along with the novel's close engagement with black cultural history, narrative action is framed within a discursive context deeply rooted in the lore sur-rounding burial rites. The novel thus opens with a childhood, eye-witness account of the hasty burial of Jerome's father, victim of a brutal father-son contest, and closes with a scene that refigures the earlier tale of entombment, but from the conjoined, adult perspective of Money and Cee. That Morrison chooses to recount the previous burial from the vantage point of youth using stream-of-consciousness underscores the mnemonic dimensions of narrative events, the way anterior occurrences remain a part of the post-trauma subject's memorial structures or "rememory" long after the originary events have occurred.[3] At the same time, the novel's evolving point of view—from childhood to adulthood—directs attention to the shifting ideological positioning on the part of the trauma survivor whose journey toward wholeness parallels the ability to confront a painful past, but in nuanced ways and in a manner suggestive of a move toward a more complex subjectivity. The clos-ing burial scene, with overtones of loss and mourning, atonement and guilt, represents the attempt to pay homage to a forgotten ancestral heritage—one that holds the key to the survivor's well-being. Money and Cee then carry out a ritual exorcism designed to put to rest the ghosts of the past and ensure the brother-sister duo's recovery.

Home therefore follows the masterplot of the ghost story, involving "a paradigmatic movement from possession to exorcism—or from bad to good forms of haunting" (Brogan 17). For Morrison, the act of writing is much like an excavation process enabling the historical reclamation that is crucial to the journey toward healing on the part of post-trauma subjects and contemporary readers who, much like the ghostly figures that people the pages of fiction, are left to bear witness to a disturbing past. Morrison's observations regarding the historical distortions resulting in the systematic removal of "the presence and the heartbeat of black people" directs attention to the 'writerly' imperative at the center of her narrative project (Davis 1986, 224-25). She points out that "You have to stake it out and identify those who have preceded you—re-summoning them, acknowledging them is just one step in that process of reclamation—so that they are always there as the confirmation and the affirmation of the life that I personally have not lived but is the life of that organism to which I belong which is black people in this country" (225). Morrison's remarks reveal the process of recovery as a guiding impulse in her evolving canon, in many respects a memorial to the buried lives of blacks in an increasingly global historiography. Her scholarly enterprise is thus resonant with the attempt on the part of indigenous cultures to recuperate an ancestral past—one that may or may not exist in its originary form—and make that past usable in light of historical erasure.

As a barometer of the need to remember and the resistance against that enterprise, Money is a figure whose ability to attest to a troubled history is complicated not only as a result of Post-Traumatic Stress Disorder manifesting itself in bouts of forgetfulness, recurring hallucinations, and acts of violence, but also the lack of documentation surrounding the events of the war. The elderly veterans who gather on Fish Eye Anderson's porch have only a grudging respect for Money by virtue of his involvement in the Korean Conflict. "They knew about Korea but not understanding what it was about didn't give it the respect—the seriousness—Frank thought it deserved" (136). Much like Morrison's rewriting of Margaret Garner's story in *Beloved*, her re-working of the little-known events surrounding "The Forgotten War" is consistent with her admonition to creative writing students that they "write about what they don't know," even as she endeavors to fill in the gaps present in extant historical records (Minzesheimer D2). It is as if the telling, or, rather, retelling of Money's story becomes a socially symbolic act—one resonant with cultural meaning—analogous with the reconstruction of the elderly man's bones at the novel's close.

The beleaguered war hero's disassociative behavior following his return from Korea reveals the psychological dualism that is both a symptom of and response to an oppressive history. While recovering from one of many drinking binges, Money sees his reflection in a store window and "thought it was somebody else" (69). At that moment he is put off by his disheveled appearance and wants to "Be something other than a haunted, half-crazy drunk" (69). Hallucinations of a mare, a severed foot, and a zoot-suited man—a potent cultural symbol for assertive black masculinity in modern America—haunt him at every turn. Aside from the hallucinations, the picture-images filtered through his subconscious serve as reminders of his disconnection from the world around him. Leah Hager Cohen rightly observes that Money's episodes of insanity are framed "within the metaphor of race" (2012, BR1). Money recalls the time when he looks outside a bus window and "All color disappeared and the world became a black-and-white movie screen" (23). Significantly, however, the focus on a range of colors following Money's discovery of the hidden truths surrounding Jerome's father's untimely death point to a multifaceted understanding of modern America that belies the apparent oppositional tension of the war hero's early, raced perspective.[4] Cee's quilt, "a shroud of lilac, crimson, yellow, and dark navy blue," figures a post racial setting where fixed notions of self no longer exist (144). Money's recovery occurs in terms suggestive of his willingness to rethink his relationship with the world around him. He must ask tough questions about the nature of manhood and victimhood as well as society's propensity for violence.

Clearly, America is undergoing a gradual shift in social attitudes and cultural values, and the image of the zoot-suited man along with the Bebop music Money hears while visiting an Atlanta nightclub help to locate narrative action within a transitional moment in time. Much like the improvisational Bebop, the novel's disjointed structure and unresolved closure mirror the tentative nature of Money's journey toward recovery. The text moves freely between stream-of-consciousness and first-person point of view, relying upon multiple and, at times, competing narrative perspectives. Such a strategy has the effect of destabilizing a totalizing, authoritative narrative and displacing the 'writerly' point of view on the part of Morrison. The reliance upon Money's eye-witness account validates Laurie Vickroy's assertion that "Traumatized war veterans are emblematic of the personal and collective losses associated with one of the most devastating twentieth-century wars, bringing with it important shifts in cultural attitudes about war, war trauma, and the reliability of authority figures" (2002, 192).

Morrison invests the war hero's testimonial account with unprecedented influence. It is as if Money takes on a life of his own similar to the ghosts who, according to Morrison, speak to her during the writing of the novel (Minzesheimer D2). At one point, Money challenges the author to render an authentic portrait of the weather in Korea, something that only he knows: "*Trees give up. Turtles cook in their shells. Describe that if you know how*" (41; emphasis in original). As memory displaces "official" or scripted history, there is a blurring of time, space, and identity. Objective truth then becomes vague, indecipherable, a matter of the readers' conjecture.

The novel privileges memory and storytelling through the use of rhetorical structures involving repetition, revision, and recursion. In this regard, tropes of doubling and the aspects of the performative offer a clue to understanding Money's uneasy adjustment to life in America following his return home from Korea. The recurrent nature of the events that Money relates validates the assertion that trauma survivors are "possessed by the past and performatively caught up in the compulsive repetition of traumatic scenes" (La Capra 2001, 21). Money's reminiscence of the altercation involving a couple on board a train *en route* to Chicago sheds light not only on the struggle to recall the past on the part of the trauma survivor, it also reveals an intricate form of rhetorical doubling or multi-voicing with regard to the representation of memorialized events. White customers at a restaurant assault the husband at one of the stops. At first, Money informs the reader that the husband will beat the wife as a way of venting frustration at the inability to protect the wife from danger. The troubled war hero therefore interprets the assault through a war-hardened lens of machismo—the same kind of code that prompts him to berate himself for his failure to save the lives of Mike and Stuff, his fallen war comrades. Later, in a scene representing a reframing of the incident and a jocular rhetorical play on Morrison's eighth novel *Love*, Money revises that account and suggests instead that the man is proud of the wife's intervention in the attack.

While the first account of the altercation offers a reading of the dynamics of the couple's marriage in terms of the male desire to conquer, protect, and rescue, the second rendering situates the anonymous man's motives within an altogether different, more redemptive context involving love. The contradictory explanations of the one event encourage a more complex reading of Money's guilt over his comrades' deaths and his apparent motivations for rescuing Cee. His heroic act of saving his sister is as much a gesture of atonement emanating out of survivor's guilt over the death of his war companions and an anonymous Korean girl as it is a show of sacrificial, unconditional affection for his sister, an alter ego or second self whose complimentary bond with her brother re-embodies the fragmented history Money must reconstruct. In his daring liberation of Cee, the war hero is instinctively re-enacting the failed rescue of his war companions.[5]

Money's testimonial story of the killing of a Korean girl offers still another instance of the influence of the spectral presence on the novel's rhetorical structure, which echoes the psychological doubling on the part of the post-trauma subject. The Korean girl is a shadowy presence whose ghostly visage hovers ominously over the narrative in ways that recall the existence of the ghost-child Beloved. In this later text, however, the spectral presence mirrors the shifting, increasingly complex identity markers of a modern world characterized by war, mass migration, and a host of human rights abuses affecting a global community of post-trauma subjects. While at a church picnic in Chicago, Money recoils in horror after seeing a young girl. As a reminder of the Korean child, the girl at the picnic not only summons repressed feelings of fear, shame, and guilt, she reveals the central character's inability to rightly mediate between life before, during, and after the war, between events transpiring then and now. In his initial account of the murder of the Korean girl, Money implicates an anonymous soldier. Later, after he learns of Cee's vision of a baby girl who "smile[s] all through the house, in the air, the clouds" (133), in a confessional gesture of self-implication, he admits that he is responsible for the young girl's death: "I shot the Korean girl in her face./I am the one she touched./I am the one who saw her smile./I am the one she said "Yum-yum" to./I am the one she aroused" (134).

Money's acknowledgement of his role in the senseless murder of the Korean girl signals a move toward wholeness as he begins to take responsibility for the girl's death instead of displacing those actions onto another individual. His tormented admission also links him in a curious way with Beauregard Scott, an Orwellian physician and "heavy-weight Confederate" who carries out his experiments on women and the poor (62). Money speaks openly about the sexual conquests he enjoys prior to marriage to Lily, telling the reader that "*I liked the small breakable thing inside each one*" (67; emphasis in original). Despite the apparent difference between the two men—one, a deranged southern doctor, the other, a tormented, alcoholic war veteran—Scott and Money are united by their adherence to a perverse sense of masculinist power and privilege.

Narrative action in *Home* occurs in an intermediate space that allows the author to refigure the past as what Bhabha refers to as "a contingent 'in-between' space that innovates and interrupts the performance of the present" (1994, 7). The novel's fictional landscape reshapes a history involving slavery, lynching, war, the share-farming system, and migration, and the text gestures toward the ancestral absence owing to the ravages of a colonizing past. The account of the migration from Texas to rural Georgia to Atlanta on Cee's part underscores the fracturing effect of race, resettlement, and economics on the family. Demands associated with the endless toil of the share-farmers' life prevent Money and Cee's parents, Luther and Ida, from offering the emotional security the brother and sister need. Much like the ghost-child Beloved, then, Money and Cee refigure the trope of the abandoned child whose domestic plight is emblematic of the ancestral loss associated with slavery and The Middle Passage. Morrison's rendering of their predicament echoes and revises the Hansel and Gretel fairytale. Lenore, a stern, abusive step-grandmother, doubles as the wicked witch obsessed with harming the brother-sister duo. It is Lenore who sets the stage for the poor self-image that prompts Cee to marry Principal, an egotistical, materialistic man intent on pursuing his own personal fulfillment. Money describes his relationship with his sister in intensely psychic terms suggestive of the doppelganger or look-alike whose presence portends illness or danger. "*Down deep inside her lived my secret picture of myself,*" he tells the reader, "*a strong good me tied to the memory of those horses and the burial of a stranger*" (104; emphasis in original). The scene in which Money attacks a man attempting to expose himself to Cee sheds light on the war hero's role as much more than just an older brother; he is a shadowy figure who offers the unconditional love, safety, and protection that parental figures fail to provide. During Cee's recovery, however, the elderly women who assist in the young woman's healing banish the older brother in ways suggestive of an exorcism—one that is a necessary prelude to Cee's cure.

Money's hesitant return to Georgia occurs in highly symbolic terms reminiscent of a ritual reenactment of childhood. Cohen correctly observes that "the very notion of home is bedeviled for Frank" (2012, BR1). In *Home*, Morrison situates the contemporary search for a utopian home within the framework of her ongoing quest for literary sovereignty both within and outside the architecture of race (Lubiano 1998, 3-12). For her, home is a fraught, contested site, much like *Beloved*'s Sweet Home plantation or Jacob Vaark's farm in *A Mercy*. In *Home*, the South's tragic history thus reveals the presence of a cultural landscape that is rich with the survival practices that have sustained African-Americans but is at the same time soaked with revengeful blood. Yet Money's ability to face his fears head-on, to return to the locus of black suffering in America, holds the key to his recovery and that of Cee. In this regard, Morrison's reliance upon the figure of the ancestor or ghost whose "curious dual force makes present what is absent" enables a recapitulation of the past in powerful ways (Brogan 1998, 29; La Capra 2001, 53, 68-9).

Nowhere is this dual force more evident than in representations of the unborn child who appears to Cee following the young woman's physical trauma at the hands of Scott. Scott's experiments on poor female subjects bring to mind the Holocaust as well as a host of human rights abuses against marginalized groups across the globe. Ron Charles is perceptive in viewing Scott as "a modern-day version of that insidious Schoolteacher in *Beloved*, a reminder of African-Americans' historically horrible relation to the science that justified their abuse from slavery to Tuskeegee" (2012, C2). That the doctors at the Seattle veterans' hospital where Money is treated for Post-Traumatic Stress Disorder sell bodies to a local hospital engaging in medical experimentation on the poor is evidence of the human rights abuses directed toward countless other marginalized individuals.

Cee's marking—the absence of a womb—serves a purpose similar to the chokecherry tree on Sethe's back and Beloved's throat scar. It is an unrelenting wound linking the young woman with a mass of scarred, dismembered, unhealed individuals within the narrative, including Money's war buddies, Mr. Crawford, Thomas, and Jerome's father. Beyond the association with these figures, the fact that "[Cee's] womb can't never bear fruit" allows Morrison to engage issues relevant to the trauma to which women in the Diaspora were often subject (128; Brogan 1998, 15). Scott's housekeeper Sarah scores a female melon in an eerie scene that foreshadows the gendered violence resulting in Cee's infertility. Like Ursa in Jones's *Corregidora,* who is physically and emotionally scarred, rendered barren as a result of an accidental fall, Cee, too, is unable to procreate and must find alternate ways of representing a heritage that refuses to release its vice-like grip on the present. With both texts, the mother-daughter relationship functions as an "intimate space of mother/daughter transmission" (Hirsch 2012, 82). Cee's mutilation, which hinders the trans-generational continuation of a memorialized period, signals a break in the continuum between past and present in ways that problematize the young woman's ability to re-embody distant memorial structures. Cee can no longer pass on the story of suffering that anchors her in a specific history. Not surprisingly, then, the vision of an unborn child who is gendered female haunts Cee so as to signify the primacy of the feminine as a source of self-identity.[6]

Of all the shadowy appearances in the novel—the mare, the zoot-suited man, the severed arm—it is the figure of the abandoned child that best represents repressed knowledge (Vickroy 2002). Morrison's readers are well acquainted with the ghost-like apparitions that people not only her fictional world, but also texts by writers across the African Diaspora. Christopher Okonkwo attributes the presence of such figures to a rhetorical practice surrounding the ogbanje or mythic spirit-child that is born to repeat a cycle of birth and death to the same mother (2008). Neither exclusively malevolent nor beneficent, the abandoned child is a mediating transatlantic figure who personifies the troubling void associated with a vanished past. Morrison's insights about how the absence of an ancestor is just as powerful an influence as the figure's presence are relevant here. Such an absence, Morrison relates, "cause[s] huge destruction and disarray in the work itself" (343).[7] Cee's vision of an unborn child is thus an intuitive response to the personal injury she suffers and, on a communal level, a means of negating the psychologically destructive effects of historical rupture. That vision serves as a means of bridging the gulf between and among Diaspora subjects across time and space owing to the absence of a maternal figure.

Cee's recovery therefore occurs in terms of her reconnection with a maternal past as she finds herself in an idealized southern setting peopled by a community of "country women who loved mean" (121). Ethel Fordam, one in a long line of indomitable mother figures in Morrison's canon, leads the way in bringing about Cee's healing. She and the other women who nurture Cee are closely associated with the folk practices that have allowed a displaced black community to survive whole. Morrison describes these country women in terms of their capacity to reverse the psychologically and physically debilitating effects associated with what the author refers to in an earlier novel as "motherloss:"[8] "Ida never said, 'You my child. I dote on you. You wasn't born in no gutter. You born into my arms. Come on over here and let me give you a hug.' If not her mother, somebody somewhere should have said those words and meant them" (129). Cee's experiences therefore support Evelyn Jaffe Schreiber's assertions regarding the necessity for "communities [to] demonstrate the importance of establishing a home—a psychic space that provides safety, self-esteem, and connectedness—in order to move beyond trauma" (2010, 53). In the urban North, this gendered space is evident in Lily's modest apartment with its female trimmings. In the South, Miss Ethel becomes the mother that Cee no longer has. Cee, in turn, recovers her lost childhood. Through the ceremonial practices associated with an agrarian homeplace—cooking, quilting, gardening, and homeopathic cures—these women provide the care that allows Cee to move closer to recovery.

The novel's final scene in which Money and Cee re-inter the elderly man's remains is not only a commemorative event, it is a timeless ritual with overtones suggestive of atone-ment as well as exorcism. Significantly, this event involves a return to an abandoned field that the brother-sister duo once visited during childhood. That Money and Cee rebury the bones of Jerome's father, attempting to "arrange them the way they once were in life," indicates a restoration of a vanished, disjointed past linked not with the brutality of the father-son duel, but with ancient beliefs about the continuity of life and the sacredness of death (143). Much like Milkman Dead who journeys to Solomon's Leap in order to inter his grandfather's bones, Money and Cee go back to the beginnings, to a site of originary individual and collective trauma, in a gesture anticipating the need to move forward from the pain each has endured.

The novel's closing scene thus bears a recursive relation to the opening. But here, a mature Cee demonstrates a level of independence noticeably absent early in life. Figura-tions of the tree "Hurt right down the middle/But alive and well" reflect the psychological wholeness toward which the young woman moves (167). Although Money has accom-plished his goal of rescue, one questions whether he or his sister can hold at bay the debilitating memories that have plagued the two. Earlier in the novel, the shadowy im-age of a zoot-suited man haunts Money. At the novel's end, however, it is Cee who sees the mysterious figure, as if to underscore the persistent, shared memories of traumatic occurrences. One might therefore interpret the presence of the zoot-suited man as an evil omen. But the fact that the man is now smiling points to a change, not so much in the ghostly images that appear throughout the text as much as in the psychology of the post-trauma subject. The move from bad to good forms of haunting is measured by one's ability to be reconciled with the past. But this reconciliation is much more doubtful than that in *Beloved*. Indeed, whereas Paul D admonishes an emotionally-distressed Sethe to forge ahead in life, insisting that "You your best thing," the future that Morrison limns in *Home* is much more tentative as she leaves the reader in an uncertain middle space of haunting and witness (273). Unlike the ghost-child Beloved who is "Disremembered and unaccounted for" following the exorcism that a community of dispossessed women carry out, the ghostly visage in *Home* refuses to be relegated to the past, stubbornly resisting ex-orcism in ways that imply a continuity between past, present, and future noticeably absent in Morrison's Pulitzer Prize-winning novel. The spectral presence in the later novel contin-ues to hover in-between worlds, beyond the end of the text itself, drawing the twenty-first century reader-audience into the narrative in creative, participatory ways. Ultimately, the reader is forced to witness the haunting experience in order to make sense of the weighty issues Morrison engages.

Morrison's *Home* reveals the profound, ongoing influence of ghostliness and tales of haunting on the art of the narrative while she endeavors to re-embody a fragmented historiography, reshaping familiar stories for a contemporary reader-audience. The novel lends emphasis to the need to remember what was dismembered. Notions of intermediacy are essential to an understanding of her narrative and rhetorical practices as she attempts to breathe new life into old legends. The unresolved closure of her latest novel suggests that she is not engaging in an uncritical recapitulation of past events, however; rather, she offers a vision of life that is 'new' in the sense that it *revises* the past so that anterior events are at once both a part of, yet distinct from, the present. The novel therefore paves the way for a fuller understanding of modern life and the individuals who both shape and are shaped by a complex history.

Notes

1. Morrison's dedication of *Home* to her late son Slade suggests her musing on death, dying, and the afterlife.
2. Toni Morrison, *Home* (New York: Knopf, 2012), 33. Subsequent references to this edition are included parenthetically.
3. Morrison once again relies upon "rememory" as an enabling narrative and rhetorical strategy which, like "post-memory," carries the sense of re-membering a past memory—one that exists apart from an originary scene, character, or place. While Marianne Hirsch offers a definition of "post-memory" in terms that differ from Morrison's "rememory," she also asserts that "'post-memory' always risks sliding into "rememory" within the context of the mother-daughter relationship. See *The Generation of Post Memory: Writing and Visual Culture After the Holocaust*.
4. Morrison's remarks regarding the pre-racial setting of *A Mercy* and her decision to situate narrative action in her ninth novel within pre-colonial America reflect the influence of the discourses of post-racialism. See, for example, "Toni Morrison Finds 'A Mercy' in Servitude," National Public Radio Author Interviews, All Things Considered. October 27, 2008.
5. In a similar sense, one can read Sethe's murder of her infant daughter Beloved upon the arrival of School-teacher as the ex-slave mother's instinctive performance of a past involving the trauma of life at Sweet Home Plantation. Sethe attempts to rescue her children from the atrocities that she experienced as a slave. Later, the scene in which Sethe attacks Mr. Bodwin with an ice pick echoes and revises the earlier scene where the ex-slave mother witnesses the arrival of Schoolteacher.
6. Hortense Spillers offers an insightful theoretical examination of the role of the feminine in black literary and cultural production. See "Mama's Baby, Papa's Maybe: An American Grammar Book," in *Feminisms: An Anthology of Literary Theory and Criticism*. Rosalyn Warhol and Diane Herudl, eds. New Brunswick: Rutgers UP, 1997: 384-405.
7. Morrison's assertions regarding the stabilizing influence on the part of the ancestor in the black narrative have implications for texts such as *Native Son*. Bigger Thomas's propensity for violence, his lack of a moral center, and his tragic fate, one may argue, stem from the absence of a stabilizing ancestral presence.
8. "Motherloss," which refers to the psychological distress associated with the ruptured mother-daughter relationship, is a term Morrison coins in *A Mercy*.

Works Cited

Bhabha, Homi. 1998. *The Location of Culture*. New York: Routledge, 1994.
Brogan, Kathleen. 1998. *Cultural Haunting: Ghosts and Ethnicity in Recent American Literature*. Charlottesville: UP of Virginia.
Caruth, Cathy. 1991. "Introduction: Psychoanalysis, Culture, and Trauma II." Special issue of *American Imago*, 48. 1: 1-12.
——. 1996. *Unclaimed Experience: Trauma, Narrative, and History*. Baltimore: Johns Hopkins UP.
Charles, Ron. 2012. "Toni Morrison's 'Home': A Restrained but Powerful Novel." *The Washington Post*. April 30.
Cohen, Leah Hager. 2012. "Point of Return: 'Home,' A Novel by Toni Morrison." *New York Times*. May 17, 2012, BR1.

Davis, Christina. 1994. "An Interview With Toni Morrison," *Conversations With Toni Morrison*. Danille Taylor-Guthrie, Ed. Jackson: UP Mississippi: 223-33.

DuBois, W. E. B. 1903. *The Souls of Black Folk*. New York: New American Library.

Gilroy, Paul. 1992. *The Black Atlantic: Modernity and Double Consciousness*. Cambridge: Harvard UP.

Hirsch, Marianne. 2012. T*he Generation of Post Memory: Writing and Visual Culture After the Holocaust*. New York: Columbia UP.

La Capra, Dominick. 2001. *Writing History, Writing Trauma*. Baltimore: Johns Hopkins UP.

Minzesheimer, Bob. 2012. "Morrison Feels at 'Home' With the Unknown," *USA Today*, May 8, D1-2.

Morrison, Toni. 1998. *Beloved*. New York: Plume-Penguin.

———. 2012. *Home*. New York: Knopf.

———. 1998. "Home." *The House That Race Built*. Wahneema Lubiano, Ed. New York: Random House, 3-12.

———. 1984. "Rootedness: The Ancestor as Foundation," *Black Women Writers: A Critical Evaluation*, Mari Evans, Ed. New York: Anchor, 339-45.

Okonkwo, Christopher. 2008. *A Spirit of Dialogue: The Incarnation of Ogbanje, The Born-to-die, in African-American Literature*. Knoxville: U of Tennessee P.

Parham, Marisa. 2009. *Haunting and Displacement in African American Literature and Culture*. New York: Routledge.

Schreibert, Evelyn Jaffe. 2012. *Race, Trauma, and Home in the Fiction of Toni Morrison*. Baton Rouge: Louisiana UP.

Vickroy, Laurie. 2002. *Trauma and Survival in Contemporary Literature*. Charlottesville: U of Virginia P.

E S S A Y

GOAT BONES IN THE BASEMENT:
A CASE OF RACE, GENDER AND HAUNTING IN OLD SAVANNAH

by Tiya Miles

I. FROM HERITAGE TO HORROR: THE SPECTRAL TURN IN SOUTHERN HOUSE TOURISM

D uring a recent visit to Savannah, Georgia, I stumbled upon an imposing old home that was advertising historic tours. I did not realize that the house was known for its resident tragic ghosts, or that by taking what would turn out to be a haunted house history tour, I was participating in a growing cultural phenomenon known as "dark tourism." As a form of touristic entertainment, "dark tourism" highlights violent and morbid subject matter by promoting visitation to sites of torture, suffering, murder, and death.[1] Sites related to the afterlife and the undead are prominent on dark tourism itineraries, as well as ghosts, zombies and vampires, entities characterized by their unnatural relationship to death. Dark tourism provides a diversification of tourism markets, broadening the appeal of travel for some and lengthening the duration of travel for others who extend day trips overnight to experience ghost tours. In an era of mega-profit global tourism, the commercial appeal of dark tourism is a key reason for its growth.[2] Geographer Glenn Gentry has emphasized this fundamentally economic aspect of dark tourism by describing the practice as "the transformation of death and disaster into saleable tourism-based commodities."[3]

Although scholars of travel trace dark tourism to religious pilgrimages stretching back hundreds of years, they date a dramatic global surge in the commercial practice to the 1990s, which is when British scholars John Lennon and Malcolm Foley coined the term "dark tourism."[4] The recent establishment of the Institute for Dark Tourism under the directorship of Philip Stone at the University of Central Lancashire in England promises an elaboration of existing findings within the field of British travel studies, where the topic has gained momentum.[5] In American scholarship, attention to "dark tourism" has been less pronounced than a broader interest in the recent rise in claimed occurrences of and references to hauntings. Scholars of American Studies using literary, cultural studies, and sociological methods have developed analyses of "ghostly matters" in temporal context, characterizing this widespread popularization of interest in the undead as a "spectral turn" linked to the late twentieth and early twenty-first century moment.[6] Scholars conducting what might be deemed an interdisciplinary inquiry into supernatural studies most often posit "millennial anxiety" as a major cause for public interest in death and post-death related experiences.[7] The theoretical consensus in this work is that the population's fear about personal demise, cultural change, and social fragmentation in a millennial moment, together with a post-modern rejection of the notion of fixed and rational truth, have fueled participation in supernatural activities. Taking up this question three to ten years after this body of scholarship emerged, I would add to this list of plausible motivators: anxiety about economic collapse in the wake of the 2008 financial recession, growing awareness of climate change and extreme weather, and the shift away from church membership in large segments of American society that has left people open to seeking new spiritual outlets.

Dark tourism and the cultural rise of what I will call "ghost fancy" converge in ghost tourism, a practice categorized by travel studies scholars as a "lighter" sub-type of dark tourism that packages death and fear as fun.[8] Ghost tourism can take multiple forms, with the haunted house tour perhaps being the oldest and most familiar. In New Orleans, for example, the reportedly haunted home of infamously cruel slaveholder Madame Delphine Lalaurie was opened to paying guests for tours as early as 1893 during the Spiritualist movement.[9] As Glenn Gentry and Derek Alderman's work in this issue illustrates, the ghost walking tour is a widespread contemporary form of ghost tourism that emphasizes mobility and flexible narrative scripts. Walking tours can incorporate historical as well as modern-era haunting stories and can include features of the landscape, such as cemeteries and spooky trees, as well as structures like pubs and houses. Haunted history tours focus on chronicling the history of places with an emphasis on death and hauntings; these tours can be stationary (located at single sites) or transitory (spread among various sites in a city). Historic tours of haunted houses include elements of both the haunted house and haunted history tour and are often stops on ghost walk tours. Although all of these types of ghost tours engage with the past through the figure of the ghost, historic tours of haunted houses focus most intensively on one or two dominant historical narratives that center on a family and dwell on the attachment of specific ghosts to specific homes. While ghost walk tours promote movement between various sites, haunted house tours capitalize on a sense of confinement for both the ghost and the guest.

In the United States, the dominance of cable television and its multiple science fiction and reality channels featuring ghost hunting programs have contributed to a cultural surround that validates the hobbyist's search for ghosts, even as more sophisticated recording and communication technologies allow amateur ghost hunters to capture and share their experiences of hauntings.[10] As ghost tours have become normative rather than fringe activities, casual tourists who would not describe themselves as "paranormal investigators" or even believers in the supernatural are beginning to seek out ghost tours as exciting alternatives to traditional history tours. On a ghost tour, history buffs and thrill seekers alike can expect to be pushed to the edges of social expectation and cultural taboo, to recapture that spine-tingling feeling of being a child in the haunted funhouse on Halloween. Ghost tours create periods of suspension from the mundane through suggestive encounters with things that go bump in the night. Beyond the thrill of hair-raising stories set in unfamiliar locales, these tours allow grown-ups to test reality, to build their own sense of the real and the possible in concert with the tour guide and fellow tourists, whose own experiences and testimonies are drawn into the tour narratives and add to the synergy of the moment. As an alternative to the staid historical tour, the ghost tour seems to provide participants elevated stimulation, access to a behind-the-scenes, secret knowledge of past events, and an authenticity of raw emotion drawn from a flirtation with the serious questions of life, mortality, and after-life. [11]

It is no wonder that ghost tourism seems to be springing up in every nook and hamlet of the United States. Whereas Salem, Massachusetts (the location associated with the famous Salem Witch Trials) has long been a magnet for tourists interested in the supernatural, now spirits of the dead are said to be manifesting almost everywhere. Many of this country's historic cities offer ghost tours and ghost experiences to visitors for a price. Each location that I have visited in recent travels through my native Midwest, from Madison, Wisconsin to Petoskey, Michigan to Cincinnati, Ohio, has advertised new cemetery tours, haunted historic road tours and haunted public building tours. While I was on the campus of the University of Wisconsin, my host, historian Stephen Kantrowitz, told me that a local paranormal group was spending the afternoon investigating an early campus building rumored to be haunted. And yet, in the midst of this widespread national flurry of ghostly activity, I posit that the American South will take the lead as a ghost tourism hot spot. The reason, I think, is that Americans hold deep impressions of a South characterized by difference and difficulty. The South, in broader American understanding, has long carried a hint of foreignness and cultural otherness, a hint of being an elsewhere within the boundaries of the nation.[12] As an "other" place closely associated with a turbulent regional history of racism, slavery, and civil warfare, the South makes for an ideal haunted setting. The tradition of southern gothic literature has long channeled notions of a tainted South into complex representations of corrupted social relations set against the backdrop of old and brooding houses. Ghost tours of southern sites tap into this pre-existing sense of the South, a fitting spatial stage for the strange and the macabre.

While promoters of southern historic sites have traditionally emphasized romantic stories of aristocratic elegance framed as cultural heritage, now a growing number of southern tourist attractions, including historic plantation homes, emphasize death and hauntings. Take Charleston, South Carolina, for example. Charleston has lately been ranked as the nation's number one tourist attraction and the world's number one destination city.[13] In tourist spots of the town, brochures for supernatural tours featuring images of haunted houses and howling ghosts now overwhelm advertisements for traditional plantation tours embellished by photos of hoop-skirted ladies and sumptuous gardens. The sheer number of available books on the subject of southern hauntings, with titles like *Haunted Plantations*, *Georgia Ghosts*, and even *Ghost Cats of the South*, as well as websites like *The Moonlit Road* and *Spooky South*, point to the breadth and mounting popularity of a commercialized haunted South narrative that borrows from southern gothic literary tropes.[14] Popular southern tourist locations like the aforementioned Charleston, as well as Savannah, New Orleans, and St. Augustine are readily linked to historical hauntings in the public imagination due to their layered histories of violence, suffering, and racial injustice. European colonization and the coerced "removal" of Native Americans, African American forced migration and enslavement, deadly tropical diseases and unforgiving storms, and the bloody conflicts of the Revolutionary War and Civil War all cast the South with a gloomy air of unfinished business, as a place to which restless spirits would readily return. So rather than selling romantic heritage packaged as an idealized past, more historic sites and independent tour companies are peddling a spectral South. I learned this first-hand during my tour of an old manor home that I stumbled upon in Savannah—the Sorrel Weed House. For the Sorrel-Weed House is not only haunted, as I will explain in more detail shortly, it is haunted by a slave woman and her mistress. My interest in this essay, then, is in exploring how enslaved people and the institution of slavery are portrayed at southern haunted house sites. In particular, I wonder how the figure of the slave as ghost affects the already troubled dynamic of black representation at historic homes.

CB

Plantation homes and manor houses of the South are a primary type of site in the practice known as "heritage tourism." They are America's version of "stately homes" tours that became popular in Great Britain in the aftermath of World War II.[15] Tourism scholars debate the strict definition of the term "heritage tourism," a form of tourism that grew in popularity in the 1990s and focused on the notion of cultural inheritance preserved in and passed on through historic places. Some scholars emphasize the nature of the site and its history as a defining factor of heritage tourism, while others emphasize the personal intention and subjective experience of the tourist who encounters the site in question. Overall, "heritage tourism" connotes an activity in which visitors connect with sites (cultural, natural, or built locations) through the hook of "heritage"—"that which is inherited from the past."[16] Visitors engage in heritage tourism to explore and reinforce their personal sense of identity as individuals and as members of cultural, social, and political affinity groups. While heritage tourism can be a positive and reaffirming experience for visitors, it can also privilege certain social identities while marginalizing others, and hence reinforce pre-existing social and cultural divisions along the lines of race, class and gender.[17]

The marginalization of black history at southern house museums is well documented. Sociologists Jennifer Eichstedt and Stephen Small conducted a large-scale study of 122 former plantation sites in the 1990s. They found that the majority of the sites practiced what they termed "symbolic annihilation and erasure" of black history, which they argued, "produced and reproduced racialized inequality and oppression.[18] In the decade since the publication of this now classic book, other scholars have also studied the racial dynamic at plantation home tours. In a 2008 study, E. Arnold Modlin, Derek Alderman, and Glenn Gentry found that tour guides at plantation house museums had begun to incorporate facts about slaves in response to academic work that had demonstrated the dearth of coverage. Nevertheless, at their case study site, Louisiana's Destrehan Plantation, these mentions of black slaves were brief, numerical, and distant, creating what the authors called an "inventory discourse." While tour guides invited visitors to connect emotionally with the white slave-owning family through moving stories about their lives told in the intimate spaces of the house, guides tended to refer to slavery as an abstract system and refer to blacks in terms of numbers. African Americans who had labored at the site were not enlivened through story and were not rendered as full human beings. The result, the authors argued, was an "affective inequality" at Destrehan Plantation, an encouragement of positive feelings for the slave-owners and a lack of that same encouragement of feeling for the slaves. The authors registered their concern about how this imbalance of caring might affect visitors' views of historical slavery and contemporary race relations, noting: "Inequality can exist on tours even at sites that are committed to more fully addressing the historical facts of slavery…The stakes of this inequality are high."[19] Christine Buzinde and Carla Santos articulated these stakes in their 2008 article, arguing that many plantation home tours "not only annihilate the histories of marginalized groups from the official heritage narrative but also foster feelings of disinheritance and exasperate historical and contemporary issues of racism."[20]

Southern plantation and house museum sites have a documented blind spot when it comes to representing slavery. As these heritage sites broaden their offerings to include dark tourism, they seem to be incorporating more stories about black slaves whose lives of suffering dramatize tour narratives. It is important to note that these enslaved people are rendered as less than full human beings (i.e. ghosts) with horrifying stories of abuse that are often rendered in cartoon fashion for the fun of the ghost tour experience. This turn from heritage to horror, I argue, does little to remedy the problem of misrepresentation and marginalization of African American history at southern historic house sites, and in fact, worsens it.

II. HAUNTED HOUSE OF BONDAGE: THE SORREL-WEED TOURS

In the remainder of this essay, I take the Sorrel-Weed House in Savannah as a case study for exploring portrayals of enslaved black ghosts at "haunted" historic homes in the South. The Sorrel-Weed House, located in the popular historic district, is publicized as "the most haunted house in Savannah," a city deemed "the most haunted city" in the United States by the American Institute of Parapsychology in 2002.[21] The house is named for Francis Sorrel, the wealthy shipping merchant and slaveholder who had it built in 1838-40, and Henry Davis Weed, a businessman and second owner of the property. The Sorrel-Weed House publicity and tours reveal a disturbing intersection between inaccurate, insensitive images of slavery and heightened commercialization for a ghost tourism market. Indeed, slave ghosts, when featured in the Sorrel-Weed House tours and other southern historic site attractions, would seem to add a double meaning to the term "dark tourism"—a meaning that is suggestive of the ways in which stories of racially marginalized subjects (and various social "others" as defined by gender, class, sexuality, religion and so on) are being leveraged to enhance this essentially profit-making activity. By exploring the layers of meaning that attention to race and gender can bring to a case study at the intersection of southern tourism and dark tourism, I hope to address the dynamic of racial projection and anxiety that persists at contemporary southern public sites. I also hope to demonstrate the value of bringing an intersectional analytical method derived from black feminist theory to bear on dark tourism studies, a field that rarely attends to issues of social power and has been described by one of its major thinkers as still "eclectic and theoretically fragile."[22] Finally, as an ancillary feature, this essay may be viewed as extending plantation house tour studies into an urban locale where domestic slavery was practiced but where scholars of public history tend not to focus attention.

The primary research on which this piece is based consists of a two-day participant-observation visit to the Sorrel-Weed House in 2012, informal conversations (in person and via phone) with Sorrel-Weed docents, an analysis of Sorrel-Weed print materials (brochure, website), and an analysis of You Tube videos and reality television representations of the home's history and hauntings. Since my initial visit, I have returned to the Sorrel-Weed House and retaken the daytime and evening tours. I have noted that the tour narrative, while consistent in its basic facts regarding main characters and events, changes in specifics, tone, and terminology depending on the tour guide, interaction from tourists, and the site staff's effort to update tour content. My analysis of the Sorrel-Weed narrative in this essay is based on my first visit there but written with the hindsight of those later observations.

I was passing through Madison Square in Savannah's historic district when a woman waved me over to an imposing manor house with chipping orange paint. She invited me to take "a historic tour" of the Sorrel-Weed, yet another classical home built by a Savannah cotton merchant in the decades before the Civil War. This was the first instance during my short time in Savannah that I had been solicited to take a historic home tour. I was intrigued by the thought of being beckoned into history and surprised that I had not heard of this home before I happened upon it. I would later learn that unlike many other historic house museums in the district that were public institutions, preservation organization projects, or association headquarters, Sorrel-Weed was held by private individuals, brothers who had purchased the home through a company they founded called Sorrel-Weed Restorations.[23] I paused to take in the dark green state historic site marker erected in front of the iron-gated yard. It read, in part:

> A fine example of Greek Revival style, this building (completed in 1840 from the plans of Charles B. Cluskey, a well-known Georgia architect) shows the distinguished trend of Savannah architecture during the first half of the 19th century… The Mediterranean villa influence reflects the French background of the original owner, Francis Sorrel (1793-1870), a shipping merchant of Savannah who was as a child saved by a faithful slave from the massacre of the white colonists in St. Domingo.[24]

Intrigued by the mention of the Haitian Revolution yet suspicious of the trope of the faithful slave, I paid for a ticket.

In the library of the home, a cheerful older couple who volunteered that they were from a nearby city sat waiting for the late afternoon tour to begin. I joined them. We were a small group. It was the slow season. But our tour guide made up for what we lacked in size with an exaggerated, if slightly sarcastic, enthusiasm. The tour began with a video profile of the house and its proprietor that had appeared on Home and Garden Television's show: "If Walls Could Talk." The clip showcased the age of the home, the owner's love of history, and the owner's discovery of artifacts and letters in the wine cellar and between the floorboards. The tour then emphasized the home's status as part of a National Historic Landmark district and as a Georgia state historic landmark, the origins and wealth of the mysterious Sorrel family, the architecture and furnishings of the house, a friendly visit by General Robert E. Lee, and an unwelcome visit by General William Tecumseh Sherman during the federal occupation of Savannah. The narrative our docent spun as we moved into the heart of the tour was immediately disturbing and even more dramatic than the historic marker had indicated. For our tour guide explained that we were standing in a haunted mansion built for a free man of color who had once owned scores of black slaves.

Francis Sorrel, the docent said, was a cotton merchant with ¼ "Haitian blood" who could and did pass for white. Sorrel was filthy rich in his time and fond of hosting lavish soirees that spilled out onto Madison square. He possessed twenty-five Haitian slaves mostly for show, as he only required five to run the house. The extra slaves had four days off during the week, working only during Sorrel's weekend social occasions. The slaves spent their ample spare time in a room in the basement that had hot running water channeled behind the fireplace, a luxury that most homes in the city lacked at that time. Next door to the slaves' "off" room was a chamber where Francis himself may have practiced Voodoo. Chicken and goat bones were found beneath the doorframe in the basement, and human remains had been discovered under the floorboards. As we toured the basement, our guide reminded us, we were walking over the still-interred bones.

Our guide explained that Francis Sorrel's strategy for hiding his true racial ancestry was to foreground his wealth. He made a habit of arriving late to his own parties, allowing the guests to soak in the grandeur of his house. He possessed a private dining room in the house that could be barricaded, and for good reason. For here is where his Haitian heritage came out into the open—in the Caribbean influenced coral toned wall color, in the pineapple shaped plaster mold on the ceiling, in the curved walls meant to ward off the ghosts, whom Francis believed lurked in corners. In the private dining room, Francis sat with his back to these protective walls, while his wife, Matilda Moxley Sorrel, sat with her back to the corners.

Wealthy though he was, Francis led a tragic existence. His young second wife, Matilda, had taken her own life, leaping from the upper floor balcony and landing in a heap on the brick courtyard below. What had driven her to this act of desperation? Francis's relationship with a slave girl. Sorrel, it turned out, was having an illicit affair with Molly, a slave who lived on the second floor of the carriage house that served as slave quarters just across the courtyard. One week after Matilda's death, Molly was found hanging from the rafters of the slave quarters. Foul play was suspected. The carriage house where Molly had lived and died was restricted during the daytime historic tour but would be open that evening during the paranormal tour, since Molly still haunted the place.

Did Molly commit suicide? People said so at the time, but the claim was doubtful. Did Francis kill Molly out of guilt? Perhaps. Did other slaves in the household murder her out of jealousy? Maybe so. Our tour guide speculated about the possibilities and explained that soon after these tragic events had unfolded, Francis abandoned the house. He moved next door into a tall, austere townhouse and had a brick wall erected between the two properties. He lived until his seventies, an old age for men in the nineteenth century. Could he have extended his life by practicing Voodoo sacrifice rituals in the basement of the old Greek Revival home? Was this the reason for the bones, both animal and human, buried in the basement?[25]

It is no exaggeration to say that the story of the Sorrel-Weed House shocked me. I had taken several historic plantation and urban slavery home tours across five states over the past ten years and read about even more in the scholarship on representations of slavery.[26] But many if not all of these other tours focused on the idealized lives of white southern elites: the beauty of their homes and furnishings, the romance of their courtships and weddings, the excitement of their economic and political triumphs, the tragedy of their loss in the Civil War. This was the first time I had heard an elaborated narrative of racial passing and sexual transgression, let alone of a slave haunting, at a plantation house or domestic slavery site. I returned again that night to take the ghost tour at a cost of fifteen dollars, noting the mark-up from the daytime price. This second tour, made even more dramatic by the cover of darkness, advanced a similar narrative as the daytime tour with variations of emphasis. A chief difference was that the so-called "paranormal tour" began and lingered in the space of the carriage house, the supposed scene of Molly's abuse and site of contemporary hauntings.

After taking both tours, I read brochures and web posts about the home, watched numerous videos on YouTube recorded by visitors to the house, and listened to recordings posted online of the supposed voices of ghosts, again, recorded by tourists. In the words of the site brochure: tourists at the home could "revisit the antebellum days of the old South! Experience this grand Savannah home that will intrigue and entice you with her rich extraordinary atmosphere of southern history, fine antiques, and outstanding architecture." The site's narrative of wealth, luxury, and famous visitors was in line with the stories told at many plantation house tours across the South. However, the daytime tour interwove details about the tragic history of the house that had led it to be haunted and directed visitors to the evening ghost tour where they would, according to the brochure, "Tour inside the most haunted home in Savannah," "learn the tragic history of the Sorrel family," and have a one-of-a-kind "experience" of the "Paranormal."[27] The Sci-Fi Channel's hit show "Ghost Hunters" had featured the house and affirmed the paranormal qualities promoted on the site brochure. The best evidence for this claim included, in ghost hunting lingo, an EVP (electronic voice phenomena) consisting of audiotaped screams. In the "Ghost Hunters" episode the Sorrel-Weed homeowner and a resident of the carriage house attributed those EVP screams to the ghostly slave girl, Molly, being attacked in the slave quarters. That scream, it turned out, was the most reproduced audio of the Sorrel-Weed House on YouTube.

Most striking to me in my visits to the house and subsequent ongoing research has been the nature of the ghost story promoted at the site and recirculated by online fans. The shared Sorrel-Weed House site interpretation centers on the suicide of the mistress of this wealthy slaveholding family in 1860, on the related brutal murder of an enslaved girl who was said to have been sexually involved with her owner, and on the "Voodoo" practices (including human sacrifice) of the master of the household, who purportedly hid his part-black racial ancestry from other Savannah elites. The story and its popularity led me to ask two related questions. What image of past lives, particularly past lives during slavery, does the Sorrel-Weed House narrative present and reinforce? What cultural work is this popular story doing in the contemporary urban South? I concluded that this ghost tour narrative belittles actual sexual violence perpetrated against enslaved black women by white male slaveholders, exploits the emotional and physical suffering of women in patriarchal household arrangements, and reproduces the stereotype of the black male threat.

The complex history and personal agency of black as well as white women in the antebellum South are undermined by the Sorrel-Weed tour narrative. Violent deaths of two women—one black, one white—animate the ghost story. These deaths are precipitated by the sexual relationship, lightly deemed an "affair," between a middle-aged white male slaveholder and an African American adolescent girl whom he owns. The story depicts this relationship as consensual and thus carries with it traces of the historical image of the seductive, over-sexed black female slave. Tour guides describe the young black woman as both a "slave girl" and "mistress" to Sorrel, language that simultaneously reveals and refuses to acknowledge the contradiction of these terms in our contemporary parlance, when "slave" denotes a lack of freedom and "mistress" connotes a freely chosen if illicit sexual relationship. Matilda, the white woman in the story and third point in this sordid romantic triangle, is represented as naive and emotionally unstable, as she takes her own life when she discovers the "affair" by walking in on Francis and Molly in the slave quarters. What is more, the tour highlights the carriage house, scene of the "affair" and murder, as a place of titillating drama, a disparagement of the actual role of the slave quarter in African American experience, as a protective space of black family and community life, and alternately, of danger when black women became vulnerable to the forced intrusions of white men. This ghost story, then, turns on violence against and experienced by women, and in particular, reproduces a female slave's suffering for entertainment value. Paying visitors can tour the room where Molly swung from the rafters and imaginatively recreate the scene of her murder. Matilda's gruesome end is exploited too, though in a less exhaustive manner, as tourists are directed to gaze or stand on the spot where she died in the palm treed courtyard.

The African American male character (passing as white) also suffers representational ignominy in the Sorrel-Weed tour narrative. Although the tour guides did not criticize the master of the house directly, Francis Sorrel emerges as the ne'er do well of this ghost story. He engaged in adulterous sex (if not explicitly named as rape), practiced black magic, and is suspected of having committed a murder. Although the "fun" of the ghost tour frame undermines the heinousness of these crimes, their inclusion in the story is significant. Rarely do southern house museums highlight corrupt acts perpetrated by elite male patriarchs. But in this narrative, Francis commits all manner of evil. His behavior can be narrated in this way in part because of the interest in the dark side of human nature that the ghost tour format invites, but also because the site story includes the intelligence that Francis Sorrel was passing for white. The secretly black Francis Sorrel spoiled his slaves, practiced Voodoo, bedded a black girl and may have killed her, and betrayed a white woman to whom, according to southern antebellum law, he should never have been married in the first place. Blackness is implicit as the base quality beneath this man's tainted characteristics, for black men are "known" in American society to be violent, sensual, devious, and predatory. This is a ghost story that can be read as an allegory of the threat of black masculinity, an allegory about urban spaces that are haunted today by the presence of black men. For in the end of the Sorrel-Weed tale, race proves fundamental and insurmountable despite Francis's wealth and social attainments. Francis Sorrel may have pulled the wool over the eyes of his fellow Savannahians, but he cannot do so to contemporary Savannah residents or paying visitors who tour his haunted house. The Sorrel-Weed story has something to tell us, and it is an age-old Southern and indeed national lesson that has been refashioned again and again in popular culture: white women are emotionally and physically fragile; black women are sexually deviant and disposable; and black men should be feared and contained. Francis Sorrel, it might be noted, does not haunt his own house. He alone among that tragic trio is dead and securely buried, a forever imprisoned black man.

The events rendered in the Sorrel-Weed tours are plausible in the history of the slave-holding South where black women had no legal protections, white women had limited rights, and a small minority of men of color owned black slaves. If taken seriously and represented accurately, the Sorrel-Weed story could be used to reveal the grossly hierarchical power relations of the past that continue to cast a shadow on our present. Indeed, the presence of enslaved characters in the story is an indirect form of acknowledging a troubled history shaped by the system of slavery. However, those who retell the standard narrative of the Sorrel-Weed House seem oblivious to or disinterested in the embedded and serious meanings of slavery, race, gender, and trauma in the material they have chosen to work with. The story told by the guides that I heard sanitized those racial and gendered dynamics, evaporating the dehumanizing aspects of slavery and suppressive aspects of patriarchy while exaggerating bits of the story that turned on illicit black sex and gender violence. The (white male) docents I encountered evidenced no shame, ambivalence, or reluctance about the human indignity of the story that they recounted.[28] The lack of genuineness or sensitivity for historical lives at this site became even more apparent to me when I learned through primary research that little evidence supports the notion that events took place at the home as described. Rather, much of the basis for the Sorrel-Weed hauntings seems to have been invented. In short, the narrative of Francis, Matilda, and Molly recreates a hierarchical racial and gendered script for the fun, comfort, and profit of it, amounting to what might be termed plantation kitsch.[29]

಄

The Sorrel-Weed House is not representative of the majority of plantation or urban southern home tours. This I readily acknowledge. Nevertheless, I offer the prediction and caution that it may soon stand as an early adopter among a crowded field of haunted southern houses and plantations, as dark tourism continues to grow with the multi-billion dollar global tourist industry. I also extend the hope that scholars, writers, and practitioners of public history will be on alert for representations of slavery that advance exploitative, and indeed farcical, narratives—and attempt to craft historically grounded, socially conscious counter-narratives to circulate in the public square. For, as many scholars of historic sites and memorials have observed, much is at stake for our contemporary social and civic lives in how we remember the racial dynamics of the past. Visitors' experiences at these locations are neither inert nor finite. Rather, the understanding that people think they have gained when they leave places of historical significance, and the feeling that motivates and shapes that understanding, can be channeled into private actions and social interactions with broader impact. Visitors to house museums—historic spaces uniquely associated with family, intimacy and safety—may be especially sensitized to the narratives they encounter there, as crossing into the private spaces of others likely encourages more lasting, emotive and conceptual links between the lives of those in the past and our own present circumstances.

Rather than giving up the ghost to movers and shakers of the tourist industry who seek to profit from misremembering the lives of the enslaved, perhaps we can imagine a different kind of social haunting. Perhaps we can bring into being—through our writing, visual art, and acts of public performance—haunting interpretations of history that chasten and enlighten our fellow citizens, compelling recollection of past wrongs and warning against the repetition of injustice in the future. This kind of radical representation using the ghost as a sign would carry with it the social meaning of haunting theorized by sociologist Avery Gordon. In her classic book *Ghostly Matters*, Gordon argues that "ghosts are urgent challenges for the politically engaged intellectual" because the presence of a ghost is an indication of "something-to-be-done." She insists that "[t]o fight for an oppressed past is to make this past come alive as the lever for the work of the present: obliterating the sources and conditions that link the violence of what seems finished with the present, ending this history and setting in place a different future."[30]

Notes

1. John Lennon and Malcolm Foley, *Dark Tourism: The Attraction of Death and Disaster* (Cheriton House, North Way, Andover, Hampshire, United Kingdom: Cengage Learning, 2010), 3. Richard Sharpley, 'Shedding Light on Dark Tourism: An Introduction," in Richard Sharpley and Philip R. Stone, eds., *The Darker Side of Travel: The Theory and Practice of Dark Tourism* (Bristol, United Kingdom: Channel View Publications, 2009) 3-22, 5-6.

   The earliest version of this essay was presented as a Plenary Address titled "Race, History, and Haunting in the Post-Bellum South" at the Southern American Studies Association conference in Charleston, January 2013. A second version titled "Haunted Emancipations: Gender, Race, and Ghostly Presences in the Modern South" was presented at the University of Wisconsin-Madison, Center for the Humanities, Emancipations Lecture Series in February, 2013. I am grateful for the research assistance of Kyera Singleton and for the astute feedback of participants at the SASA conference as well as special issue editor Sarah Juliet Lauro, and colleagues Stephen Kantrowitz at the University of Wisconsin and Paulina Alberto and Farina Mir at the University of Michigan.

2. Elizabeth Becker, *Overbooked: The Exploding Business of Travel and Tourism* (NY: Simon and Schuster, 2013) 16.

3. Glenn W. Gentry, "Walking with the Dead: The Place of Ghost Walk Tourism in Savannah, Georgia," *Southeastern Geographer*, vol. 47, no. 2, November 2007) 222-238, 223.

4. Lennon and Foley, Dark Tourism, 3-4. Malcolm Foley and John Lennon, "JFK and Dark Tourism—a fascination with assassination," International Journal of Heritage Studies, Vol. 2, No. 4 (1996): 198-211; Malcolm Foley and John Lennon, "Dark Tourism—an Ethical Dilemma," in Malcolm Foley, John Lennon, and Gillian Maxwell, eds., *Strategic Issues for the Hospitality, Tourism and Leisure Industries* (London: Cassell, 1997): 153-164.

5. "Tragedy, suffering and pain are the new way of travel: 'Dark tourism' getting Popular: Study," *New York Daily News*, April 26, 2012, http://www.nydailynews.com/life-style/tragedy-suffering-pain-new-travel-dark-tourism-popular-study-article-1.1067904. Accessed 8/17/2013. "'Dark Tourism getting even more popular," *New York Daily News*, April 26, 2012, http://www.nydailynews.com/2012-04-26. Accessed 12/13/2012; link discontinued.

6. Avery F. Gordon, *Ghostly Matters: Haunting and the Sociological Imagination* (1997; reprint, Minneapolis, MN: University of Minnesota Press, 2008); Jeffrey Andrew Weinstock, ed., *Spectral America: Phantoms and the National Imagination* (Madison: University of Wisconsin Press / Popular Press, 2004; Maria del Pilar Blanco and Esther Peeren, Popular Ghosts: The Haunted Spaces of Everyday Culture (NY: Continuum, 2010); Judith Richardson, Possessions: The History and Uses of Haunting in the Hudson Valley (Cambridge: Harvard University Press, 2003).

7. Catherine Spooner, *Contemporary Gothic* (London, United Kingdom: Reaktion Books, 2006) 8. Jeffrey Andrew Weinstock, "Introduction: The Spectral Turn," in Jeffrey Andrew Weinstock, ed., *Spectral America: Phantoms and the National Imagination* (Madison: University of Wisconsin Press / Popular Press, 2004) 3-17, 5.

8. Philip R. Stone, "'It's a Bloody Guide': Fun, Fear and a Lighter Side of Dark Tourism at The Dungeon Visitor Attractions, UK," in Richard Sharpley and Philip R. Stone, eds., *The Darker Side of Travel: The Theory and Practice of Dark Tourism* (Bristol, United Kingdom: Channel View Publications, 2009) 167-185, 169.

9. Carolyn Morrow Long, *Madame Lalaurie: Mistress of the Haunted House* (Pensacola, FL: University Press of FL, 2012), 161.

10. For more on ghost hunting shows and the use of technology, see Sarah Juliet Lauro and Catherine Paul, "'Make Me Believe!': Ghost-hunting technology and the postmodern fantastic," *Horror Studies*, Vol. 4, Number 2 (2103): 221-239.

11. My observations about tourists' emotional reactions at ghost tours were informed by remarks made on the following panel: Jill Ogline Titus, moderator, David Glassberg, Robert Thompson, Glenn Gentry, Richard Sharpley, "Ghosts and Generals: Theatricality, Dark Tourism, and the Ghost Tour Industry," The Future of Civil War History: Looking Beyond the 150th (symposium), Gettysburg College, Gettysburg, PA, March 15, 2013. For a closer look at ghost tour participants and their diverse motivations, see Glenn Gentry, "Walking with the Dead."

12. For discussions of the South as regional "other" see James C. Cobb, *Away Down South: A History of Southern Identity* (New York: Oxford University Press, 2005), introduction, chapter 1; John D. Cox, *Traveling*

South: Travel Narratives and the Construction of American Identity (Athens, GA: University of Georgia Press, 2005), 8-9, 144.

13. Warren L. Wise, "Conde Nast declares Charleston top tourist city in the world," *The Post and Courier*, October 17, 2012. http://www.postandcourier.com/article/20121017/PC05/121019368. Accessed 8/29/2013.

14. Geordie Buxton, *Haunted Plantations: Ghosts of Slavery and Legends of the Cotton Kingdoms* (Charleston, SC: Arcadia Publishing, 2007). Nancy Roberts, Georgia Ghosts (1997; reprint, Winston Salem, NC: Blair, 2008). Randy Russell, Ghost Cats of the South (Winston, Salem, NC: Blair, 2008). http://themoonlitroad.com. Accessed 12/13/2012. http://americanfolklore.net/folklore/2010/07/spooky_south.html. Accessed 12/13/2012.

15. Pat Yale, *From Tourist Attractions to Heritage Tourism* (1990; second edition, ELM Publications, Huntingdon, Great Britain, 1998) 69.

16. Yaniv Poria, Richard Butler, David Airey, "The Core of Heritage Tourism," *Annals of Tourism Research*, Vol. 30, No. 1 (2003): 238-254, 239. Quotation: David T. Herbert, "Preface," in David T. Herbert, ed., Heritage, Tourism and Society (London: Mansell Publishing Limited, 1995): xi-xii, xi.

17. Yaniv Poria, Gregory Ashworth, "Heritage Tourism: Current Resource for Conflict," Annals of Tourism Research, Vol. 36, No. 3 (2009): 522-525, 524.

18. Jennifer L. Eichstedt and Stephen Small, *Representations of Slavery: Race and Ideology in Southern Plantation Museums*, (Washington DC: Smithsonian Institution Press, 2002), 10, 3.

19. E. Arnold Modlin, Derek Alderman, and Glenn Gentry, "Tour Guides as Creators of Empathy: The Role of Affective Inequality in Marginalizing the Enslaved at Plantation House Museums," *Tourist Studies*, Vol. 11, No. 1 (2011): 3-19, 5, 8.

20. Christine N. Buzinde and Carla Almeida Santos, "Representations of Slavery," *Annals of Tourism Research*, Vol. 35, No. 2 (2008): 469-488, 483-4.

21. Russ Bynum, "Savannah to Be Named 'Most Haunted," *Associated Press Online*, October 12, 2002. Accessed 1/9/2013.

22. Kimberle Crenshaw, "Demarginalizing the Intersection of Race and Sex: A Black Feminist Critique of Antidiscrimination Doctrine, Feminist Theory and Antiracist Politics," *University of Chicago Legal Forum* (1989): 139-167; Kimberle Crenshaw, "Mapping the Margins: Intersectionality, Identity Politics, and Violence Against Women of Color," *Stanford Law Review*, Vol. 43, No. 6 (July 1991): 1241-1299; Sharpley, "Shedding Light," *Darker Side of Travel*, 6.

23. "Building History," Savannah Now.com, *Savannah Morning News*, p. 5. http://savannahnow.com/stories/050700/LOCsorrelweed.html. Accessed 3/1/2012.

24. "Old Sorrel-Weed House," The Historical Marker Database. http://www.hmdb.org/Marker.asp?Marker=5628. Accessed 7/26/203.

25. Historic Sorrel-Weed House, Historic Day Tour, Feb. 27, 2012.

26. Eichstedt and Small, *Representations of Slavery*; Modlin Jr., Alderman and Gentry, "Tour Guides as Creators of Empathy: The Role of Affective Inequality in Marginalizing the Enslaved at Plantation House Museums"; Christine N. Buzinde and Carla Almeida Santos, "Interpreting Slavery Tourism Representations," *Annals of Tourism Research* 36: 3 (2009): 439-58; Buzinde and Santos, "Representations of Slavery," (2008); James Oliver Horton and Lois E. Horton, eds., *Slavery and Public History: The Tough Stuff of American Memory* (New York: New Press, 2006); Tiya Miles, *The House on Diamond Hill: A Cherokee Plantation Story* (Chapel Hill, NC: University of North Carolina Press, 2010); Jessica Adams, *Wounds of Returning: Race, Memory, and Property on the Postslavery Planation* (Chapel Hill: University of North Carolina Press, 2007); Gerald and Patricia Gutek, *Plantations and Outdoor Museums in America's Historic South* (Columbia, SC: University of South Carolina Press, 1996).

27. Sorrel-Weed House print brochure, front and back sides, winter 2012.

28. For more on the social and moral dynamics of shame see Erika Doss, *Memorial Mania: Public Feeling in America* (Chicago: University of Chicago Press, 2010), 260-62.

29. For an engaging analysis of the role in kitsch (the notion of the cheapening effect of consumer culture) in dark tourism, see Richard Sharpley and Philip R. Stone, "(Re)presenting the Macabre: Interpretation, Kitschification and Authenticity," in Sharpley and Stone, eds., *Darker Side of Travel*, 109-128.

30. Gordon, *Ghostly Matters*, xix, xvi, 66.

BURIED BODIES, BURIED TREASURE:
COAL MINES AND THE GHOSTS OF APPALACHIA

by Brent Walter Cline

In Talcott, West Virginia, a rockslide kills an entire train crew of workers, and a tunnel must be completely rebuilt. During the reconstruction, a brick mason sees the ghost of an enormous man swinging two hammers. Instinctively, he knows it is Appalachia's most famous folk hero, John Henry, who has, in the words of the narrator, "returned to the scene of his triumph" (Roberts 1978, 113). As a ghost story, it is a fairly simple one to characterize: the ghost returns to his place of death. Yet the structure of the story suggests a complicated relationship with dangerous labor. The tunnel is the site of a catastrophe, yet the mason sees the ghost of John Henry as a victor. The mason's understanding of triumph ignores the traditional narrative that John Henry's legendary defeat of the mechanized steam drill cost him his life, as well as the fact that his ghost does not seem to sympathize with any ghosts that might exist from the recent rock slide. Within the same story, the labor of clearing a tunnel has the potential to be so triumphant that one's spirit remains to joyfully continue in the work, while that same labor is an existential threat to any living persons.

If the danger of work on the railroads in Appalachia spurred ghost stories like this one of John Henry, it should come as no surprise that the coal mining industry has created a catalogue of ghost stories that document the fear and anxiety inherent to the profession. Of course, the conditions of the underground mines suggest an ideal location for ghost stories. There is the threat of imminent death from cave-in, explosion, or asphyxiation. Since the 1880's (when records began), over 100,000 miners have been killed, with millions injured (Lockard 1998, 53). There is the pitch darkness, as Michael Guillerman shares in his memoir of working in the Eastern Kentucky coalfields: "I could envision every sort of monster lurking in the darkness, ready to pounce. At the time, I thought of myself as tough, energetic, and agile—able to handle almost any situation, except for a confrontation with a monster…Many a time, I felt relieved to get back into a fast man-trip and speed away from a jinxed unit" (155). This darkness must be coupled with the labyrinthine nature of the mines, which even as early as the turn of the 20th century could stretch up to fifteen miles long (Long 1991, 26). Ruth Ann Musick, West Virginia's most important folklorist, understates the matter when she writes, "The work of the miners, even in times of prosperity, may have something to do with their love of wonder and magic. Theirs is a life of contrast and uncertainty" (1970, xii). The instability of this life obviously manifested itself through the labor movement in the first half of the 20th century, but it is also revealed in the ghost stories of the Appalachian coalfields. William Lynwood Montell, arguably to Kentucky's ghost stories what Musick is to West Virginia's, writes that folklore is "a key means of getting at attitudes, values, and world view, those intangibles of historical experience that rarely show up in historical documents" (Montell 1988, 63). How the miners narrated the afterlife of their killed comrades reveals the same ambivalent, contradictory relationship toward a potentially deadly, exploitative profession that a labor history might reveal—or a folk story of John Henry's ghost.

When one reads the collected ghost stories of Musick and Montell—which spans the rise of the coal mining industry in the late 19th century until the pervasive rise of strip mining after World War II—the unique role that coal mines have within Appalachia begins to form.[1] The coal mines are more than the simple location of death and hauntings, like some country graveyard or abandoned home; the coal mines are both the location and *cause* of death and hauntings. Yet unlike the other causes of unnatural death throughout the region's ghost stories—whether owing to cruel slave masters, murderous thieves, or abusive husbands—the coal mines (and their operators) are immune from the retribution of ghosts seeking vengeance and justice. The ghost stories of Appalachia afford these mines a unique place in the folklore of the region.[2] The mines are instruments of destruction, but also an economic necessity for both those destroyed and those who survive. This tension in their depiction assumes a position above justice and reflects Appalachia's past and current relationship with the mines, which endanger environmental stability and human health, while at the same time provide—no matter how short-sighted—an economic stimulus, and perhaps more importantly, a narrative identity. If ghost stories are an opportunity through narrative for a community to perceive and manage its anxiety, then the ghost stories of Appalachia reveal ambivalence toward the mines, a primary provider of the collective anxiety—along with economic and cultural capital—of the region.

Rather than finding the meaning of how these ghost stories of the mines are told by settling them into a larger genre of American folklore, this study will compare the mines as they exist as elements of the ghost stories, especially in comparison to similar elements in other ghost stories of the region.[3] Folklorists such as George Korson have long identified that ghosts in the mines generally serve a series of purposes, all of which can be found in the aboveground ghost stories: revenants returned to finish jobs, to console, or to save the living (Santino 1988, 209). When the coal mines as narrative elements are specifically compared to other elements of Appalachian ghost stories, then more can be said about how the mining stories speak (and fail to speak) of resistance to the fear and necessity of the mines in the region. These mines ultimately serve two functions in these ghost stories, as setting and agent of unnatural death. When compared to the region's other folk settings and agents, the mines claim a distinct place. More than geography but less than an agent deserving of retribution, the ambivalence of the region's relationship to Appalachia becomes clear.

MINES AS LOCATION

In her dissection of what constitutes a narrative, Mieke Bal (1997) in *Narratology* writes that one of the basic elements of the story is location, which is "given distinct characteristics and [is] thus transformed into specific places" (8). One need not take a strictly structuralist perspective—and that is certainly not the position of this current study—in order to accept that location is an integral part of the story. Seymour Chatman aggregates the possible uses of setting in a story, stating that they can be utilitarian, symbolic, or simply irrelevant (143). The locations within Appalachian ghost stories are generally understood to be utilitarian or irrelevant; their use is to help establish a mood or provide the necessary physical scenery for the story to take place. Even when the ghost stories occur in actual places in Appalachia, these places only help locate the story, or perhaps provide a distinct mood to a literal place.

Similar to ghost stories from other regions, the most popular location for Appalachian ghost stories is also the most frequented location: the home. Throughout Musick's and Montell's collections, the home is the most basic and often-times irrelevant feature in the stories, whether the ghost be out for justice or lingers without a distinct motivation. While the house may be the site of an unnatural death, and at times might conceal the victim of that death, the house itself is not the cause of the death. It is only a location for the plot to occur, and the ghost's presence is primarily due to its mortal presence in the same home.

Montell dedicates an entire volume to stories of domestic ghosts, and the narrative purpose of the home is nearly always the theatrical stage for the haunting. In a story from Pike County, Kentucky, an old woman's ghost runs young girls off her property when they attempt to pick flowers from near the house. The ghost is unidentified as anyone other than the former owner of the house; in this case, the house is simply the necessary setting. In Montell's story of "The Tan Man," however, the ghost is the result of unnatural death and haunts a Pike County home near where its body had been disposed by an FBI agent. "The Tan Man" harasses the owners of the house by causing bizarre sounds to emanate from the family piano or spinning the lights on the wall. Despite the fact that the murder of "The Tan Man" seemingly connects the house to a nefarious deed, the house remains nothing more than a location, providing the material for the ghost's harassment (Montell 2001, 165, 7). In a Knox County, Kentucky story, a house was even an explicit part of the death, when a newborn child was shoved behind a wall and suffocated, only to return generations later to scrape and tap until the current owners opened the wall to find the skeleton. The house, the instrument of destruction to the baby, is nevertheless not considered part of any agency in the unnatural death; this lies strictly with the child's alcoholic mother. Montell records the informant's ending, suggesting that all can be well with the house as it is only a location of wicked doings: "The strange rapping was never heard again, and the Dizneys still live there" (84).

While the domestic space is the most common location for Musick's and Montell's stories, scenes in nature occur frequently and, much like the haunted house, witness the appearance of ghosts simply because they are the site of death. In *Ghosts Across Kentucky*, Montell (2000) tells a story of a woman who is raped and murdered by Union soldiers at the base of a cliff. When the informant himself comes to the cliff he can hear the woman screaming for help from below (224). While the site is clearly haunted, the location is not signified as a participant in the violence, as the Union soldiers clearly are. The base of the cliff is haunted because the assault happened to occur there, not due to any inherent wickedness in the site. As in the stories of haunted houses, even when nature *causes* unnatural death, the storyteller assigns no maliciousness to the location. In *Green Hills of Magic*, Musick's (1970) collection of European ghost stories told to her by West Virginia miners, she records the story of Frank McKenna, who in anger resisted his friends' advice to come in from a hunting expedition and is killed in a snowstorm. Not only does the snow eventually kill him, but when they find his body, "His prayer book lay opened upon his mouth, and his hat was pulled down, so as to cover it and his face" (194). Nature conquers McKenna's petitions to God, but what is understood to cause McKenna's death, as well as result in his curse to be a revenant, was his anger toward his loved ones: "The ghost answered that he was not allowed to speak with any of his friends, for he had parted with them in anger" (195); nature's destructive power is strictly an amoral force.

Although the snowstorm that kills McKenna receives no blame for his death, this is not to suggest that there were not locations within Appalachia that embodied destruction and wickedness by corrupting both the home as well as nature through unfair labor practices: not coal mines, but slave plantations. While West Virginia and Eastern Kentucky had far fewer slaves than more southern states, plantations do appear in the region's ghost stories. If any location might be understood as embodying evil, and therefore participatory in either unnatural death or unsettling hauntings, it is the site of chattel slavery. In Musick and Montell, however, the evil is always contained within the slave master rather than the plantation, even if the work itself is what either killed the slave or drove him to suicide. When a slave is killed by his master in Musick's (1965) *The Telltale Lilac Bush*, he promises to return to kill the master. In the mean time, slaves begin to get sick and die, and the master's house is burned down (91). Eventually the slave's ghost drags the screaming master off the land never to be seen again; the ghost does not reappear. Despite the location becoming the arena for horrifying exploitation, the land itself does not inherently contain evil. The site of the slave's murder is only significant because of the presence of the master and his wickedness.

In all of these locations, two categories of space can be identified. The first is that space is simply a geographic and narrative necessity, and the appearance of ghosts occurs there only because of what happened on that space. This is the case in the story of the old ghost protecting her home's flowers from being picked, or of the murdered woman's screams due to the violence of the Union soldiers. If the site is evil, it is because the site had evil literally enacted upon it. It is a kind of victim, as can be seen in stories when the revenant is dispatched to the afterlife and the location returns to a place of pleasure or peace. The second is that space sometimes participates in unnatural death and causes a revenant to appear, but this participation is either considered amoral, as in the story of Frank McKenna, or secondary to the wickedness of a human being, as is the case in the slave story above.

The coal mines of West Virginia and Kentucky are, like domestic spaces and open swaths of nature alike, common sites for ghosts in the region. The mines, however, do not fit easily into the two aforementioned categories of location. They are not geographical accidents; their very existence is what causes the unnatural deaths to occur. And unlike the second category, there is no amoral participation in the deaths, nor is there an immediate villain to be pinned with guilt. Ghosts who remain in the mine do so not only because it was the place of their murder, but because the place itself is the malevolent force which caused it.

Nearly every ghost story in Appalachia that involves a coal mine is rooted in a deadly mine accident. This may seem to go without saying, but it suggests an immediate, important difference with the locations listed above. The coal mine is not scenery for thieving or murdering; the mine itself is virtually always the agent of death. Even in the above stories where location was the instrument of death, as in the story of the newborn baby stuffed in the wall or of Frank McKenna dying in the elements, there is an external, villainous force causing the unnatural deaths to occur: in the former, the baby's mother, and in the latter, McKenna's anger. The coal mines, however, are both the agent and the weapon. It is the mines themselves that destroy the miners, and there are no outside forces apart from the existential reality of the mines and the economic reality of needing work, which cause the unnatural deaths to occur. In the story "The Old Horse" from Musick's (1965) collection *The Telltale Lilac Bush*, the informant speaks of the connection between a miner and his beast of burden: "The horses were the men's best friends, and it was a sad day when they were taken out of the mines" (108). The sentiment in the relationship is perhaps oddly matched with the reality of the mortal danger of the mines; the storyteller says of his father and a workhorse, "[they] had to pass a section that had had a cave-in just a few days before" (108). The reality of the cave-in is stated as a matter of fact, with nothing to sentimentalize or bemoan because the danger is inherent in the mines themselves. In *Coffin Hollow*, Musick (1977) records a story of two friends, one of whom is falsely accused of sleeping with the other's wife. When both are caught in a mine collapse, the accused friend is crushed to death, but his ghost returns to hold the bracing while the husband can escape (82). The imminence of collapse is the known reality of life in the mines, and only the presence of the supernatural can stave off its killing of miners. The ghost of a betrayed friend is no less an expectation than a mine safe from collapse. The ghost stories of cave-ins do not concern themselves with corrupt mine operators; supervisors are a rarity within the ghost stories, and the owners themselves are universally absent. There is no overt economic or social concern in the stories. The ghost stories are concerned with the immediate confrontation of the conditions of the mines, the very existence of which suggest the cause and means of unnatural death.

Throughout Appalachia's ghost stories, coal miners must find means of escaping the expected—but nevertheless unnatural—death within the mines. In a common motif, Nancy Roberts writes of a ghost story where a miner hears hissing through the pipes and knows it to be all of the dead miners' ghosts sealed into the tunnels (104). Within the ghost stories (and arguably in real life as well), superstitions abound to counter the reality of impending death, such as keeping women out of the mines, befriending three-legged rats and supernatural cats who bestow safety to those miners who pass on a bit of kindness (Musick 2004, 11, 15). The miners of the ghost stories await doom the way a cursed man in other stories might flee from the furies.

MINES AS VILLAIN

If the coal mines have been shown to be more than a geographic neutrality in Appalachia's ghost stories, and are instead agents (as well as means) of unnatural death, then they can be fairly compared to the other common agents of unnatural death such as thieves, murderers, and debauched husbands. These agents of unnatural death are most often the very cause of the appearance of the ghosts who seek to right some wrong, whether that be restoration or retribution. Patrick Gainer, one of West Virginia's most important academics working on the Appalachian folktale, writes, "Most ghosts who appear in folktales are really revenants—unlaid ghosts, who have remained on earth to give a message to the living. As a rule, these ghosts are the spirits of people who have met violent deaths at the hands of murderers, and they wish to disclose the identity of the murderer. These ghosts usually remain on earth until some wrong is corrected" (35-36). That the mines have such a prevalence of ghost stories suggest that the miners themselves see the deaths as an injustice which demands restitution. As will be seen, however, what cries for justice the mining stories seem to demand sound sadly muted when contrasted with stories of vengeance outside of the mines.

One of the most common reasons for revenants is murder, and either the ghost lingers as though cursed, or specifically returns in order to point the misty finger at the criminal. The former occurs in stories such as Montell's tale of Billy Damorn, a young man killed for turning over a moonshine still to federal agents. There is nothing in the story to suggest Damorn's supernatural appearance will bring justice to his murderers, who are never specifically named in the story. Billy's ghostly presence is limited to his prayer in which he begged his murderers not to kill him (Montell 2000, 140). More often, however, the revenant does seek (and inevitably finds) some kind of justice against the murderer. The eponymous story of Musick's *The Telltale Lilac Bush* tells the story of exposing a husband who attempts to conceal his murdered wife's remains.

The wronged ghost may be seeking vengeance against a random attacker, as in the subgenre of stories where a traveling peddler is murdered, or against a betraying business partner, a man who steals a friend's spouse, or a murdering thief. Importantly, family is by no means off-limits for these bouts of justice. Musick records one story of a father who, while in a drunken rage, beats his son to death. The son returns to the father and torments him by repeating the phrase, "Thirsty, Pop?" until the father smashes the bottle against his own body. As he dies, the son whispers to him, "I'm still here, Pop" (Musick 1965, 35). The sanctity of the family bond is severed with the initial murder, therefore the revenant has no duty to anything but, in this case, "an eye for an eye" retribution.

In cases of mass cruelty and death, such as the institution of slavery or the Civil War, revenants return for justice against those who break a kind of code of honor. Slave owners aren't murdered by slave ghosts simply for being slave owners, but because they were excessively cruel or sadistic. In *Coffin Hollow*, Musick (1977) records the story of an escaped slave who is "willing to risk death itself rather than continue life under these wretched conditions" (61). The slave, still a young boy, escapes only to be caught by his master's hounds and nearly torn apart. Musick writes, "As the master arrived, he called off the dogs, and in front of many a watching slave (for the field was in sight of the huts) he drew his sword and with one mighty blow cut off the young boy's head" (61). The master's exhibitionism is soon turned against him as he is afterward tormented by the boy's voice. Eventually, as though in an irresistible trance, the master returns to the site of the murder; when the master's body is found by searchers, "they noticed he had no head, and beside the body lay the very same sword he had used to murder the slave boy" (62). In the same volume, a Union soldier murders a Confederate soldier by a bullet to the head after the latter was taken as a prisoner of war. After the war, when the Union soldier passes through the area where the Confederate was eventually buried, the former is seen speeding away on his horse, chased by the Confederate ghost and his "blood-curdling rebel yell." Eventually the Union soldier is found dead with a bullet in his head that matches the Confederate's gun, and when they open the Confederate's grave, "They found there, to their horror, that the bullet was gone from the reb's head and in his hand was a still-smoking revolver" (12). The subgenre of Civil War and slavery ghost stories suggest that even within dangerous conditions such as war or chattel slavery, there is a place for retribution. The horrifying conditions do not excuse the cruel and irresponsible behavior of those in power.

Throughout Appalachia's ghost stories then, the demand for justice or restitution from those who have wrongfully been killed proves to be a primary rationale for the appearance of a revenant, so much so that when revenants appear, often times the living simply assume that something must be fixed. The mines, however, stand apart from all of these murdering agents. Not only is there no active human agent in any of the unnatural deaths of miners, there is no attempt by ghosts to seek retribution. The role of the mines has already been established as being more than a geographic setting for a generic ghost story in that it actually creates unnatural death, but these same mines receive decidedly less anger or vengeance by the supernatural than other agents of death. Musick records a story of a small boy who dies, through no fault of his parents, yet returns to haunt them by playing the trumpet at night that they refused to let him play during his life. The parents are tormented, and "The mother told the father they were the cause of the boy's death" (Musick 1965, 32). The parents are in no way understood by the audience to be the actual cause of the boy's death, but it is still enough for his ghost to haunt them as retribution. The mines, the setting and cause of much more dangerous and negligent behavior than denying a boy his trumpet, are the site of no such acts of retribution. They are recognized as deadly as a thief's knife, but provide no possibility for a ghost to take vengeance. What *is* allowed to these returning ghosts is a muted form of retribution; the miner cannot escape the reality of the mines, but the revenant can help him survive what is his occupational destiny.

As seen in the above story of the woman who is raped and murdered by Union soldiers, there is a category of ghost whose torment cannot be ceased. This is a common occurrence in the mines, as miners hear the screams of their fallen colleagues and must simply accept them as a reality. In one story recorded by Musick, a man named McCormick, who died in a car wreck outside the mines, nevertheless returns to the mines to continue to work, causing miners who see him to flee or black out (Musick 1965, 115). While McCormick does not attempt to torment the miners or howl in damnation, he is ostensibly the same as the disembodied voices of the miners which travel through the ventilation pipes: his torment and labor will never cease. In these situations, the response is often to avoid the area: "[the miners] would not go near the section and made another route around it" (110).

One of the most common motifs in the coal mines is the revenant demanding or assisting in a pyrrhic type of retribution. Supervisors or safety inspectors are never involved, corrupt union bosses are far too removed from the immediate environment to appear, and a haunting driven by the desire for more money for living colleagues is unknown. Instead, revenants seek two pitiful forms of restitution against the mines as agents of death: the restoration of the dead miner's body, or the survival of the living miner. In the story "The Blue Flame," a man is killed by an explosion in the mines, and his body is never recovered. In one of the few mentions of economy in the coal mine ghost stories, "The son was forced to go to work in the same mine to make a living for the family" (Musick 1965, 112). While in the mine, the son sees a blue flame and begins to follow it as it takes him deeper into the mine. Eventually he hears a voice call his name and sees his father in the blue flame. As he runs toward his father he falls into a hole and finds his father's body.

The story ends on this note, because the revenant has completed his job. There is no hope for the son to do anything but work in the mines. Twice the short story recounts the son's fear of the mines, a fear that cannot be resolved. All that can be won back from death is the body of the fallen miner. Another story recorded by Musick recounts the death of a "Mr. Jones" who was killed in the mines. His corpse, apparently horrifyingly damaged, is transferred to his home where a hand falls off. Jones's ghost wanders until a child finds the hand under the house's porch. Once reunited with the rest of the body, the miner can rest in peace in the afterlife (Musick 2004, 10). A final example is that of "Big Max," an African-American miner known for his John Henry-like proportions. Big Max volunteers to repair a cave-in site where several miners had been killed. Big Max is joined in the reconstruction attempt by a miner who was able to do as much work as the living miner, but "was just a bag of bones" (Musick 1965, 113). When Big Max attempts to set a beam, the skinny miner begins to shout to set the beam somewhere else, madly pointing to a different spot. Big Max places his shovel on the new spot, and finds the body of the skinny miner revenant. Such stories of revenants needing to reclaim their bodies are in no way exclusive to the mine stories, but they are a part of a larger pattern of muted vengeance. Musick records the story of a husband who deposited his murdered wife in a spring house; the wife's revenant gains peace not only by the reclamation of her body, but in the meting out of justice against the agent of her death. In the mines, there are no examples of ghosts causing a supervisor or operator to be brought to justice, or even a dangerous mine to be shut down. For the revenant's benefit, all that can be gained is the restoration of the body for a proper burial.

If reclamation of the body is all the revenant can hope for himself, there is survival to hope for amongst the living, and ghosts assisting the survival of colleagues is common enough for Musick to list "helpful mine ghosts" as a genre motif (Musick 1977, 185).[4] This assistance to the living is, like the ghost's demand for its own body, something of a pyrrhic victory as it can only ensure that the miner survives a single day. The reality is that the miners who are saved by the good works of revenants must return to the mines to face the same danger the next day. Musick records a story in *Coffin Hollow* of a family of brothers who all work in the West Virginia mines. Ben, the eldest, is killed in the mines, and later when a cave-in occurs, the brothers hear the voice of their famously protective kin, "Follow me, brothers, follow me" (81). Ben not only shows them the right way out, but when the brothers return to show inspectors how they got out, they find that there was no physical way for them to have escaped. A ghost is therefore able to direct his brothers through impossible seams to escape, but he can only save them from immediate danger. As the abrupt ending of the story suggests, these brothers must return to the site of mortal danger as though nothing had happened.

There are occasional stories of true retribution in the mines, but these stories are of vengeance directed against figures other than those responsible for the condition of the mines. Ultimately then, these stories of vengeance only highlight the other revenants' lack of ability to end the threat the mines represent. For instance, Musick's *Coffin Hollow* contains a story where a miner killed in a cave-in seeks revenge after his death, but only toward his wife who was cheating on him. It is as though he cannot conceive of vengeance against the mine operators who ensured the disastrous working conditions. Montell records a story where a miner, apparently in an odd attempt at wooing a potential lover, breaks the superstitious prohibition of bringing a woman into a mine. When a cave-in occurs, the miner survives but his companion does not. The grandmother of this nameless young woman curses the miners to have more cave-ins should her granddaughter's name be mentioned (Montell 2010, 188-89). The mines can therefore be made *more* dangerous through supernatural force, but they cannot be made consistently safer. The miners telling these ghost stories, of course, seemingly cannot abide by tales where the mine conditions improve; they can only imagine ways in which the mines become even more of an existential threat to them.[5]

Of Musick and Montell's collected ghost stories, only a few times does a revenant appear to address an overt economic need. This is despite the fact that poverty pervades the region of the coalfields, where even after temporary post-war booms, "Almost 60 percent of the housing units in eastern Kentucky lacked indoor plumbing...[and] the median value of such housing was 27.7 percent below the national average" (Eller 2008, 32). When revenants do address economic need, however, it is never with a salvific deux ex machina, but a humble grasp at the most basic financial goals. In the above story of "Big Max," the eponymous miner is met at his door the following day after his discovery of the body. The revenant has returned, and thanks Big Max for finding his body as it will now allow his wife to get the payments the mine operator owes her. In another story, perhaps as sentimental as it is financial, a miner named Horace is killed in a cave-in. His revenant begins to sit on the machinery dressed in white, causing the workers to refuse to work. In one of the few cases of an appearance of an authority in the mines, a foreman is forced to find Horace's watch and return it to his wife so the revenant might find peace (Musick 2004, 15). Perhaps the most common form of a revenant addressing the economic reality of the miners is when ghosts appear in order to help miners work faster and more effectively. Since miners were paid by the tonnage, a revenant who assisted in the loading of coal would not only make the day's work lighter for his living comrade, but make his paycheck increase as well.

Rare is the miner who flees the mines after an experience with the revenant, even if the experience is a negative one. This lack of change in the miner should not be unexpected, however, as the role of the mines in the stories parallel their place in reality, in which economic circumstances are virtually impossible to change. The ghost stories are not optimistic daydreams but, like most folktales, "illustrate a truth or...a moral" (Brunvand 1968, 103). Because of this, the ghost stories of Appalachia do not accept that the coal mines are simply another location in which the narrative occurs. As a location, the coal mine is an agent, a devious one, which consistently acts as the malevolent force in the miners' lives. Unlike other agents of destruction, however, no sense of retribution can be mustered against the mines. They are classism and economic inequality made carbon, and unlike other agents who receive their comeuppance and fall to justice, the mines can only be combatted in small victories that merely delay hardship.

THE MINE GHOSTS REMAIN

The conditions of the coal mines and the prospects of miners have obviously changed since these ghost stories were created and began to circulate. There is perhaps a danger of ossifying both the industry as well as the region by suggesting that ghost stories from early to mid-20th century Appalachia, when animals could still be found in the mines and the unions were still gaining power, continue to represent the region's feelings toward the industry. Clearly, in both underground and surface mines, safety has drastically improved: according to the West Virginia Office of Health, Safety, and Training, the most dangerous year to be in a West Virginia mine was 1925; the safest was 2009.[6] The idea of static images of Appalachia has been the concern of classic scholarly works on the region. In *The Invention of Appalachia*, Allen Batteau (1990) writes that in the 1920s, "A national image…had been created of industrial serfdom and political corruption in the Mountain State. The homonym of 'feud' and 'feudal,' and the imagery of overbearing power intent upon crushing all beneath it, were permanently attached to the state, to the mountaineers, and to the coal industry" (115). Yet the archivist of Musick's manuscripts at Fairmont State University and editor of a journal on West Virginia folklore states that even with diminishing numbers of miners and an increase of surface mining, these stories continue to be passed on to this day (Judy Byers, phone conversation with author, August 8, 2013). What then can be fairly said in 2013 of these ghost stories' representation of the mines?

While mules have long since been evicted from the mines and safety precautions receive much more oversight, the fear and anxiety present in the ghost stories of the coal mines nevertheless remain in the lives of those surrounding the coal fields, whether they work in the mines or not. Mining, especially in its aggressive form of mountaintop removal, continues to force locals into the same ambivalent relationship of indebtedness and resentment toward the industry that the ghost stories reveal. Rebecca Scott writes, "Appalachians are constantly asked to sacrifice for the nation to which they belong, but this belonging is problematic. As prototypical white rural citizens, they are in some senses ideal Americans, but at the same time they are culturally and economically marginalized, and the national/corporate interests they are asked to serve are not necessarily compatible with the survival of their communities and practices" (31). The cynicism in which the miners approached their safety in the ghost stories is reflected in a region's acquiescence to be, in the words of Scott, "a sacrifice zone," which assumes the same lack of choice that a miner has in stories where his safety is dependent upon any number of superstitions. In 2011, a poll of Appalachian voters showed that 50% were against the surface mining practice known as mountaintop removal, with 27% in favor, and 23% unsure (Lake Research Partners and Bellwether Research 2011). Few of these respondents would actually be surface miners themselves, yet the ambivalence is clear. Those who are against mountaintop removal are worried about their health as much as the miners in the ghost stories, though their deaths will not come from cave-ins but toxic levels of arsenic and selenium. And those who are in favor of mountaintop removal are assuredly not in favor of environmental degradation, but prioritize an industry that promises economic sustainability for the region. Art Kirkendall, the County Commissioner of Logan County, West Virginia—at the very heart of coal mining—states, "It's been well documented that every coal mining job creates six to seven additional jobs. This area is rich with direct coal support jobs, people who fix the equipment, sell the supplies, everything the coal companies need, and they pay a decent wage while employing a decent number of people" (Buchsbaum 2010, 56). Even in 2013, with machines rather than mules, and sometimes on the surface rather than in the darkness and absence of the underground mine, the danger, the inescapability, and the promise of success of the coalfields carries on.

These stories have undoubtedly lost some of their verisimilitude to contemporary mining practices, but their persistence in print as well as in oral communication suggests that the relationship between the region and the mines remains what the ghost stories reveal. Until the day, nearly impossible to imagine, when the coal industry does not demand the sacrifice of the region—both of miner and civilian, and of personal safety and environmental integrity—in order to be lifted from poverty, these ghosts of Appalachia will continue to be passed on. In Musick's *Telltale Lilac Bush*, an unusual tale perhaps speaks to this consistent truth within the ghost stories. A miner named Fred Brown, alive at the time of Musick's recording, was possessed by the ghost of an Italian miner who had asphyxiated two years earlier in the mines. After the miner exhibits bizarre behavior, a local woman, Mrs. Rose Cooper, comes to perform an exorcism. When she learns that the ghost is Sam Vincci, a miner she once knew, Mrs. Cooper asks him why he would ever possess another man. The ghost tells her that he wants a mass said in his name, and if this is done, he will leave the possessed's body. Mrs. Cooper obliges and sends word back to Italy for a mass to be told, and the ghost, true to his word, departs. Practically as a postscript, however, the informant states that Mrs. Cooper needed to return because Vincci's ghost had once again possessed Fred Brown's body. There is no rationale for the return of Vincci's ghost. Whatever the Catholic mass was meant to do was simply not enough, and the ghost made his presence felt once more. Mrs. Cooper writes for another mass, and Vincci's ghost departs, with no suggestion as to whether he will return again to be exorcised once more. Perhaps the ghost stories of Appalachia's coal mines are like Vincci's ghost, who will continue to return to the coalfields until their full needs have been met, and the region is not forced to exist in tension between degradation and economic development.

Notes

1. Besides the breadth of their catalogues of ghost stories, I primarily use Musick and Montell because they are trained folklorists. While recent collections of ghost stories are often published by vanity presses or unknown publishing houses, both Musick and Montell were published by the University of Kentucky. Their stories are catalogued according to accepted academic folklore, providing motif listings and available information on the story's provider.
2. "The mines" must be understood as a collective whole, as the vast majority of Musick's and Montell's stories do not refer to a specific mine, or even a specific location.
3. There is no attempt to analyze these stories along lines of type or motif index. This is not to suggest that types and motifs do not serve a very real purpose, but for present purposes they are less relevant than dividing the stories by the presence of the mines rather than any more specific categorization technique.
4. See for instance, Musick's stories, "The Ghost of Jeremy Walker," "Big John's Ghost," and "The Invisible Friend," all of which involve ghosts aiding in the escape or continued labor of the miners.
5. This impossibility of imagining a safer mine can be seen thanks to one of the more bizarre stories of Musick's collection. A German immigrant miner has three children, one of whom was born with the vestige of a bat wing, which the miner had a company doctor remove. Before the child had been born, however, the German miner had killed a "renegade" bat that had torn out his eye.
6. These changes can be overstated as well. For instance, the rise of surface mining (in the form of mountaintop removal) since the 1970s has been an enormous part of the evolution of the industry. Yet according to the West Virginia Office of Miner Safety, Health, and Training, underground mines still double the amount of coal produced by surface mines. Because of surface mining's massive mechanization, nearly three times as many miners still work at underground mines than surface mines. And one year after 2009, the safest on record for West Virginia mines, 29 miners were killed in an explosion in Raleigh County, the worst disaster in 40 years.

Works Cited

Bal, Mieke. 1997. *Narratology: An Introduction to the Theory of Narrative.* Toronto: University of Toronto Press.

Batteau, Alan. 1990. *The Invention of Appalachia.* Tucson, AZ: University of Arizona Press.

Buchsbaum, Lee. 2010. "Falling on Deaf Ears," *Coal Age* 115:48-57.

Brunvand, Jan. 1968. *The Study of American Folklore: An Introduction.* New York: Norton.

Chatman, Seymour. 1980. *Story and Discourse: Narrative Structure in Fiction and Film.* Ithaca, NY: Cornell University Press.

Eller, Ronald. 2008. *Uneven Ground: Appalachia Since 1945.* Lexington, KY: University of Kentucky Press.

Gainer, Patrick. 2008. *Witches, Ghosts, and Signs: Folklore of the Southern Appalachians.* Morgantown, WV: West Virginia University Press.

Guillerman, Michael. 2009. *Face Boss: The Memoir of a Western Kentucky Coal Miner.* Knoxville, TN: University of Tennessee Press.

Lake Research Partners and Bellwether Research. 2011. "Survey Findings on Mountaintop Removal Strip Mining." August 3. Accessed September 26, 2013. http://www.lakeresearch.com/news/mtr/LRP-Bellwether%20Memo%20on%20MTR%20Survey%20Findings.pdf.

Lockard, Duane. 1998. *Coal: A Memoir and Critique.* Richmond, VA: University of Virginia Press.

Long, Priscilla. 1991. *Where the Sun Never Sets: A History of America's Bloody Coal Industry.* St. Paul, MN: Paragon House.

Montell, William Lynwood. 1988. "The Folklorist and History: Three Approaches." In *100 Years of American Folklore Studies: A Conceptual History,* edited by William M. Clements, 61-64. Washington, D.C.: The American Folklore Society.

——. 2000. *Ghosts Across Kentucky.* Lexington, KY: University of Kentucky Press.

——. 1975. *Ghosts Along the Cumberlands: Deathlore in the Kentucky Foothills.* Lexington, KY: University of Kentucky Press.

——. 2001. *Haunted Houses and Family Ghosts of Kentucky.* Lexington, KY: University of Kentucky Press.

——. 2010. *Tales of Kentucky Ghosts.* Lexington, KY: University of Kentucky Press.

Musick, Ruth Ann. 1977. *Coffin Hollow and Other Ghost Tales.* Lexington, KY: University of Kentucky Press.

——. 2004. "Folklore of Coal," *Traditions: A Journal of West Virginia Folk Traditions and Educational Awareness* 9:8-15.

——. 1970. *Green Hills of Magic: West Virginia Folk Tales from Europe.* Lexington, KY: University of Kentucky Press.

——. 1965. *The Telltale Lilac Bush and Other West Virginia Ghost Stories.* Lexington, KY: University of Kentucky Press.

Roberts, Nancy. 1978. *Ghosts of the Southern Mountains and Appalachia.* Columbia, SC: University of South Carolina Press.

Santino, Jack. 1988. "Occupational Ghostlore: Social Context and the Expression of Belief." *The Journal of American Folklore* 101:207-218.

Scott, Rebecca. 2010. *Removing Mountains: Extracting Nature and Identity in the Appalachian Coalfields.* St. Paul, MN: University of Minnesota Press.

West Virginia Office of Miner Health, Safety, and Training. "2011 Calendar Year Statistical Report." Last Modified October 10, 2012. http://www.wvminesafety.org/2011statisticalreport.htm.

E S S A Y

"A City Built Upon its Dead": The Intersection of Past and Present through Ghost Walk Tourism in Savannah, Georgia

by Glenn W. Gentry and Derek H. Alderman

"...the dead can often be more powerful than the living..." (Derrida 1994, 48)

"Haunted places are the only ones people can live in" (deCerteau 1984, 108)

INTRODUCTION

On a warm July evening in 2003, the humidity made the soft streetlamp light hang like Spanish moss from the live oaks. Hearing heavy footfalls and hard breaths, we turn to see a man whom we had met two squares and two hours before while interviewing ghost walk participants before their tours of Savannah's historic district. He completes his awkward jog and puts hands to his knees to catch his breath. A Methodist minister from Mississippi, the gentleman had traveled to Savannah to introduce his young family to his childhood home. As the minister straightens up, his breath returns to a more natural cadence and he says: "I am glad I found you." We smile and wait, letting him catch a few more breaths. The minister continues, "I wanted to tell you why I wanted my kids to take a ghost tour." He looks at us square in the eyes, bright and intense. "If you want to know Savannah you have to know her ghosts." With that the minister gives a nod and turns to return to his family; disappearing back into the night through the oaks, mist and moss.

This memory of the Mississippi preacher returns to us often, singular in occurrence but not in message. Ghost experiences, or aspirations of them, play an important part in the motivations and experiences of the many ghost walk tour participants who have spoken to us over the years. In 2003, we undertook a major study of Savannah walking ghost tours, leading to interviews with tour guides from a number of companies and a survey of over a thousand tourists participating in a ghost walk (see Gentry, 2007). Our findings and observations led us to recognize the important role that ghosts play in people's interactions with Savannah as a place. Ghosts, for some of these participants, shape the perceived landscape. The haunted aspects of the city resonate with residents as well as visitors, representing more than a mere tourist gimmick. As some locals responded to the question that night, *do you believe in ghosts?* "We don't not believe...we've got one."

When visiting and touring Savannah, Georgia, it does not take long before you hear someone proclaim that it is "a city is built upon its dead." The phrase often references the yellow fever epidemic of 1854, which claimed six percent of Savannah's population and forced city authorities to dig mass graves beyond the public cemetery, as well as supposedly "secret" tunnels that run underneath the city where yellow fever sufferers are reported to have been herded, left, and de facto buried. Other accounts stress how public officials relocated an early burial ground for African slaves to make room for the expansion of housing in Savannah, although it is often said that the bodies in many unmarked or poorly marked graves were never moved. The "fact" that more bodies are buried in the Colonial Park cemetery than there is room for is a popular item that Savannah tour guides make note of, often pointing out that the cemetery's original footprint includes the surrounding roads. Some former cemeteries are far from hidden. At the intersection of Bull Street and Oglethorpe Avenue stands the Jewish Cemetery Memorial, marking the city's original Jewish cemetery and now a median between two major streets in the historic district. Not far away on a building at the southwest corner of Reynolds Square is where another "found" cemetery is marked. Not surprisingly, it is said that the dead lie beneath the busy streets, parks, and homes of the coastal city's historic district. Walking on graves is unavoidable in Savannah. Not left to the past, and refusing to be forgotten, these abandoned souls supposedly haunt Savannah, to such a large degree that the city has become a popular destination for paranormal researchers and ghost hunters.

No city in the American South has cornered the market on death and tragic epidemics. Arguably, many places can recount tales of paving over graves in the name of urban development, especially the graves of people with relatively little power within their communities. Every city is built upon its dead, literally, in terms of the way cities occupy and appropriate the spaces of the nonliving in order to live. Yet, cities also engage death more deeply by remembering (or forgetting) the dead and constructing the social meaning of earlier generations in order to make sense of the present. In this sense, all cities are built upon their dead because they are repositories of memory and sites for enacting certain identifications with the past, whether in terms of creating public memorials or monuments, or through more ghostly narrations and interactions. It is in the latter sense that a study of Savannah is significant.

While being built upon the dead is not unique to one city, Savannah has done more than most urban areas to retell and even market its history of death, ghosts, and the macabre. The widely successful book and film *Midnight in the Garden of Good and Evil* did much to put Savannah on the map in the 1990s as a haunted place as well as a city of murder, voodoo, and eccentricity. Joining what has become the global phenomenon of dark tourism, Savannah now hosts numerous ghost tours in which visitors are led through the streets, neighborhoods, and squares of the historic district by guides telling stories of the supernatural. While one can take these ghost tours in vans, trolley cars, horse-drawn buggies, or even in hearses, many visitors elect to participate in a walking tour. Death has clearly been made into a commodity in Savannah, and the city's economy continues to build heavily upon its dead, but in ways that remember rather than forget the departed. Savannah's dead are active in how the city is understood by visitors and locals alike.

In addition to entertaining and educating the public, Savannah's death-related tours actively construct the identity of Savannah, shaping the sense of place of tourists and residents and the way they interpret and navigate the urban terrain. Beyond this, at least for some, Savannah's death-related tours become a site of self-exploration, affirmation and community. The purpose of this essay is to delve into Savannah's ghost tourism industry, particular walking tours, in order to understand the role of ghosts, ghost-tourism, and ghost tour providers and participants to show how Savannah is represented, experienced, developed, negotiated and even debated.

SAVANNAH IN *MIDNIGHT IN THE GARDEN OF GOOD AND EVIL*

Savannah, Georgia is nestled up against the Savannah River and is a short drive from the Atlantic Ocean. The city is the site of the earliest settlement of the Colony of Georgia, founded in 1733 by James Edward Olgethrope (Russel et al. 1992). Despite its age, the town has remained insular throughout most of its history. The "State of Chatham" has been content with itself, developing a rich local culture spiced by a colorful and traumatic history. An important port on the eastern coast of the United States, the city of Savannah has survived the Burning of Georgia by Sherman (the town was presented to President Lincoln as a Christmas gift), three major fires, and numerous epidemics. The legacy of war, slavery and death has left its mark on this congenial city, leading to the title "America's Most Haunted City" (Marino 2002), an appellation that can be found on tourist brochures and bumper stickers.

Despite a history of insular tendencies, tourism is an increasingly important component of Savannah's economy, contributing 12.1 million visitors and $1.95 billion in tourism spending in 2011 (Van Brimmer 2012). These 2011 figures represent a 6% increase in visitors and a 15% increase in spending as compared to 2010. There are several factors that explain the growth of tourism in Savannah—from the wholesale redevelopment and preservation of the city's downtown by SCAD (Savannah College of Art and Design) beginning in the 1980s to the more recent rise to stardom of Paula Deen. The owner of Savannah's Lady & Sons restaurant, Deen was a Food Network star until pulled from the air after she acknowledged using racial slurs in the past. However, the first major boom in Savannah tourism and ghost tourism specifically came with the 1994 release of John Berendt's nonfiction book, *Midnight in the Garden of Good and Evil*. "The Book," as it is referred to by locals, became a "place-defining" piece of literature for Savannah and significantly raised public interest in the once hidden city.

Midnight in the Garden of Good and Evil, and the subsequent 1997 movie by the same name, which was directed by Clint Eastwood and filmed on location in Savannah, contributed to the representation of the city as a site of beauty, mystery and darkness. "The Book" retells the story of the 1981 murder of "redneck gigolo" Danny Hansford and the legal trials of his accused murderer, wealthy antiques dealer Jim Williams—all while writing vignettes about Savannah's unique social life and history, including its graveyards. Perhaps the most memorable characters of the book and movie are Minerva, the voodoo doctor employed by Jim Williams to curse the prosecutor of his case and other enemies, and the Lady Chablis, a local drag queen who does his/her part to steal the show. *Midnight* is very much a narrative about death: a tale of not just Hansford's shooting but also Savannah's broader fascination with and fixation on death. Berendt discovered this fixation on the southern gothic when talking with many locals. For instance, he quotes Mary Harty as saying: "The dead are very much with us in Savannah.... Everywhere you look there is a reminder of things that were, people who lived. We are keenly aware of our past" (Berendt 1999, 31).

"The Book" spent a record 216 weeks on the *New York Times* Best Seller List. Its popularity and the resulting film drove an increase in tourism that is still felt in Savannah today. The mass media has long been important in constructing a sense of place, relaying a range of cultural meanings and values to those who were unable to travel to locales and sometimes motivating people to visit those very locations (Squire 1994). Place images in literature and other forms of media, such as film, are recognized as playing a pivotal role in the development and definition of places (Hanna 1996). The appearance of a location within a novel or a movie has had a significant influence on travel to many places, at times shifting the local economy to one that is more tourism-based and influencing the material construction of destinations (Squire 1994; Hanna 1996; Herbert 1996 2001; Riley, Baker, and Van Doren, 1998; Kim and Richardson 2003; Inglis and Holmes 2003). This was especially the case with *Midnight*, which helped spur the physical renovation and revitalization of the downtown and riverfront areas, an increase in the number of bed and breakfast accommodations in the historic district, and the creation of theme-related memorabilia shops and organized tours of places from the book and film, including ghost walk tours.

It is important, we believe, that the events highlighted in *Midnight* are relatively recent in occurrence. The "heritage" is fresh and many of the places are relatively unchanged since the original events occurred. Tourists come to see the actual locations of the story and murder in very much the same state as mentioned in Berendt's book and as portrayed in Eastwood's film. The tourist not only seeks these places, but also wishes to experience the sense of mystery is that supposedly connected with those places. Indeed, some of the personalities and locations in *Midnight in the Garden of Good and Evil*, especially Jim Williams' homes, have become important stops along ghost walks. This is very much the case with the Mercer House, William's most famous residence and the location of the Hansford shooting. Ghost tourists are also often taken to another house owned by the antiques dealer and house restorer, the Hampton Lillibridge House, the scene of several tragic deaths and supposedly the most haunted house in Savannah. When paranormal activity scared off workers and slowed the house's renovation, Williams arranged to have the structure exorcised, but this proved unsuccessful. It was these experiences with the Hampton Lillibridge House that supposedly inspired Williams' interest in psychic phenomena and voodoo (Ramsland 2013).

While *Midnight* and the story of Jim Williams remains an important part of ghost tourism in Savannah, these tours are by no means limited to sites associated with "the Book," and they cover more ground—historically and geographically—allowing the public access to a larger portion of the city's landscape, image, and historical narrative. And while ghost tourism has an especially popular place in Savannah, such tourism is found across the South (including in nearby Charleston, SC), the U.S., and the globe, as tourist destinations change the way they deal with and talk about trauma, death and the past.

DARK AND GHOST TOURISM

Within the tourism industry, there is a growing recognition that death and disaster are saleable commodities that can be marketed (Ruane 2004). Places are thus promoting the "darker" or more underground aspects of their history as a way of offering a greater selection of unique tourism experiences. Termed "dark tourism," this form of tourism represents a "fundamental shift in the way in which death, disaster and atrocity are being handled by those who offer associated tourism" (Lennon and Foley 2000, 3). Dark tourism destinations feed a growing public fascination with death and are often used to encourage somber reflection and grief about tragic aspects of history as well as entertainment and voyeurism.

Dark attractions lie along a "fluid and dynamic spectrum of intensity" in terms of design and purpose that is just beginning to be categorized typologically (Philip 2006, 145). Traditionally sites of tragedy have a long history as popular tourism destinations (Foote 1997). As Seaton comments: "Death is the one heritage that everyone shares and it has been an element of tourism longer than any other form of heritage" (Seaton 1996, 234). Familiar sites of dark tourism include the Tower of London, Taj Mahal, the catacombs of Rome and Paris, battlefields, the graves of famous people, and now even the devastation of Hurricane Katrina along the U.S. Gulf Coast.

Previous studies of dark tourism have focused on what Edensor (2000, 2001) has called "enclavic spaces," attractions that tend to place strict boundaries around the movements and interpretations of tourists (Inglis and Holmes 2003; Strange and Kempa 2003). These places have distinct (or at least understood) entrances and exits that separate them from the public space beyond the bounds of the tourist site and regulate the tourists' experience, instilling visitors with a shared sense of history and tragedy while avoiding conflicting images and messages from the outside world. To date, most studies of dark tourism have tended to focus on places with these clearly demarcated boundaries (Strange and Kempa 2003; Inglis and Holmes 2003).

Ghost-walk tours, as exemplified in Savannah, represent an interesting and significant variation in which dark tourism takes place in open, heterogeneous spaces (Edensor 2000, 2001), allowing us to expand our understanding of the spatial uniqueness of this emerging form of tourism. Rather than traveling to enclavic sites of known "darkness," the ghost-walk tour introduces representations of darkness into dynamic everyday spaces, thus adding elements of surprise, uncontrollability, and potential controversy to the urban heritage experience.

The structure of ghost tours vary, but generally the tour guide escorts a tour group to various sites while narrating stories of ghosts, hauntings and previously forgotten or unpleasant aspects of the locations. The degree of "darkness" within these tours varies, with some operators and guides attaching parental advisories to their tours while, in other instances, the title of "ghost tour" is simply window dressing for a normal history tour conducted at night. In general, however, most ghost tours fall somewhere in between.

In addition to its heterogeneous spatial nature, ghost walk tours differ from other forms of dark tourism in another important way. While traditional dark tourism focuses intently on sites associated with turmoil, tragedy, and suffering, much ghost walk tourism is geared more toward the paranormal and the supernatural. For many tour participants, ghost tourism is a source of entertainment, and they are often lighthearted compared to the topics they cover (Seeman 2002; Inglis and Holmes 2003; Ruane 2004). This does not, however, reduce ghost tourism to a culturally and historically insignificant practice. Presenting tragedy in a light-hearted manner does not "preclude the presentation of counter-hegemonic stories or tales of injustice" (Strange and Kempa 2003, 387). In the words of Seeman (2002):

Compared with most heritage tourism, ghost tours—by turns campy and didactic—offer visitors unblinking and, no doubt, at times unwelcome views of the skeletons in the closet of early American history: slave coffles, Indian massacres, debtors' prisons, and the sundry other sad and sorry fates of people you might expect would want to haunt America's cities.

Thus, ghost walk tourism differs greatly from other forms of dark tourism, not in failing to present atrocities but through a mixture of humor and poignant reflection and juxtaposition with the everyday.

Ghost walk tourism therefore offers an alternative both to traditional dark tourism and more standard tourism. Indeed, scholars such as Holloway (2010) have documented the varying ghost tourism experiences available in England. One attraction that ghost tours boast is revealing the dark or hidden aspects of a place, the back stage of historic sites, and the dirty laundry of a city's history. Ghost tourism allows places to be explored and lived beyond the glossy tourist ads and crafted tourism facades. Of course, there is no guarantee that ghost tours always challenge conventional historical narratives. Tiya Miles illustrates this point well in this issue when she exposes how the ghost tours of Savannah's Sorrel-Weed House continue to present the past in racialized and gendered ways even as they claim to offer the tourist a different experience with the past. In other cases, however, ghost tourism adds depth to the tourist experience, and central to this is the airing of ghosts, of giving them presence and agency in how place is known and its memories created and explored.

Some would argue the ghosts are, in fact, necessary to fully experience places. Ghost stories, like folklore, are one way the past works to define the present. On this point, Bell claims that "the rise of the heritage industry is that we are coming to miss our old ghosts, to resist the loss of sentimental and social connection to place and thus, ultimately, to ourselves—and our selves" (Bell 1997, 830). While Bell makes clear that he is speaking more metaphorically than as one who believes in ghosts, he makes a powerful case for ghosts in the landscape. He states that ghosts in the landscape are a result of social interactions with space, making abstract space into meaningful place. Bell (1997, 816) argues that ghosts are:

> central [to] the social experience of the physical world, the phenomenology of the environment. Such experience arises in part from the social relations of memory, and the memory of social relations. But the ghosts of place should not be reduced to mere memories, collective or individual. To do so would be to overlook the spirited and live quality of their presence, and their stubborn rootedness in particular places.

Karen Till (2005) and Steve Pile (2005), agree, contending that landscapes are haunted with collective memories expressed in the present and these memories carry with them both a sense of the past as well as a sense for the future. Cities are "places of memory... created by individuals and social groups to give a shape to felt absences, fears, and desires that haunt contemporary society" (Till 2005, 9). Memory and meaning are both fixed and unfixed, embodied in physical structures as well as people. Pile (2005) encourages us to approach the meaning of heritage sites from multiple directions and in ways that may challenge our modern conceptions of urban spaces. This includes ideas of the supernatural, and he reminds us that we do not have to believe in ghosts for them to exist for others.

Although ghosts are often first treated as historical, remnants of times past, it is also necessary to consider ghosts as in the present and having a presence, as very much active participants in the experience, representation and memories of place. This is perhaps a controversial idea, yet it was the central topic of heated debate in Savannah in 2003, which will be explored later in this paper.

Ghost walk tourism, at least from what we have seen in Savannah, differs from other types of dark tourism and even other types of heritage tourism in how memories, especially those of some tour participants, are performed. Performance here is not just how tour guides act and the costumes they wear. Rather, the term "performance" also encompasses the bodily reenactment and narration of memory. For many ghost tour participants, ghost tours are an intersection of their own ghostly encounters brought forth for sharing and validation. There can be a swapping of ghost stories before the tour. In some cases that we have observed, tour participants have actually led part of the tours and woven their own stories into the tour narrative. In this case, the ghost tour is not simply a scripted recounting of history, but rather an active performance of memory by tour guides, tour participants, and even at times, locals met along the way. For example, on one tour Glenn attended, a homeowner confessed of an exorcism performed by an inebriated priest who rented a room in the house. Ghosts in Savannah are a dynamic part of the ghost tour experience and they "appear" from multiple sources and sites. Ghosts, while perhaps unexpected (though not to say unsought), are present center-stage within Savannah.

Ghost Walks in Savannah

The publication in 1984 of *Savannah Spectres and Other Strange Tales* by Margaret DeBolt marks the official beginning of ghost tourism in Savannah, Georgia. The book retells stories of ghosts and local hauntings as reported and investigated by the author and her psychic assistant, although DeBolt took care not to reveal the locations of the hauntings in order to protect her sources. While *Savannah Spectres* is not a ready guide for visitors wishing to explore the haunted landscape of Savannah, the book is the basis of several ghost walk tours currently operating in the city. As we mentioned earlier, however, ghost tourism flourished in earnest with the release of John Berendt's *Midnight in the Garden of Good and Evil* (Wittish 2002). Even though tourism related to "The Book," and later the film adaptation, peaked in 1998 (Bynum 2004), ghost tourism continued to increase in popularity. The sustainability of Savannah's ghost tourism can be explained, in part, by a trend in television programming toward promoting ghost tourism nationally. The Discovery Channel has even published a book entitled *Haunted Holidays*, which includes information on Savannah and thirteen other cities in the United States. We would suggest, however, that the continuing allure of ghost walk tourism in Savannah is also linked to the way these tours share space with the dead and open up alternative ways of navigating the city.

Ghost walk tours travel through many parts of the historic district of Savannah, generally focusing on the squares in the oldest part of the city. James Edward Oglethorpe, the city's founder, originally designed Savannah's squares in 1733 for quick defense, intending each square to have mixed use, including governmental offices, religious buildings, business and private housing (de Vorsey 2012). Many of the squares maintain a mixed use today, although some have acquired a more business or residential character. The squares are heterogeneous spaces for visitors and locals alike. The squares help facilitate pedestrian travel, are thoroughfares for visitors and locals walking the city, and thus serve as an ideal space for the intersection of the past and present through a ghost tour. The squares are also destinations, with memorials, large oak trees and green space for public enjoyment. The multiple sites (and sights) in the squares and the ample park benches support a leisurely pace, and tourists to Savannah often become familiar with the city's squares early during their visit.

Many of the ghost walk tours use the squares as a starting point. The tours generally begin with a brief explanation of Savannah and some of the more curious habits of the locals. Plagued through the course of its history by war, fire and disease, and known as a site of piracy and slavery, Savannah is not short on stories of mystery, murder, disaster and atrocity. After the tour guides place Savannah within a broader cultural and historical context, the ghost walk begins in earnest. Some ghost walk tour guides utilize books on the subject; others perform their own investigations, using local libraries, archives and residents as sources. Another source for stories, utilized by nearly all tour guides that we have interviewed, are previous tour participants. Obviously, these participants are new visitors to the city, but they can also include some locals and even previous residents turned tourists.

Over the course of ghost walk tours, tour participants will often travel through the very same streets they have traversed on other tours and during their own exploration of the city. Many of the tour groups will visit popular squares full of other tourists and locals. Ghost walk tour guides, however, introduce tour participants to the "invisible" landscape within Savannah. Using a mixture of stories and recorded historical facts, the ghost walk tour guide engages in an important creation of place and memory. Savannah's guides point out long since paved and planted over graveyards, the past living quarters of slaves (more commonly referred to as "carriage houses"), and the location of crimes and other tragedies where ghosts are said to haunt. Often there is little or no evidence available for the tour participant to have discerned these occurrences from the landscape. The Colonial Park Cemetery, a popular stop on Savannah's ghost tours, is identified with many hauntings, none more harrowing than the story of Rene Asche Rondolier. A tall and hideous figure, Rondolier was thought to have brutally killed two young girls and dumped their bodies in Colonial Park. A Savannah mob captured and lynched the supposed killer in the surrounding swamps, although locals suggested that the ghost of Rondolier was responsible for later victims found in the Colonial Park Cemetery. The re-telling of the Rondolier tale, the facts and dates of which can vary from tour guide to tour guide, offers a place narrative that makes visible a city's fears, discrimination, and vigilantism and re-identifies Colonial Park as "Rene's Playground."

Ghost walk tour guides thus offer access to hidden and unseen aspects of Savannah's landscape and local color. This can, and often does, challenge the dominant and more visible place images used in promoting Savannah. History is important to Savannah's tourism industry. The City of Savannah requires all tour guides to pass an extensive test on local history before receiving a tour guide license. Stories and images communicated through ghost tourism, however, often fall outside the realm of 'documented' history, leaving tour guides at great liberty to tell unregulated historical and place narratives. Indeed, one of the most established of Savannah's ghost walk tour guides, Shannon Scott, provides the following disclaimer on the web page advertising his ghost-walk tour: "Each story teller reserves the right to pursue their own story telling paths."

While standard historical tours tend to follow well-established paths and major routes, the ghost walk tour often tries to introduce visitors to alternative views and stories of the city, blurring the boundaries between public and private spaces as well as tourist and non-tourist places. Indeed, in Savannah, the ability of ghost walks to engage in heterogeneous space increases the likelihood of conflict because they often pass through the territory and activity spaces of local residents. Rather than relegating ghosts and hauntings to abandoned places: prisons, old hospitals and houses outside of town—places that are socially and often physically distant—ghost walk tourism defies this distance by placing stories of ghosts and dark history along the same streets and in the same buildings walked, visited and, at times, occupied by locals and tourists.

Ghost-walk tours in particular accentuate the geographically dynamic and potentially unbound nature of dark tourism. Geography, rather than chronology, determines tour paths (Seeman 2002), in the attempt to maximize the amount of storytelling in a limited amount of travel time. Walking removes the tourist from physical and emotional shelters and forces the engagement of place through ambulation. Paul Adams (2001) expanding on Yi-Fu Tuan's (1974) theory on walking, states the "multisensory apprehension of one's surroundings is qualitatively different than vision or mediated visions—it is a more profound mode of experiencing place." Adams takes the idea further by stating that walking can lead to a greater sense of place than bus or car travel alone. "Habituation to a 'motorized metal box' reduces one's environment to a visual tableau" leading the occupant to be "entirely separate from his or her surroundings" (Adams 2001, 189). By walking, the participant is engaged in the multisensory experience of potential hauntings, sudden chilled air and rotten smells, mixed with the timbre of the tour guide's voice. A waitress "interviewed" while Glenn was getting a burger in Savannah spoke about the difference between a walking and riding tour. The waitress said she could not go on a walking tour, despite the fact she walked by many of the haunted sites on her way between work and home. She needed glass, something to separate her from the stories, from the possibility of ghosts. The waitress was so moved by the discussion, she shook when confronting the possibility of ghosts existing around her. The separation from, or presence near, is important in understanding the ghost walk experience as well as the politics around them, which we will return to soon.

Storytelling is central to the role of the tour guide in Savannah ghost walks. Walking tours enable greater elaboration because the possibility to dally at particular sites, and the skipping of later sites, leads to an individuality of each tour. In some instances, tour paths and stories told are in part due to the preference of the guide and in part guided by reactions of the group. Many sites in Savannah have multiple stories, each with multiple versions attached to them. The guide then selects from the possible tales to unveil a picture of Savannah meant to entertain, enlighten and titillate the tour participants. Storytelling, however, is not for the tour guide alone, for as we mentioned before tourists often become active participants as authors and editors of stories presented on the ghost tour, by adding their stories from other places and sometimes even their experiences in Savannah. Ghost-walk tours fill spaces with stories, tales and legends, enabling the tour participant to more fully inhabit the landscape, rather than just pass through it.

Ghost tourism positions ghosts not as something lost to the past but as active agents of the present. Ghosts become present as possible sights (tour guides tell visitors that they may very well see a ghost) and as sites of discussion and commonality for those who believe in and/or have experience with ghosts. This is an important role for ghosts during the tour but not the only. Ghosts also become present in how place is understood and marketed; they gain a politics, a power. This can be seen by looking at the controversy over ghost tours in Savannah, beginning in the spring of 2003. While much of it appears to be about how the ghost tours were held, at the core it was a debate over the expansion of ghost tours beyond the tourist times and spaces. It can be seen as an attempt to limit the (possible) presence of ghosts in Savannah and how the city's heritage is currently understood and represented. Graham, following Lowenthal, states that heritage is the "contemporary use of the past, and if its meanings are defined in the present, then we create the heritage that we require and manage it for a range of purposes defined by the needs and demands of our present societies"(Graham 2002). The argument is then whether or not ghosts are needed in Savannah.

TELLING THE STORY OF GHOST TOURISM IN SAVANNAH I: THE POLITICS

Controversy arose over ghost walk tours in the spring of 2003 when a complaint was filed by a Tourism Advisory Committee (TAC) member who lives in a neighborhood frequented by tours in Savannah. He drafted regulations for walking tours to address problems he felt these tours created. According to him "walking tours near his home create unsafe situations with tourists wandering into the streets" with tours that "run [operate] too late." The TAC member also believed that tourism in Savannah was outgrowing the city. "It's the 800 lb. canary—it does whatever it wants," said the complainant. "It's not a bad thing, but how many tourists come past your house all day (before) it becomes a theme park?" (Murdock 2003a). His proposed regulations would have excluded tours from some of the historic neighborhoods located near downtown Savannah, not allowing more than one tour group at a time in a square, limiting tour sizes, and not allowing walking tours to operate after a set time (some suggested as early as 8 p.m.). These regulations were selective, targeting walking tours but not affecting motorized tours that travel over the same streets and visit some of the same locations (Murdock 2003a). This involved restricting access to the most infamous and popular streets on ghost-walk tours.

Other TAC members did not perceive walking tours in the same negative light and were less willing to impose regulations, preferring self-regulation among the tours rather than city control. Some local people found the tourist crowds at night "reassuring," "encouraging" and "positive," for they felt more people on the streets at night made them safer for walkers and residents (Murdock 2003a). Shannon Scott, one of the most vocal and active ghost-walk tour guides involved in the debate, was against any additional regulation. He was quoted as saying:

> It's [Savannah] not Disneyland, and it's not Hilton Head, gated and elitist...But are we going to dunk Savannah in formaldehyde and charge admission or are we going to allow Savannah to be a city that can be enjoyed in real time—and have people not leave when the museums close?...Stories are like energy that open the neighborhood and bring these buildings alive. (Murdock 2003a)

Other guides questioned the ability of the city to enforce proposed regulations, especially the one tour group per square rule. Other obstacles included large groups of conventioneer and Girls Scouts (who have their national headquarters and founder's home in Savannah) who did not like being broken up into smaller groups. One of the biggest arguments against the regulations was the popularity of midnight tours. In this respect, limiting the time tours could be offered would take money away from the ghost-walk tour guides (Murdock 2003a).

The proposed regulations drew immediate public and media response. In the "City Talk" section of the *Savannah Morning News*, journalist Bill Dawers addressed the regulations in terms of safety, commenting that: "There hasn't always been a consensus about how best to address downtown crime. But there's one thing everyone seems to agree on: busy streets are safe streets"(Dawers 2003). Dawers talked about the reassuring feeling of seeing a tour group approach as he stood alone in a darkened square at 10 p.m. one evening. "The tour guide was soft-spoken and the group moved as quietly as the ghosts it was seeking." Dawers (2003) then turned his attention to the walking tour controversy.

> It's easy to understand why some downtown residents are concerned about the number of nighttime tours. Longtime residents are still adjusting to Savannah's relatively new designation as a tourist mecca and college town. The recent controversy about limiting walking tours, and banning them from certain streets after a certain hour, seems to us…to be another example of local residents and government trying to limit otherwise legal activity.

Only one ghost-walk tour was featured in the Dawers' article by name, Shannon Scott's Sixth Sense Tour. Scott would be quoted later in an article related to safety, but this time about street lighting. One of the issues exposed by the walking tour regulation controversy was the lack of a tourism office in Savannah (Bell 2003). Scott again tried to affect public opinion. He supported the creation of such an office, speaking as a representative of the Savannah Walking Tour Association (Bell 2003). In a newspaper article, Scott is quoted as saying, "If we are going to keep people in love with this place, a tourism office could show that there is a strong arm for tourism in Savannah" (Murdock 2003b).

In a letter to the editor printed on June 19, 2003 entitled "City should be helping local tourist industry, not hindering its success," Scott sought to combine all the issues into a single and understandable package (Murdock 2003a). He also introduced himself to the public, establishing his history in Savannah, the legitimacy of ghost walking tours, and his vision of how the city's tourism industry should be constructed and regulated.

Scott implored the local media to keep the issue alive and to prevent policy decisions from being made without the input of local tour guides. Ironically, the day following Scott's letter to the editor, a city-led meeting was held to discuss trial regulations for walking tours. The meeting and regulations were immediately controversial. Rather than the meeting serving as an open forum, it was used to disseminate guidelines to the tour guides without discussion. "We were handed this," said David Pinckney, a guide with Coastal Tours, shaking a paper with the guidelines. "They said it was a workshop, but they didn't do that. They give us this paper and said that's all we are going to do" (Murdock 2003c).

The following week, the city's newspaper again reported about ghost tours, this time not about the controversy, but of the tours' increasing popularity and their usefulness in successfully in selling Savannah (Murdock 2003d). During this same period, Shannon Scott was in the news for openly resisting the trial walking tour guidelines. In an editorial letter, an angry citizen commented:

Shannon Scott of Sixth Sense says his company choose [sic] not to participate in the voluntary regulations. If he's trying to force the city into turning the voluntary guidelines into mandatory law, he's doing a good job with that cavalier attitude. (Editorial in *Savannah Morning News* 2003a)

While the commentary predicted dire results for Scott's action, it did not prove to be the case. This description does not tell the case entirely. Sixth Sense is the only tour company operating in the more southern part of the historic district. His tour did not travel in the restricted areas. The operating time limit was the most important factor, considering Scott operates one of the few midnight ghost-walk tours in Savannah.

By early August of 2003, public support for ghost-walk tours and the visible opposition from guides, especially Scott, had forced a solution to be reached in dealing with the regulation of walking tours. After a meeting with "plenty of applause" and "people patting each other on the back," city officials and tour companies were able to come to agreement on what regulations were needed. This agreement was a product of several factors, including the support of some municipal leaders. Savannah's mayor came out in favor of tourism at the meeting, reminding attendees, "Tourism is a good money-making industry and I want to keep tourists coming here…people who are complaining about tourists need to realize they help keep their property taxes down" (Murdock 2003d).

At the same time, however, ghost tour guides such as Scott could certainly take some credit for the negotiated agreement, even beyond the political pressure they exerted through the media and the ignoring of the trial regulations. According to Jim Gilliamsen, parking services coordinator, "the city took undercover tours to get a first-hand perspective" on the issue when the controversy over ghost walk tourism escalated. The city's judgment, according to him, was that "walking tour groups are managing their businesses" (Murdock 2003d).

Three major changes to walking tours resulted from the meeting between the city and tour companies. The first eliminated restrictions on operating hours for walking tours. The second change defined when a motorized tour became a walking tour and the responsibilities therein. The last change limited the area of minimal tour guide use to two residential blocks in the most controversial zone. Beyond the regulations was the acknowledgement that Savannah's image needs to be beyond those as defined by an individual or two, and that ghosts have a place up front in the various ways Savannah has become imaged to others.

TELLING THE STORY OF GHOST-TOURISM IN SAVANNAH II: THE STORYTELLING

As owner and guide of Sixth Sense Savannah, Shannon Scott has played an active role in the development and popularity of ghost tourism in the city. Scott also became a public face for ghost tourism at this time through letters to the editor in the local newspaper and as a frequent target for journalists and critics of ghost tours during in the events of 2003. While Scott was not alone in actions by tour guides and owners during the events of 2003, he was the most visible player in a loose association of ghost tour guides who united to protect their economic and cultural stake in saying how Savannah's tourist places should be constructed, represented, and ultimately regulated. Scott was seen as controversial not only to the opposing side, but also within the tour guide ranks. In fact, many guides we have spoken with believed that the events of 2003 were directly tied to a few politically powerful citizens within Savannah attempting to close down Scott's tour. Shannon Scott was kind enough to share with us his philosophy of telling the ghost stories of Savannah. This affords us the chance to look further into the role of the ghost story in ghost tourism, not just those told by guides, but also by tour participants, alluding to the role of performing memory and narrative in understanding ghosts and dark tourism.

Scott attempts to "paint" Savannah to ghost tour participants as something more than just the "Old South" but also as "its own place with its own definite ways…attempting to keep that intact but also rounding out that meaning by presenting companion viewpoints." According to him, he offers an "individual interpretation of its history, current culture and aesthetic atmosphere" (interviews with Scott 2003). Interpretation and negotiation of place are important to Scott, an aspect of tour guiding that he feels separates him from other, more conventional tour guides. He finds many other tours "classically antiquarian" with a focus on facts and accepted history. For Scott, it is the active reinterpretation of the facts that helps develop a sense of place at the personal, rather than marketed, level. A former student of the Savannah College of Art and Design, Scott suggests that his tours are "a bit like looking at art but also about returning to the painting at different times and seeing something new. I think for many historians and locals it is about fighting to see things only one way and unfortunately never adding anything that is new, which is sad seeing that history itself [e]volves as we do." Scott actively promotes the understanding of an evolving history through both reinterpretations of standard history but also by introducing tour participants to aspects of Savannah they would not receive on other, non-ghost walk tours and travels through the city (Scott interviews 2003).

While Scott uses art as his metaphor for presenting and representing Savannah, his desire to introduce tour participants to a richer, rather than just different, presentation of Savannah is consistent with the attitudes held by other ghost-walk tour guides.
Walking and storytelling combine to make an important medium for presenting Savannah to tour participants. Ghost-walk guides agree that walking is paramount for the development of storytelling and provides a medium in which the oral tradition is best shared. According to Scott, when walking "storytelling [is] at its height…[where] a deeper relationship between the guide and the city is at hand." Walking allows for a different experience of place, and since most ghost tours occur after dark, a different atmosphere as well. Walking provides "shadowy lanes and corners of town…close-up perceptions of buildings and people at night…a town after hours, if you will." For Scott, storytelling is the "connection and affirmation" of person to place and person with belief. Storytelling takes a primary role exemplified through the medium of walking. Scott attempts to combine walking and storytelling to separate his tour from other tours by providing the "psyche" of Savannah. This goal then separates him, and potentially other ghost-walk tour guides, from guides of other types of tours.

> Ghost tour guides can be like a town's psychoanalyst if you will. You're often taking people into what's shaped the place by way of tragedy: Death the inevitable. You're also getting personal gossip and dirt on the history of the place.

Scott believes that the investigation into the often hidden and secret places in Savannah mirrors the individual's desire to investigate one's own being. The journey through Savannah potentially satisfies, though perhaps only briefly, the tour participant's search for an "Other" to facilitate self-discovery. In other words, by exploring and directly engaging Savannah's ghostly landscape, people search for narratives that work to frame their place within a broader world. It is here that Scott stresses the role of storytelling: "Storytelling is connection and affirmation. It's a mental and conceptual adventure." In this way Scott views ghost-walk tourism as not only a way to gain a greater sense of place, where place is defined as a physical location, but also place as defined socially (see Tuan 1974).

While many ghost-walk tour guides do not grant their tours such analytical powers, some long-time ghost walk tour guides point out a connection between their tours and questions about an afterlife. The more veteran guides such as Scott recognize that tour participants seek more from their tours than just entertainment. Here we can see how ghost stories broaden and enrich the heritage landscape, and for some, do more intimate work in understanding their own memories. Memories, as we will see, are not merely moments of the past revisited, but also moments of the present. In this way ghosts and their stories in Savannah, created there or brought in by others, are not relegated to history but are actors in the present.

CONCLUSION

In July and October of 2003, we conducted research on Savannah's ghost walk tourism, focusing of four of the city's most popular and oldest tours at the time. Surveys were administered to 411 tourist groups as they waited to disembark on walking tours from several of Savannah's famous public squares. The number one question asked of us during our surveying of ghost tourists was "Do you believe in ghosts?" Generally, this occurred right after asking them the same question. Our answer did not waiver and went something like the following "It does not matter if I believe, what is important is that others do." Steve Pile (2005) encourages such an approach in *Real Cities*. He considers the very real presence of alternative beliefs through an investigation of dreams, magic, vampires, witches, and ghosts in urban spaces. Pile is not encouraging us to believe but pointing out that our beliefs (and our memories) are not needed for these beliefs (and others' memories) to exist in city spaces.

The existence of ghosts as subjects in literature, fodder for TV and movie entertainment, and as subjects of tourism is beyond doubt. So, too, they are real for those who claim to have experienced them. Though not in the majority, roughly 20 to 25% of the participants in ghost walk tours we surveyed said they were taking the tour to see ghosts and/or learn about supernatural events. That number however sells short the belief in the possibility of ghosts for tour participants. Just over half of the tourists we interviewed stated they believe in ghosts (usually followed with a story about their own encounters with ghosts) and even more tourists said they were open to the possibility of the existence of ghosts. The more veteran ghost walk guides say that questions about an afterlife were common among tour takers along with the sharing of participants' own supernatural experiences. For some participants then, the ghost tour becomes a safe space of sharing and validation, perhaps even hope and reaffirmation. Guide Shannon Scott (2003) put it this way:

People are definitely seeking affirmation for their own experiences of ghostly kinds. And often they're very personal questions. Or that they perceive these things as being almost secrets. In fact many times they ask their relatives or friends to wait outside while they consult me or another tour guide. Typically they just want to know if they're alone (in their experiences) and when they discover that they're not they leave much more content as people I would say.

To ignore ghosts, to call them merely figments of imagination ignores the work they do as well as the experiences of tour participants within and outside of the ghost tour. Ghosts are controversial subjects, as beings and as representations of memory. And perhaps surprisingly, they have a politics. The city of Savannah and its tourism industry afford an opportunity to look at how ghosts become public and even part of public policy. We can also begin to see how ghosts are also private and intimate regarding how individuals interact with and experience places. While the American South cannot claim to be the only site for ghosts or for seeing hosts, ghost tours and the place-based interactions they encourage appear to be a particularly active part of the regional culture and illustrate how people consume and engage that culture. So possibly worst of all, to ignore ghosts would be to ignore part of the legacy of the South.

Works Cited

Adams, P.C., 2001. *Peripatetic Imagery and Peripatetic Sense of Place*. In Adams et. al (eds.), Textures of Place: exploring humanist geographies. University of Minnesota Press, London, Minneapolis, pp.183-206.

Bell, B., 2003. Savannah in the Spotlight. 02 June 2003. Savannah Morning News, available online at SavannahNow.com.

Bell, M. M., 1997. The Ghost of Place, *Theory and Society* 26(6)

Bynum, R., 2004. Savannah still in spotlight 10 years after 'Midnight'. 24 January 2004. The Daily Reflector.

Dawers, B., 2003. City talk: Are the safest streets empty ones? 13 April 2003. Savannah Morning News, available on line at SavannahNow.com

de Vorsey, L. 2012 The Origin and Appreciation of Savannah, Georgia's Historic City Squares Southeastern Geographer, Volume 52, Number 1, Spring 2012 pp. 90-99

Edensor, T., 2000. Staging Tourism: Tourists as Performers. *Annals of Tourism Research*. 27(2): 322-344.

Edensor, T., 2001. Performing tourism, staging tourism: (Re)producing tourist space and practice, *tourist studies*, 1(1): 59-81.

Foote, K. E. *Shadowed Ground*, (Austin: University of Texas Press, 1997)

Gentry, G.W., 2007. Walking with the Dead: The Place of Ghost Walk Tourism in Savannah, GA, *Southeastern Geographer*, 47(2):222-238

Graham, B., 2002. Heritage as Knowledge: Capital or Culture? In *Urban Studies*. 39(5-6):1003-1007

Hanna, S. P. "Is it Roslyn or is it Cicely? Representation and the Ambiguity of Place," *Urban Geography*, 17, no. 7 (1996): 633-649.

Herbert, D. T., 1996. Artistic and literary places in France as tourist attractions. *Tourism Management*. 17(2): 77-85.

Herbert, D., 2001. Literary Places, Tourism and the Heritage Experience. *Annals of Tourism Research*. 28(2): 312-333.

Holloway, J. 2010. Legend-tripping in spooky spaces: ghost tourism and infrastructures of enchantment. Environment and Planning D: Society and Space. 28: 618-637

Inglis, D. and Holmes, M., 2003. Highland and Other Haunts: Ghosts in Scottish Tourism. *Annals of Tourism Research*. 30(1): 50-63.

Inglis, D. and Holmes, M., 2003. Highland and Other Haunts: Ghosts in Scottish Tourism. *Annals of Tourism Research*. 30(1): 50-63.

J. deCerteau, *The Practice of Everyday Life*, (Berkley and Los Angeles: University of California Press, 1984).

J. Derrida, *Specters of Marx: The State of the Debt, the Work of Mourning, & the New International*, (Routledge: New York and London, 1994).

John Berendt, *Midnight in the Garden of Good and Evil*, (New York: Vintage, 1999).

Kim, H. and Richardson, S.L., 2003. Motion Picture Impacts and Destination Images. *Annals of Tourism Research*. 30(1): 216-237

Lennon, J. and Foley, M., 2000. *Dark Tourism: The Attraction of Death and Disaster*. Continuum, London, New York.

Marino, J.R. "Savannah's Unseen Inhabitants." *Savannah Morning News*, October 31, 2002. http://savannahnow.com/stories/103102/LOCghosts.shtml (accessed August 26, 2013).

Miles, W.F.S., 2002. Auschwitz: Museum Interpretation and Darker Tourism. *Annals of Tourism Research*. 29(4): 1175-1778

Murdock, K., 2003a. Walking tours may need to live by new rules. 07 April 2003. Savannah Morning News, available online at SavannahNow.com

Murdock, K., 2003b. One-stop tourism shopping: Business owners, residents say Savannah should consider a city-run tourism office. 19 April 2003. Morning News, available online at SavannahNow.com.

Murdock, K., 2003c. City hopeful tour companies will cooperate with trail ordinances. 20 June 2003. Savannah Morning News, available online at SavannahNow.com.

Murdock, K., 2003d. Sides find common ground on walking tours: Latest meeting to review tour guidelines was more amicable than previous meeting. 08 August 2003. Savannah Morning News, available online at SavannahNow.com.

P. Russel, and B. Hines, *Savannah: A History of Her People Since 1733*, (Savannah: Beil, 1992), 3.

Philip Stone Dr. "A Dark Tourism Spectrum: towards a typology of death and macabre related tourist sites, attractions and exhibitions" *TOURISM: An Interdisciplinary International Journal* 54.2 (2006): 145-160.

Pile, S., 2005. *Real Cities: Modernity, Space and the Phantasmagorias of City Life*. London: Sage Publications

Ramsland, K http://www.trutv.com/library/crime/notorious_murders/classics/hampton-lillibridge/1_index. html last accessed 17 September 2013

Riley, R., Baker, D. and Van Doren, C.S., 1998. Movie Induced Tourism. *Annals for Tourism Research*. 25(4): 919-935

Ruane, L., 2004. Ghost tours mix history, lore. News-press.com (accessed 03 March 2004)

Squire, S.J. "The Cultural Values of Literary Tourism," *Annals of Tourism Research*, 21, no. 1 (1994): 103-120.

Savannah Morning News, 2003a. Editorial: Treading lightly. 20 June 2003. Savannah Morning News, available online at SavannahNow.com

"Savannah still in spotlight 10 years after 'Midnight'." *USA Today*, sec. Travel, January 12, 2004. http://usatoday30.usatoday.com/travel/destinations/2004-01-12-savannah_x.htm (accessed August 26, 2013).

Seaton, A.V., 1996. Guided by the Dark: from thanatopsis to thanatourism. *International Journal of Heritage Studies*, 2(4): 234-244.

Seeman, E., 2002. Spooky Streets. *Common place*, 3(1). http://www.common-place.org

Strange, C. and Kempa, M., 2003. Shades of Dark Tourism: Alcatraz and Robben Island. *Annals of Tourism Research*. 30(2): 286-405

Till, Karen E., 2005. *The New Berlin: Memory, Politics, Place*. University of Minnesota Press: Minneapolis/ London

Tour guide interviews with authors, 2003.

Tour owner interviews with authors, 2003.

Tuan, Y.F., 1974. Space and place: humanistic perspective. *Progress in Geography*. 5:233-246.

Tuan, Y.F., 1977. *Space and Place: The Perspective of Experience*. Minnesota Press, Minneapolis.

Van Brimmer, Adam. "Tourism Leaders: Record visitor numbers bode well for Savannah's future." *Savannah Morning News*, June 10, 2012. http://savannahnow.com/exchange/2012-06-10/tourism-leaders-record-visitor-numbers-bode-well-savannah-future

Wittish, R., 2002. BOO! All the Way to the Bank: There's Gold in Those Thrills. In Business Report & Journal. www.savannahbusiness.com/archieves (accessed 23 March 2003).

E S S A Y

Confronting the "Ghosts" of Southern Masculinity in Stephen King and John Mellencamp's
Ghost Brothers of Darkland County

by Cameron E. Williams

In the spring of 2012, Atlanta's Alliance Theater hosted the world premiere of the Southern Gothic, supernatural "musical horror story," *Ghost Brothers of Darkland County*. A collaboration between Stephen King, John Mellencamp, and T Bone Burnett, *Ghost Brothers* follows the struggles of Frank and Drake McCandless, two brothers whose competitive relationship is intensified during a trip to their family's isolated Mississippi lake house. Interwoven with Frank and Drake's story is that of their uncles, Jack and Andy, two *other* brothers who died tragically in 1967 and return to the present as *ghosts*, "haunting" the stage and the family's cabin by the lake, ethereally wandering in and out of the action. As the narrative unfolds, the similarities between the lives of the two sets of brothers become increasingly and frighteningly apparent. Joe McCandless—father to Frank and Drake and youngest brother of Jack and Andy—must finally confront the demons of his past and reveal to his sons the true story of their uncles' deaths. The play concludes in true, grisly King fashion, confirming that Frank and Drake have been fated to repeat the terrible, violent history of their family's past.

Ghost Brothers is a complicated and unusual kind of musical; as Ryan D'Agostino points out, musicals typically are not "a guy thing." *Ghost Brothers* is a musical "written by men for men," a Southern Gothic play chiefly concerned with representations of white, heterosexual masculinity. Moreover, as the title of the musical clearly indicates, the brothers at the center of the play's narrative are ghosts. In *Spectral America: Phantoms and the National Imagination*, Jeffrey Weinstock explains that ghosts are "symptom[s] of repressed knowledge" that raise questions about "the possibilities of a future based on avoidance of the past." Ghosts are also symptoms of their time and place; they "reflect the ethos and anxieties of the eras of their production" (6). Notably, Jack and Andy's deaths occur at a time when Southern men were plagued by a peculiar "crisis of masculinity" brought about by the radical social changes of the 1960s. Jack and Andy are killed in 1967, but their ghostly presence lingers forty years later; King's musical takes place in 2007 and it premiered in Atlanta in 2012, where it ran for just over a month. This essay will look at how *Ghost Brothers* reveals the "ethos and anxieties" of its cultural time and place—of its setting and production—by focusing on the play's predominant concern with white, heterosexual masculinity. I will explore the ways it invokes many of the South's deeply entrenched mythologies of manhood and womanhood. Ultimately, while *Ghost Brothers* challenges our perception of Southern norms, it fosters many of the South's deep-seated anxieties about gender, sexuality, class, and race.[1]

The idea for *Ghost Brothers of Darkland County*—set in fictional Lake Belle Reve, Mississippi—was originally conceived by John Mellencamp and is based on actual events that transpired years ago in Mellencamp's very own "haunted" cabin in Indiana. "Two brothers and a girl, in 1935, were talking and drinking and…the two boys got mad at each other," Mellencamp says in an interview with Stephen Colbert, "and one of them hit the other one over the head with a poker in front of the fireplace" ("Stephen King"). In a tragic turn of events, the other brother and the girl were involved in a fatal car accident while on their way to get help. Even though the original event that inspired the musical took place in Indiana, it's certainly worth noting that Mellencamp and King chose to set *Ghost Brothers* in the South. As musical director T Bone Burnett explains, the creators were "infatuated with the idea of the Southern Gothic" (Brock). The South provided the "'dark, foggy' atmosphere" that the creators were looking for and therefore proved to be the perfect place for both the musical's setting and its production (Harris).

The South's long, sordid history of violence also makes it the ideal setting for Mellencamp and King's dark musical. Out of its uniquely tragic experiences with the horrors of slavery and the gruesome carnage of the Civil War—that famously pit brother against brother—many of the South's "ghosts" have been born, "visible and recurring manifestations of the past, history constantly present and influential" (Martin 303). While ghosts and ghost stories are present in almost every culture, they are for this reason an especially persistent presence in the South's folklore and literature. Indeed, as many scholars have contended, the South (and particularly its fiction) is very much *haunted* by the past. Allen Tate, for instance, has considered the South as past-haunted, calling its long-standing "obsession" with the past "the defining trait of modern southern writing" (qtd. in Jones 619). Lewis P. Simpson similarly observes the tendency of Southern fiction "to see the life of the individual southerner as always in a dramatic tension with history"; citing Robert Penn Warren, Simpson suggests that the South is forever "trapped" in the past (77). In Southern fiction, ghosts and ghost stories serve as a means by which to confront the burden of the past, often functioning "as a metaphor" for characters who surrender to "the repetitive re-creation" of history (Martin 306).

Quite a few ghosts haunt the stage of King and Mellencamp's musical. As patrons file into the theater, waiting for the house lights to go dark, so too do townspeople—many of them seemingly materializing out of thin air—take their places on different parts of the stage, sitting or standing "mostly motionless, as though in limbo" (Osborne). Every now and then, a towering, spectral figure appears, a visual projection that creeps slowly across the stage and vanishes. This projection is only the first of the play's many ghosts; Act I Scene 3 introduces brothers Andy and Jack McCandless, the object of their mutual affections, Jenna, and Dan (bartender of the Dreamland Café and singular African American character), all of whom traverse the stage encapsulated in blue light. They are enshrouded in blue light to indicate that they are spirits, ghosts of characters who died in 1967 and return to 2007 to preside over the action of the musical's present time period. There is one other, more sinister ghost or specter that haunts the stage: a menacing figure—tattooed, leather-clad, and referred to only as The Shape—serves as a sort of rockabilly ringmaster who moves across the stage illuminated by a red glow and guides the performance by both introducing aspects of the storyline and by influencing the other characters' behavior.

Notably, the ghosts (and indeed the very cast) of *Ghost Brothers* are predominately male. *Ghost Brothers* has been called "the first-ever musical written by men for men." As a genre, musicals are often considered "feminine" or are associated with homosexuality, but *Ghost Brothers* is careful to shirk the conventions of the typical Broadway-style production. At the outset, the play asserts itself as decidedly "hetero" and "masculine" when The Shape takes the stage to introduce the overlapping storylines of the two generations of

McCandless brothers. The Shape performs the first musical number; the song "That's Me" is dark, "haunting and all-American" (D'Agostino), and it immediately sets the tone for the musical numbers to follow. There is no elaborate orchestra anywhere to be found, just a simple rock-and-roll band set up in "The Dreamland Café" that "floats in mid-air over the cabin" onstage (King 10). The first act of the play also makes it clear that the narrative is primarily focused on representations of heterosexual white masculinity. Frank first takes the stage when he arrives at the cabin with Anna, both his and his brother Drake's love interest, for a romantic rendezvous. After entering the cabin, the two almost go directly to the bedroom where they begin having sex.

Because of the Southern setting, it is therefore important to consider the musical's treatment of masculinity in relation to the South's historical concepts of manhood. Situating Southern men within what Craig Thompson Friend calls the "metanarrative" of American masculinity—from which Southern masculinity deviates inasmuch as it also intersects—is helpful in understanding how *Ghost Brothers* engages, reflects, and challenges some of the South's ideas and anxieties about gender, class, and race. E. Anthony Rotundo's seminal 1993 study *American Manhood: Transformations in Masculinity from the Revolution to the Modern Era* identifies the new appreciation for what he terms "passionate manhood" that came about toward the end of the nineteenth century (227). Passionate manhood—which Rotundo also calls "primitive masculinity"—valued traits that throughout the nineteenth century had been considered "fundamental qualit[ies] of the male sex," such as "lust, greed, selfishness, ambition, and physical assertiveness" (227). As Friend affirms, passionate manhood did not eclipse other forms of masculine expression, but rather, by celebrating male emotions "through acts of competition, aggression, force, sexuality, self-fulfillment, and a new attention to the male body," reshaped prevailing attitudes in the South about the traits that characterized "proper manliness" (ix). With it came also what Gail Bederman observes as "a primal virility," a renewed attachment to nature and a desire to participate in "savage activities" that directly opposed earlier versions of "civilized" manhood (qtd. in Friend ix). Michael Kimmel adds that the industrialism of the late nineteenth century—the turn away from agriculture and "frontier life"—forced a reconsideration of how men could demonstrate their masculinity. Men looked to sports and leisure then for the "boost [they] needed…to develop some all-male preserves" (9-10). Expressions of passionate manhood continued into—and ultimately thrived in—the mid-twentieth century, when war, economic fluctuation and depression, shifting gender roles, sexual revolution, and the Civil Rights movement precipitated a "crisis of masculinity." As Fred Fejes writes, for most Americans, such changes "disrupted their sense of a coherent, national moral order" (3). Nowhere was this truer than in the South, where the vestige of "genteel society" still demanded of its men and women what Angelia Wilson calls gender and sexual "clarity" (3). Passionate masculinity, with its emphasis on aggression, competition, and sexual prowess, encouraged a "return to sheer primitivism" and thus became the reigning response to the South's ever evolving socio-cultural scene (Friend ix).

Also according to Friend, the release of *Gone With the Wind* in 1939 inspired men to see competition as a new way to display honor and power. Hunting or shooting, in particular, became what historian Ted Ownby describes as a Southern "cultural institution" at the beginning of and on into the twentieth century (qtd. in Friend xviii). *Ghost Brothers* similarly makes conspicuous the role that competition and shooting play in demonstrating manliness. In life and as ghosts, brothers Jack and Andy are fiercely competitive. Joe describes witnessing his older brothers fight frequently "over anything and everything" (King 50). As Joe reveals at the end of Act I Scene 3, it is ultimately the Minutemen's annual Hawkeye Shooting Competition that precipitates Jack and Andy's final and fatal encounter (51). Up until the shooting match, Andy had the honor of being considered the superior brother. While Andy made all A's in school, got his driver's license "first crack," and courted Jenna's affections with little effort, Jack struggled to live up to his brother's accomplishments. But at the shooting match (staged as a "flashback" to where Jack, Andy, and Jenna are alive and are no longer enshrouded in the blue light that marks them as ghosts) Jack proves to be the more talented rifleman. Andy, fingers "wet with sweat," "trembles" with his rifle, nearly dropping it between the first and second rounds (54). Jack, on the other hand, remains steady and confident throughout the competition.

Not only does *Ghost Brothers'* shooting match ominously foreshadow the musical's grisly conclusion, it furthermore underscores the ways that violence—particularly for Jack and Andy—is evidence of masculinity. Following the Hawkeye Competition, Jack, Andy, and Jenna return to the cabin and proceed to get drunk. Bitter about losing the competition and his girl, Jenna, to his younger brother and spurred on by too much liquor, Andy attempts to emasculate Jack, as he has been similarly emasculated by his very public defeat at the shooting match. When Jack drops the liquor bottle, Andy angrily calls him a "pansy," then continues to insult Jack's sexual prowess (80). The two continue to exchange invective remarks, verbally emasculating one another in a way that emphasizes how Jack and Andy's white, heterosexual masculinity is formed through denigration of homosexuality or homosexual behavior. Through the musical interlude "So Goddam Good," Andy relentlessly taunts Jack, badgering him to demonstrate his masculinity and prove his skills with a rifle by shooting an apple off of his head. Jack finally snaps and shoots; however, instead of hitting the apple, Jack hits Andy right between the eyes, killing him instantly. Jack and Andy's nephews, Frank and Drake, eventually meet a frighteningly similar end. But before Frank shoots and kills Anna, Drake, and Joe in the play's penultimate scene, he and Drake regularly come to verbal and physical blows. On one particular occasion, Frank emasculates Drake by suggesting that he'll never be successful. Drake retaliates, and in the fray breaks Frank's arm (32). Even in the absence of physical brutality, the threat of violence looms heavy over the entire narrative. The ironically titled song "Brotherly Love," performed by Frank and Drake in Act I Scene 3, illustrates the intensity of the brothers' hatred for one another. Frank sings: "Cain and Abel ought to be our names / If it weren't for the murdering charge / I'd put you in your grave" (31). Without missing a beat, Drake replies: "I'd beat you like an old mule / And leave you like an old wet sack / Spit in your face and blacken your eyes / And leave you on the river bank / Let them crows pick your bones / Let the wolves chew off your head / Then I'd make you dig your own grave / Till I'm sure that you was dead" (31-32).

The shooting match furthermore demonstrates the ways in which Southern conceptions of manhood comprise an element of public performance. As Friend explains, white Southerners have always felt "the need to publicly demonstrate manliness"; since before Reconstruction Southern manhood "required regular public performance" as a way of maintaining social, gender, and racial hierarchies (x). Kris DuRocher elucidates the function of public rituals—specifically lynching—as "culturally constructed spaces

that communicate social realities by defining and setting a common cultural agenda."
Southern men were obliged to participate in such rituals because of the way that public
performance "allow[ed] participants to assert a conception of identity to themselves and
to those around them in the larger social context." For Southern men confronting certain
post-bellum challenges—economic depression, Populism, and women's suffrage among
them—lynching became a primary way for white men to maintain supremacy. Lynching
sent "a message to the black community as well as white women and children to obey
boundaries set up by white males" (47). More frighteningly, it was through the destruction of black bodies in the lynching ritual that white men measured and affirmed their
own masculinity. A sadistic and shockingly common element of the ritual involved the
torture, mutilation, and castration of African American victims. The purpose behind this
was to humiliate and emasculate the victims, all for the sake of white male demonstrations of manliness. The terrible violence committed against black men and women during
lynchings operated as a means through which white Southern men "defined and defend-
ed" heteronormative masculinity (47). DuRocher's analysis makes apparent the extensive
and horrifying role that violence played in both "creating" and "exhibiting" Southern
masculinity (47). *Ghost Brothers* does not include any kind of lynching sequence, yet
DuRocher's insightful description of the very public context of Southern manhood sheds
light on much of what is at stake in the musical's shooting match scene, a competition
which, in the South, in many ways evolves from such earlier rituals as lynching.

DuRocher's analysis of the lynching ritual can also help to make sense of the treatment of the few female characters in *Ghost Brothers*. Like concepts of manhood, notions
of white Southern womanhood also developed out of ante- and post-bellum efforts to
maintain structures of white patriarchal power. Many lynchings were "justified" in the
name of pure white womanhood, but the concept of "pure white womanhood" itself arose
out of white men's desire to demonstrate manliness by controlling female sexuality. Out of
fear that sexual relations between black men and white women would "destroy the white
race," white patriarchy turned to fiction (Hodes 147). They disseminated "discourses of
nostalgia and threat" that vilified black men as "bestial" and placed white women on a
pedestal to be worshipped as a mythic symbol of the South's virtue, honor, and chastity
(Roberts 104). As W.J. Cash suggests in *The Mind of the South* (1941), beginning before
the outbreak of the Civil War, Southern women were invested with "the very notion"
of the South itself (Gray 189). The Southern woman was hailed as "the shield-bearing
Athena gleaming whitely in the clouds, the standard for its rallying, the mystic symbol of
its nationality in the face of the foe"; she was worshipped as "[t]he center and circumfer-
ence, diameter and periphery, sine, tangent and secant of all…affections" (Cash 86-87).
The Southern woman was expected to be a "stainless" symbol of the South's ideal (Gray
189). She was the center of the domestic sphere; she catered to her husband and bent to
him "in all manners," bearing him children to whom she tended with love and care. She
was "pious, self-effacing, and kind, and was therefore an indispensible figure of the patriarchy (Scura 413). Her sexuality minimized to the point of complete absence, she was an
angelic emblem of perfection and purity.

Through the ghost of Jenna (and also through the "live" character, Anna) *Ghost Brothers* makes visible the anxieties (and fantasies) that continue to surround ideas about female
sexuality in the South. Jenna is overtly sexual and in this way defies the expectations of

Southern womanhood. In "Jukin'," Jenna describes her ability to "be a lady / Or a snake in the bedroom" (74-75). She sings: "I can turn off the lights / with a flip of my hip / I can kiss your lips real hard" (75). Jenna here also appropriates conventional masculine characteristics by actively exhibiting an assertive sexuality, acknowledging her unique ability to negotiate male and female spaces and thereby collapsing gender binaries when she croons: "I can drink you under the table / Leave you weak out in the backyard" (75). Described as "a gawky-legs tomboy" (51), she can drink excessively, as good as or better than any man around, and is still "ladylike" enough to be crowned Miss Darkland County 1967 (53). Anna—Jenna's present day doppelgänger and object of Frank and Drake's romantic rivalry—is similarly overtly sexual. When she first comes onstage in Act I Scene 3, she not only initiates sex with Frank but shortly after introduces herself to Monique, Frank and Drake's mother, wearing nothing but Frank's shirt and shamelessly admitting with "an irritating little sub-deb giggle," "We...um...broke the bunk" (22). Like Jenna, Anna also acknowledges her sexuality and her aptitude for vacillating between feminine and masculine domians. In "That's Who I Am," she refers to herself as "a whole lotta big little girl" who knows "what men like": "Look out boys 'cause here comes Anna / With her skirt hiked up high" (12). She then explains her understanding that there is a certain time and place for embracing the codes of womanhood and for pushing against them: "I can be as nice as pie / Whenever I need to / Put my hand in your front pockets / And tighten up your screw / Make you feel like a big man / Walkin' with your Barbie Doll / Put you down when you ain't around / And kick you when you fall" (13).

"That's Who I Am" furthermore evinces Anna's seeming awareness that white female sexuality in the South is more threatening than enticing. Anna and Jenna both may rail against the time-honored notions of female purity, but the two are ultimately vilified for embracing their sexuality. Indeed, throughout *Ghost Brothers*, Anna's and Jenna's sexuality is construed as dangerous, even frightening. When Drake discovers that Anna has left him for Frank, he evidently insults her, as Anna indicates when she and Frank first enter the lake cabin together. Her response is to further her relationship with Frank: "Do you know who calls me a bitch and gets away with it?" she asks Frank. One of the libretto's stage notes also refers to Anna as a "bitchkitty" (22), "one Southern belle you do not want to cross" (12). In Act II Scene 2, Andy similarly insults Jenna by calling her an "open-legs little slut" (80). For Andy and Drake, Jenna and Anna must occupy a negative feminine space; to reinscribe them as *sluts* and *bitches*—names that represent a marginal femininity—is to place them as inferior to what Andy and Drake deem their hegemonic masculinity.

The stage notes affirm that we as an audience are also supposed to understand Jenna and Anna, with their threatening sexuality, as villains. Andy blames Jenna for the dissolution of his relationship with Jack just as Drake blames Anna for his problems with Frank. Joe too holds Jenna (along with the Hawkeye shooting competition) accountable for the fatal feud between his older brothers (51), suggesting that her presence only exacerbated their jealousy toward one another:

> For quite a while, [Andy, Jack, and Jenna] went everywhere together. Jenna insisted. Andy went along with it, prob'ly thought she was being nice to his little brother because Jack had a crush on her. When they were together, they got

along as sweet as pie. When she wasn't there, though, the fights started gettin' hotter. Maybe Andy was startin' to get a clue—he was sure of himself, but not dumb. (53)

As Eve Sedgwick explains in *Between Men* (1985), Rene Girard's notion of the erotic triangle involves two men competing for the affections of one woman. In these triangulations, as "in any erotic rivalry, the bond that links the two rivals is as intense and potent as the bond that links either of the rivals to the beloved." Girard's *Deceit, Desire, and the Novel*, she writes, traces "a calculus of power" that is structured by "the relation of rivalry between the two active members of an erotic triangle" (21). Concentrating on "the immanence of" male same-sex bonds and their "prohibitive structuration" to bonds between men and women, Sedgwick—taking as her starting point Girard's theory as well as what Gayle Rubin terms "the traffic in women"—claims that male bonds are formed through the symbolic exchange of women. The erotic triangle often makes conspicuous the frequent erasure of women, obscuring the female role either by writing the woman out entirely or by simply writing her off as the villain. As Sedgwick concludes, men, when "in the presence of a woman who can be seen as either pitiable or contemptible," are able to "exchange power and…confirm each other's value even in the context of the remaining inequalities in their power" (160). The conflicts between the two sets of McCandless brothers are the result of a classic case of romantic rivalry, or erotic triangle, and the stage notes and Joe's assessment of Jenna underscore the fact that Jenna's and Anna's primary function in the musical is to destroy the already tenuous bond between two generations of McCandless brothers. The bond between brothers is the far more important bond in *Ghost Brothers*, and the rivalry between Jack and Andy and Frank and Drake ultimately obfuscates any bond one of them may have had with a girl. Because of the ways that Anna and Jenna are vilified—"written off as contemptible"—we as an audience are able to recognize the profound "immanence" of the brothers' bonds.

A violent death concludes the storyline for Frank and Drake who, much like Jack and Andy, were killed ultimately because they let their conventional "male passions"—jealousy, competitiveness, aggression, violence, sexuality, and self-fulfillment (Friend ix)—get the best of them. However, Jack and Andy—and Jenna—who died in 1967 and are already dead when the narrative begins, are able to return to 2007 as ghosts where they must watch helplessly as their nephews (re)live the sins of their family's past, right down to their feud over basically the same girl. And that's all they can do: watch. As ghosts, they are unable to talk to the living characters onstage, and though the living characters onstage might seem to discern their phantom presence, at no point do they interact with one another. As ghosts, Jack, Andy, and Jenna are doomed to watch history repeat itself. As Jeffrey Weinstock suggests, ghosts—like Jack, Andy, and Jenna—disrupt the "presentness of the present" and serve as a lingering reminder of the past: "As a symptom of repressed knowledge, the ghost calls into question the possibilities of a future based on avoidance of the past. Millennial specters ask us to what extent we can move forward into a new millennium when we are still shackled to a past that haunts us and that we have yet to face and mourn fully" (6). Despite their efforts to demonstrate their superiority through displays of manliness, both sets of brothers still wind up dead, and what's more, they inflict pain and suffering on others in the process. The ghosts of Jack, Andy, and Jenna, then, serve as a warning, a reminder of how dangerous it is when we let our past consume our present. The present day generation of McCandlesses, haunted by their family's violent past, surrender inevitably to "the repetitive re-creation" of history and themselves become ghosts (Martin 306).

Ghosts are furthermore "always constructions embedded within specific historical contexts and invoked for more or less explicit political purposes." They are products of their time and place and as such, they "participate in, reinforce, and exemplify various belief structures." As Weinstock suggests, "Examining our ghosts tells us quite a bit about America's hopes and desires, fears and regrets—and the extent to which the past governs our present and opens or forecloses possibilities for the future" (8). The context of *Ghost Brothers*' 2012 staging is therefore especially significant and can perhaps provide additional insight into the way the play confronts Southern views of heterosexual masculinity and female sexuality. A heated election year, 2012 witnessed quite a few conservative reactions to political discussions of women's sexual health and reproductive rights. Abortion and contraception became major campaign issues in the 2012 presidential bid, and much of the resistance to women's freedom on these issues was concentrated in the South. Southerners comprise a prominent portion of the nation's conservative base, Tracy Thompson confirms in *The New Mind of the South* (2013):

> Southerners are conservative people. Everybody knows this is true, but not everybody—including many of my fellow Southerners—understands why it's true, which is that the South is a region that has known more massive, wrenching social change than any other part of the nation. If Southerners place a high value on tradition, it's because tradition in the South is like beachfront property in an era of global warming: as much as you love the view, you live with the knowledge that some morning you will wake up and find it gone. (10)

By no means am I suggesting that *Ghost Brothers* is pushing any kind of political agenda. I am, however, suggesting that the South's ideas about appropriate gendered and sexual expression are themselves—like Jack, Andy, and Jenna—*ghosts*: they are concepts that developed out of ante- and post-bellum efforts to maintain structures of white patriarchal power, that have, to be sure, evolved over time, but that are so deeply ingrained in the Southern cultural consciousness—and indeed, in the *American* consciousness—that they continue to haunt us decades later. In its consideration of masculinity, *Ghost Brothers* engages and in some ways pushes against the anxieties attached to manhood in the South, specifically those codes of masculine behavior that value violence, competition, and aggression. Jack, Andy, Frank, and Drake—two generations of brothers—demonstrate the extent to which, as Friend and Glover explain, "the power of that hegemonic version of southern manhood"—a version cemented in our cultural consciousness by W.J. Cash and Bertram Wyatt-Brown and which values honor, individuality, "valor through vengeance," mastery, violence and vigilantism—"has persisted in the historiography" (viii). And perhaps that's what we should take away from this: that *Ghost Brothers of Darkland County* is a comment on the ways in which the South is itself a sort of specter, a "dark, foggy" entity there to remind us what happens when we let our past continue to haunt our present.

Note

1.In my analysis of Ghost Brothers of Darkland County, I reference the 2013 libretto penned by Stephen King.

Works Cited

Brock, Wendall. "Stephen King, John Mellencamp unveil 'Ghost Brothers' in Atlanta." *Culture Monster*. Last modified April 13, 2012. http://latimesblogs.latimes.com/culturemonster/2012/04/stephen-king-john-mellencamp.html#sthash.A9yk7fdl.dpuf

Cash, W. J. *The Mind of the South*. New York: Vintage, 1991.

Cohen, Jeffrey Jerome. *Monster Theory: Reading Culture*. Minneapolis: U of Minnesota P, 1996.

D'Agostino, Ryan. "No. 88: A Musical for Men." *Esquire*. Last modified September 18, 2007. http://www.esquire.com/features/esquire-100/ghostbrothers1007

DuRocher, Kris. "Violent Masculinity: Learning Ritual and Performance in Southern Lynchings." In *Southern Masculinity: Perspectives on Manhood in the South Since Reconstruction*, edited by Craig Thompson Friend, 46-64. Athens: U of Georgia P, 2009.

Fejes, Fred. *Gay Rights and Moral Panic: The Origins of America's Debate on Homosexuality*. New York: Palgrave Macmillan, 2010.

Friend, Craig Thompson. "From Southern Manhood to Southern Masculinties: An Introduction." In *Southern Masculinity: Perspectives on Manhood in the South Since Reconstruction*, edited by Craig Thompson Friend, vii-xxvi. Athens: U of Georgia P, 2009.

Friend, Craig Thompson and Lorri Glover. "Rethinking Southern Masculinity: An Introduction." In *Southern Manhood: Perspectives on Masculinity in the Old South*, edited by Craig Thompson Friend and Lorri Glover, vii-xvii. Athens: U of Georgia P, 2004.

Gray, Richard. *Writing the South*. Baton Rouge: Louisiana State University Press, 1998.

Harris, Manning. "Theatre Preview: 'Ghost Brothers of Darkland County' at The Alliance." *Atlanta In Town*. Last modified December 30, 2011. http://www.atlantaintownpaper.com/2011/12/theatre-preview-ghost-brothers-of-darkland-county-at-the-alliance/

Hodes, Martha Elizabeth. "Politics: Racial Hierarchy and Illicit Sex." In *White Women, Black Men: Illicit Sex In The Nineteenth-Century South*, 147-175. New Haven: Yale University Press, 1997.

Jones, Diann Brown. "The Past." In *The Companion to Southern Literature*, edited by Joseph M. Flora and Lucinda H. MacKeithan, 619-20. Baton Rouge: Louisiana State U P, 2002.

Kimmel, Michael. *Manhood in America: A Cultural History*. Oxford: Oxford U P, 2011.

King, Stephen. *Ghost Brothers of Darkland County: Libretto*. Beverly Hills: Concord Music Group, 2013.

Leonard, Arthur S. *Homosexuality and The Constitution, Vol. 4; Vol. 7*. New York: Taylor & Francis, 1997.

Martin, Charles D. "Ghost Stories." In *The Companion to Southern Literature*, edited by Joseph M. Flora and Lucinda H. MacKeithan, 304-06. Baton Rouge: Louisiana State U P, 2002.

Osborne, Bert. "'Ghost Brothers of Darkland County' a musical horror story that twists and turns." *Access Atlanta*. Last modified April 13, 2012.

Roberts, Diane. *Faulkner and Southern Womanhood*. Athens: University of Georgia Press, 1994. http://www.accessatlanta.com/news/entertainment/music/ghost-brothers-of-darkland-county-a-musical-horror/nQzSp/

Rotundo, E. Anthony. *American Manhood: Transformations in Masculinity from the Revolution to the Modern Era*. New York: Basic Books, 1993.

Scura, Dorothy M. "Lady." In *The Companion to Southern Literature*, edited by Joseph M. Flora and Lucinda H. MacKeithan, 413-14. Baton Rouge: Louisiana State U P, 2002.

Sedgwick, Eve Kosofsky. *Between Men: English Literature and Male Homosocial Desire*. New York: Columbia UP, 1985.

Simpson, Lewis P. *The Fable of the Southern Writer*. Baton Rouge: Louisiana State University Press, 1994.

"Stephen King, John Mellencamp, and T Bone Burnett." *The Colbert Report*. By Stephen Colbert. Comedy Central. June 6, 2013.

Thompson, Tracy. *The New Mind of the South*. New York: Simon & Schuster, 2013.

Weinstock, Jeffrey, Ed. *Spectral America: Phantoms and the National Imagination*. Madison: University of Wisconsin Press, 2004.

Wilson, Angelia R. *Below the Belt: Religion, Sexuality, and Politics in the Rural South*. New York: Continuum, 2000.

ON THE PLANTATION WITH GHOSTS:
ANTAGONISMS OF SLAVERY TOURISM

by Benjamin D'Harlingue

"[T]he 'time of slavery' negates the common-sense intuition of time as continuity or progression, then and now coexist; we are coeval with the dead."
—Saidiya Hartman, "The Time of Slavery"

Along Louisiana's River Road, plantations established prior to the United States Civil War are now tourist destinations. Folklore and tourism industry have it that some of these plantations are haunted. An entry on Loyd Hall, from the guidebook *Louisiana's Haunted Plantations*, focuses on the ghost of someone named Sally Boston.[1] The author, Jill Pascoe, gives very little biographical information about Boston: "She was a slave nanny who lived in the house with the Loyd family. The exact cause of death is shrouded in mystery, but it is thought she was poisoned" (45). Pascoe has Boston haunt thusly:

> There are times when people in the house have caught a fleeting glimpse of a black woman dressed in white. When this specter is seen there is an overwhelming feeling of comfort and an aroma of food cooking. Sally also seems to manifest herself in the back parlor. [...] One of the ladies who worked in the house once saw a translucent black woman slap the candles off the mantle. [...] And what problem does she have with the candles? Could this be the room in which she was poisoned? (47-48)

This guidebook's entry on Loyd Plantation is typical of haunted plantation tourism in several ways. First, this guidebook proposes that, at historical plantations, employees and tourists interact with ghosts of individuals who lived before the United States Civil War. Second, when this tourism conjures ghosts of the enslaved, it reinforces the slave's enslavement, as if for perpetuity. In the Loyd Hall example, Sally Boston appears in ongoing captive servitude. Boston, now spectral, perpetually cooks and waits on the parlor. She is without kin or peers, called forth only for the sake of another, for the white slave owner and later the tourist. Ghosts of the enslaved are trapped in the social death they suffered in life, after their biological lives have already ended. Third, haunted plantation tourism proposes that violence is a cause of haunting, but understands violence only as individual acts, and thus obscures the systemic gratuitous violence that is slavery. Hence the Loyd Hall narrative speculates that Boston's "problem" must be that she was poisoned, and does not ask whether enslavement might be a problem. This point segues with the fourth point, that is, the slave's possible rebellious action is a site of narrative anxiety, surveillance, and containment. Fifth, the tourist is invited to enjoy slavery's manifestations. This is evident in the passage above, wherein Boston's servitude is associated with "an overwhelming feeling of comfort." Pascoe describes Loyd Hall as "a perfect setting for family celebrations"

(44), thus coupling hospitality with the spectacle of slavery. Sixth, as evidenced by Pascoe's suggestion that families visit the "grand plantation" (44) to celebrate and enjoy hospitality typified by the servitude of the ghosted slave, it is clear that Loyd Hall, like other plantation tourist destinations, encourages tourists to identify with white slave-holding families, thus structuring kinship on the basis of black enslavement.

Like the tourism of Loyd Hall's haunting, the broader phenomenon of haunted plantation tourism mobilizes slavery's ongoing anti-black violence. By "haunted plantation tourism," I mean the tourism of historical plantations that focuses on ghosts that supposedly lurk at these places. This article asks: How does haunted plantation tourism organize contemporary encounters with slavery? In what ways is slavery's structural violence enacted through this haunted plantation tourism? Unique to this tourism is its central figure, haunting, which is set up in such a way as to propose, desire, stage, or, we might even say, acknowledge a contemporary co-presence with slavery. Haunted plantation tourism presupposes that through visiting these plantations, people today can time travel back into the Antebellum American South. According to the main premise of this tourism, slave-holding whites and enslaved black people from that earlier era ostensibly linger as ghosts in our time, at plantations. Tourists and employees supposedly interact with the ghostly incarnations of white enslavers and enslaved black people. By deploying the structural positions of "master" and "slave" in the contemporary field of subjectivity, haunted plantation tourism activates slavery's enduring, violent power relations—or what Frank Wilderson, III calls "antagonisms."[2] As Wilderson argues, the positions "master" and "slave" are antagonistic, in the sense that they are not involved in a contingent conflict with one another, but instead are structurally completely at odds with one another, until the dissolution of one or both positions. While the master exercises domination, the slave is reduced to "social death"—Orlando Patterson's term, referring to the condition of being exposed to gratuitous violence, generally dishonored, disallowed kin and contemporaries, and detached from the human community.

Antagonism driven, haunted plantation tourism encourages people to identify with, feel empathy for, and even imagine that they are elite whites holding enslaved black people in captivity. Stories recounted at and about these places offer black enslavement as a point of ghostly amusement and historical interest, through accounts of anti-black violence, black servitude, repressed revolts, and the ghosts that supposedly arise from these happenings. Kitschy ghost entertainment's spectral replay of gratuitous violence occurs alongside invitations to enjoy the beautiful grounds, mansions, and hospitality of these plantations, thus valorizing the time, place, and system of slavery.[3] If haunted plantation tourism invites tourists to identify with or even as slave masters, this interpellation is geared toward white tourists, and is perhaps more generally available to tourists who are, at the very least, not black. In contrast, haunted plantation tourism discourse does not craft out a place for black tourist subjectivity. It is not simply that this tourism does not specifically announce a role for the black tourist to play. This tourism figures black people as objects, socially dead in the past and present. For this tourism is pitched as a journey into the time of slavery, as an entry into slavery's antagonisms. Within such an imaginary, there is no black tourist, only black enslavement.[4]

While substantial research has been conducted on plantation tourism, existing scholarship has not theorized the significance of the niche of plantation tourism that focuses on ghosts. Attending to haunting will require a mode of analysis slightly different from that offered in existing scholarship, which has tended to critique representations for their inaccuracy and partiality.[5] One of the field's more influential scholarly works, which exemplifies this emphasis on skewed representation, is Eichstedt and Small's *Representations of Slavery: Race and Ideology in Southern Plantation Museums.* Eichstedt and Small's important intervention is based on the authors' exhaustive survey of U.S. Southern plantation tourism in all its variety. The authors visited over one hundred plantations, yet the book offers only a couple of pages discussing plantation tours with ghost stories. Moreover, the authors do not treat the ghost as a figure requiring any significant alteration of their overarching argument. Throughout the work, Eichstedt and Small's main concern is over "rhetorics that [...] confine to oblivion, the system of slavery and the presence of those enslaved. [T]hese rhetorics are part of a racialized regime of representation that valorizes the white elite of the preemancipation South while generally erasing or minimizing the experiences of enslaved African Americans" (Eichstedt and Small, 2). Eichstedt and Small point to instances where plantation museums (their term for historical plantations offering tours, lodging, restaurants, or exhibits) fail to mention slavery, minimize slavery's violence, or present plantation life primarily from the perspective of and in sympathy with white "master enslavers."[6] Their study provides an important precedent for the more narrowly focused study on haunted tourism that I conduct here. My analysis aligns with theirs on the point that plantation tourism (including *haunted tourism*) typically "valorizes the white elite of the preemanicipation South." Yet, Eichstedt and Small's mode of analysis—common to much scholarship on plantation tourism—which is to critique representations for their historical inaccuracy or partiality, falls short with regard to specifically *haunted* plantation tourism, for several reasons. First, in haunted plantation tourism, the rehearsal of stories of violence against enslaved black people makes up a crucial component of the occult entertainment. Inasmuch as tourism emphasizing haunting typically proposes that particular violent incidences give rise to ghosts, it might be said that haunted tourism inaccurately represents slavery, by failing to show that its violence is unremitting. That is, haunted tourism's fixation on particular *acts* of violence might suggest that violence is contingent to rather than definitive of the system of slavery. Nonetheless, haunted tourism's focus on signs of violence, such as killing and dismemberment of enslaved black people, does make it unique amongst the broader array of plantation tourism, from which representations of violence have ostensibly typically been omitted. Second, the main draw of haunted plantation tourism—ghosts, which are inherently fantastic entities—frustrates attempts to measure representations for their historical veracity. Third, haunted plantation tourism is not simply claiming to depict the past. Instead, it proposes to transport people into the time and place of slavery, amidst its characters and events, and thus amidst the violence that this tourism thematizes and offers up for touristic amusement.

This article keeps at the forefront a question posed by Saidiya Hartman: "to what end is the ghost of slavery conjured up?" (Hartman 2002, 763). While the plantation tourism I examine invokes haunting in such as way as to perpetuate slavery's violence, scholars such as Toni Morrison, Avery Gordon, Ian Baucom, David Marriott, Jenny Sharpe, Christopher Peterson, Hershini Bhana Young, and Sharon Patricia Holland have employed haunting tropes to critically interrogate slavery's ongoing effects. For example, Avery Gordon, who uses haunting both literally and metaphorically, argues in her reading of Toni

Morrison's *Beloved*, "paying attention to ghosts can, among other things, radically change how we know and what we know about state terror and about slavery and the legacy of American freedom that derives from it" (Gordon, 27-28). Sharon Holland's *Raising the Dead: Readings of Death and (Black) Subjectivity* conducts an inquiry into "the other side of that finite line" between life and death, such that "the line would no longer represent a demarcation but a suturing" (Holland, 2000, 4). For Holland, recognizing the dead links black subjects to ancestors, cutting through social death's refusal of black generationality. If, as Holland suggests, white American culture never stopped imagining black subjects as enslaved, and thus, in a certain sense, always already dead, Holland proposes that "embracing the subjectivity of death allows marginalized peoples to speak about the unspoken" (Holland, 4-5). Thus, scholars introduce haunting to demonstrate how slavery violently makes the modern world, and to undermine slavery's continuing and pervasive impact on living and dying. In contrast, haunted tourism looks nostalgically to earlier instantiations of slavery that this tourism considers past, except at rare places retaining that past. However, in order for this tourism to appear attractive as leisure or vacation activity, the force of slavery must be operative beyond the boundaries of these tourist sites, in the routes and cultural formations that embed this tourism. If, as scholars in black studies have demonstrated, slavery is constitutive of modernity, and continues to make the U.S. nation-state and its transnational world, this haunted plantation tourism is one instance where these effects unfold, and do so through the trope of haunting. To return, then, to Hartman's criteria for evaluating instances of slavery's haunting, the "ends" of the haunting in this plantation tourism are the remobilization of slavery's violent social formations, still with us today.

This article contributes to scholarship on slavery's contemporary violence, by examining how anti-blackness[7] is elaborated through an understudied kitschy popular culture form.[8] While this tourism may seem a relatively minor or obscure cultural phenomenon, and while this tourism vaunts the exceptionality and uniqueness of its ghostly sites, tourism relies on routes. Inasmuch as tourism circulates people, commerce, marketing, memorabilia, discourse, and affect, haunted plantation tourism indexes a racial violence that is not so much isolated as it is connected to broader social structures. But if this tourism is indexical rather than aberrational of racist culture, the peculiar mode of commodified haunting, which is variously playful, sardonic, campy, fantastic, and enchanted, allows for a kind of unguardedly frank expression of nostalgia for, and fantasy about, slavery in all its gratuitous violence. Perhaps this tourism has not undergone greater scrutiny because of its appearance as backward, cheap, crass, or ironic. Kitsch forms, Marita Sturken argues, operate through combining experiences of proximity and distance, as with haunted plantation tourism, which spectrally positions slavery as present yet past, as an experience unique to plantation tourism yet accessible for mass consumption. Sturken also points out that kitsch offers easy emotional formulas for complex histories, and thus sidesteps critical politics. Following Milan Kundera, Sturken suggests that kitsch sentimentality registers two affective moments: the first is through an emotion at the object of kitsch contemplation; the second is appreciation that the emotion is shared by humanity (22). I argue that haunted plantation tourism typically proposes that tourists experience emotions comparable to those of white slave masters. As such, this kitsch form offers an emotional connection routed through a slavery-circumscribed version of the human.[9]

By analyzing haunted plantation tourism discourse as it appears in official tour promotional materials, tourist guidebooks, news media coverage, and ghost hunting enthusiast groups' literature, I interrogate this tourism's violently subtended power relations as they manifest in racialized arrangements of space and time, horror and pleasure, ethical and aesthetic judgment, subjection and identification, kinship and enmity, and life and death. In what follows, I examine two plantations, as case studies demonstrating tendencies shared by other haunted plantation tourist sites. Myrtles and Destrehan appear more frequently in haunted tourism guidebooks than do some other sites. Here, each plantation is treated in a separate section, thus replicating typical guidebook organization by place entry, so that each description gives a sense of place for the particular site under scrutiny. At the same time, in this article, the entry headings for each plantation are subtitled in such a way as to identify the violence of the tourism, which while fascinated with violence, does not typically identify the violence of its own practices and epistemologies.[10] While Myrtles and Destrehan overlap with each other thematically and each evidences the themes shown through the Loyd Hall example given at the beginning of this article, the Myrtles case study focuses on the ways that haunted tourism deploys ghosts to stage an encounter with the time and space of slavery, wherein beauty, the good life, hospitality, and enjoyment are supposed to be the hallmarks of the plantation, while the entertainment on hand is the torture and bondage of enslaved black people. The Destrehan case study focuses on haunted plantation tourism's valorization and reproduction of white kinship, maintained through containment of slave revolt. I conclude the essay with a discussion of the manner in which the structure of haunted plantation tourism contributes to black social death by figuring contemporary black people as fungible objects, interchangeable with ghostly slaves.

THE MYRTLES PLANTATION, ST. FRANCISVILLE, LOUISIANA: AESTHETIC JUDGEMENT AND VIOLENT ENJOYMENT OF SLAVERY

The Myrtles Plantation has been a site of ghost tourism since at least the mid-twentieth century.[11] American surrealist photographer Clarence John Laughlin's 1948 *Ghosts Along the Mississippi*, a book that helped prompt plantation preservation, mentions that several ghost stories about Myrtles abound, but does not detail specifics. Between 1960 and 1964, the Louisiana Department of Commerce and Industry produced and circulated the booklet *Louisiana Plantation Homes*, an early example of tourism industry promotion of haunting at Myrtles. The booklet states that Myrtles "is popularly reputed to have at least one 'ghost'" (59). More so than other allegedly haunted plantations, today, Myrtles' official marketing foregrounds this plantation's haunted status. Myrtles has more entries in guidebooks of ghost hunting and haunted places than do other plantations. Even those guidebooks, news, and other popular media venues that are not primarily oriented toward a ghost touring audience and genre tend to put haunting narrative at the center of their accounts of Myrtles.[12]

To place tourists and potential or virtual tourists amidst ghosts, Myrtles proposes to be a place still in Antebellum time. The homepage of Myrtles' official website shows a photo of the plantation, with the following text superimposed over it:

Official Website
The Myrtles Plantation
circa 1796
"One of America's Most Haunted Homes"

The caption over the digital image acknowledges the existence of the internet medium and webpage genre, yet positions Myrtles as an epicenter of a national haunting within 1796. The fold in time, in national time, which this mise-en-scene suggests, recurs throughout Myrtles's promotional materials. The "History" page of the website reads: "The Myrtles Plantation, circa 1796, invites you to step into the past to experience antebellum splendor. You will see fine antiques and architectural treasures of the South and discover why The Myrtles has been called one of 'America's Most Haunted Homes.'" More than merely nostalgia, this passage proposes that the tourist will actually "step into the past," be transported back in time, or perhaps simply be in a place that is timeless, frozen at an earlier moment. To produce this temporal placement, this "experience" of "antebellum splendor," Myrtles directs tourists to antiques and architecture, "treasure of the South." One is invited to discover haunting itself embedded in these material artifacts. It is these material remains, at this site over time—though certainly altered by wear, preservation, refurbishment, duplication, transplantation, simulation—that link moments so as to freeze space and place. While haunting as spectrality often implies a kind of absence of physical form, here it is material culture that ultimately provides the evidentiary grounds, the conditions of possibility, for a discourse of haunting.

Aesthetic judgment defines the experience of these material artifacts, their past, and their staying power. "Treasured" architecture and antiques function as signs of the good life that "antebellum splendor" presumes and denotes. Thus, the call to the tourist to occupy, to experience, to be in the antebellum South apparently still lingering, entails that the tourist take on an axiological position. Even as the tourist is called upon to realize the character of staged plantation artifacts, the value judgment asked of the tourist is posed as a non-question. The beauty, the splendor, the treasure of plantation experience—exemplified and carried by haunted material culture—are to be taken as already apparent, true, and self-evident.

To measure the beautiful and related terms in the aesthetic register, this tourist discourse relies on a particular sensibility of the good and desirable. Couching evaluative terms in the language of historical fact, Myrtles' "History" webpage reads:

The history of the South will always provide us with tales of romance and mystery. The saga of the Antebellum South and a lifestyle that will never be forgotten lives on at this grand mansion. A first glimpse of the mansion with its magnificent double dormers and lacy grillwork of the 120-foot veranda envelopes [sic] one with a complete sense of peace and tranquility.

"Romance" and "mystery"—categories that can easily accommodate haunting and ghostly allures, while also gesturing at love, intrigue, sentimentalism, and heroism—set the mood and desire that frame architectural description and stories of persons and ghosts populating the plantation. Aesthetic judgment is linked to moral and ethical judgment. Valued are not simply the material artifacts, but particular Antebellum social forms to which the artifacts are tethered. Positively evaluated architecture—termed "grand," "magnificent"— is mobilized to construct a memory of a "lifestyle." Inasmuch as this lifestyle-imbued mansion "envelops" the tourist into a "complete sense of peace and tranquility," the ideal tourist is called upon to take on these sensibilities.

The aesthetic assessment of the building and romanticized plantation favors the worldview of the master. For on the plantation of chattel slavery, peaceful life comes in short supply. Life is a domain reserved for the master and those recognized as his family. Hierarchy amidst the life-infused white family does not distribute its tranquility equally amongst its gendered membership. The master governs his family, his house, and people deemed his property. The converse of the valorized master and family are the enslaved, subjected to unremitting gratuitous violence, including being possessed by and captive to another. Plantation tourism's discourse of aesthetic appreciation thus functions as a vehicle bearing relations of force and rule. Consideration of the ghost stories most often rehearsed and the ghosts most noted to lurk within the plantation clarifies the regime of life and death that clings to and forms the condition of possibility for the discursive construction of romantic life and splendorous architecture.

The "Mystery Tours" at Myrtles discuss several ghosts, as do guidebook entries. Chloe is the ghost most regularly mentioned in guidebook entries and the only ghost named on the official website.[13] The following account, from Jill Pascoe's guidebook, *Louisiana's Haunted Plantations*, condenses the crucial details typically rehearsed:

> In 1818 The Myrtles passed to Sarah Matilda (General Bradford's daughter) and her husband Judge Clarke Woodruff. While living in the home they owned a house slave named Chloe. She was apparently very curious and wanted to know the affairs of the house. She is also said to have been Judge Woodruff's mistress, a common practice at the time. In the early 1820s Chloe was caught eavesdropping outside either the gentleman's parlor or the dining room by Judge Woodruff. In his fury over Chloe's misbehavior Judge Woodruff ordered her left ear cut off. She was also banished from work in the house and forced to a life of labor in the fields. [...]
>
> In an attempt to make amends to the family and regain her position in the house Chloe baked a birthday cake for one of the Judge's daughters. However, this was no ordinary birthday cake. It contained oleander leaves, which produce a poison like arsenic. Some believe Chloe did not wish to kill anyone in the family, but merely make them sick. What's more, since she knew the cause of their ailment, she could cure them and regain her stature in the house. It is of course possible that she baked the cake as an act of terrible revenge to the Judge, but The Myrtles' staff prefer to think she had good intentions. Chloe's plan failed miserably. The women of the family fell deathly ill and Chloe could not cure them. A terrified Chloe confessed to the other slaves in the hope that someone wiser than she would be able to cure the ailing family, but it was too late. Sarah Matilda and her two daughters were dead by daybreak. In their horror over what she had done, the other slaves hanged Chloe and threw her corpse into the river. (Pascoe, 15)

This scene, central to the stories that draw tourists and mark this plantation as haunted, is articulated alongside the earlier mentioned aesthetic appreciation of the "romantic" plantation lifestyle. The two renderings are constitutive of one another. The discourse of romance structures this passage, as evidenced by use of a euphemism like "mistress" to describe the position of an enslaved black woman in a sexual encounter with the white man who owns her. This is characteristic of what Saidiya Hartman terms, "the discourse of seduction in slave law," which consists in "confusion between consent and coercion, feeling and submission, intimacy and domination, and violence and reciprocity" (1997, 81). Language such as that used to describe Chloe's position in relationship to Woodruff mystifies the complete subjection that slavery required, and like slave law, disavows the routine rape of black women under slavery. Hartman explains:

> The discourse of seduction obfuscates the primacy and extremity of violence in master-slave relations [...] Seduction makes recourse to the idea of reciprocal and collusive relations and engenders a precipitating of black female sexuality in which rape is unimaginable. As the enslaved is legally unable to give consent or offer resistance, she is presumed to be always willing. (81)

The discourse of seduction is prevalent throughout accounts of this story. An online news magazine, *nola.com: Everything New Orleans*, which does not even refer to Chloe as a slave, but as a "house servant," characterizes Chloe's position as the result of her decision: "Legend has it that Judge Woodruffe [sic] took up with Chloe, who gave in to the Judge's advances to keep her position in the house rather than working out in the fields." This passage offers decision constrained amidst power imbalance (notably, that of a judge and "servant," a misnomer blatantly concealing slavery). But the passage misses the fully antagonistic struggle between master and slave by framing this scenario as a negotiation around workplace assignment—Chloe "gives in" as a choice of labor relation. By what means could the enslaved woman's choice, agency, or consent be discerned in a situation such as this? Consequences for an enslaved woman resisting a master could consist of far worse than work relocation, as the slave was unremittingly subjected to the slave owner's unimpeded gratuitous violence. Law did not require that a white man who owned a slave seek the slave's permission to do anything. Under slavery, black women were not able to take a case of rape by a white man to court. White men's violence was seen as caused and necessitated by the sexuality of black women. According to Hartman, "Not only was rape simply unimaginable because of purported black lasciviousness, but also its repression was essential to the displacement of white culpability that characterized both the recognition of black humanity in slave law and the designation of the black subject as the originary locus of transgression and offense" (79-80). Myrtles tourism thus replicates nineteenth century dominant cultural and legal prescriptions. The versions of agency, desire, and relation that law and cultural norms mandated and allowed to appear are condensed into Myrtles's narrative description, which transforms slave law's projections into essential characteristics of the figures in this storied master-slave encounter.

Paradoxically, this story poses the enslaved Chloe's own actions as precipitating the series of events that ends in her eventual death. While she is depicted as ostensibly choosing to engage in a sexual relationship with Woodruff, eavesdrop on Woodruff's conversation, and poison Woodruff's family, it is only this last action that makes her legible as a ghost. This is no doubt haunted tourism's delayed cultural corollary of a legal situation, described by Hartman, wherein black women's agency did not appear before the law except by way of criminality. That is, enslaved black women were at times brought to trial for murder of a white man, whereas in most other instances, slave owners punished transgressions on their own without seeking redress to the court.[14] While Myrtles discourse treats Chloe as the driving force of an entire series of events, Chloe appears as an agent only to the extent that her will seems to diverge from that of the master. Until this moment of perceived defiance that begins the story, Chloe's will is presumed to be in line with that of the master. Chloe's transgression and the killings that result are the crux of this story—not slavery's regularized sexual violence, or even white masters' typical arbitrary bodily mutilation of enslaved people, which here appears as just a detail.

The story provides a lesson about the place of the slave, the sanctity of the heteropatriarchal white family, and the force of the law.[15] While some accounts treat Chloe's transgression as intentional revolt, such as Michael Norman and Beth Scott's *Historic Haunted America*, which narrates that "Chloe plotted to avenge the judge's ghastly punishment" with "a deadly treat" (Norman and Scott 187), Pascoe's version curbs that possibility, stating, "It is of course possible that she baked the cake as an act of terrible revenge to the Judge, but The Myrtles' staff prefer to think she had good intentions" (Pascoe 15). Apparently a slave's act of revenge does not signify "good intentions." Pascoe and the tour guides she describes align the sovereignty of the master and the law with the good, and would have tourists do the same. The law of the master acts in the name of white women and children, who, Tara McPherson notes in her work on plantation tourism, function as objects of protection and rescue in plantation tourist discourse. Myrtles discourse positions the killed white family members as tragic figures, with whom tourists can empathize. According to Pascoe's account as well as plantation tour narrations, the ghost of Sarah Matilda is occasionally heard crying in the house. Sarah Matilda's daughters' ghosts sometimes appear playing with phantom dolls, or they play with lights, amusing guests on the "mystery tour." At other times the children can be noticed reliving the drawn-out agony of their deaths from poisoning. These are unobtrusive, basically benign ghosts. In contrast, Chloe is a threatening ghost. Pascoe writes, "Guests have reported a sense of dread as if someone was watching over them while in bed. When they open their eyes, a woman with a green turban is peering intently at them. Sometimes guests report being tucked tightly into bed as if they were children"(16). The ideal tourist is to assume the position of the white family, to reside in the place of the ghostly white family, alternatively threatened and served by Chloe.

The force of the law is further displaced insofar as it is other slaves that punish Chloe for killing the family. The black woman in revolt is portrayed at odds with the interests and affect of the black slaves who avenge the white family. By Norman and Scott's account, "the Woodruffe [sic] slaves were outraged at Chloe's deed. They dragged her to a tall tree near the Mississippi River and hanged her. Her corpse was thrown into the river" (Norman and Scott 187). According to Pascoe's version, in "horror over what she had done, the other slaves hanged Chloe and threw her corpse into the river" (Pascoe 15). The Myrtles entry on the website *Angels and Ghosts* contends that slaves hung Chloe to avoid mass retribution from Woodruff. In each version, the law of the master is carried out, as the punishment for transgression is achieved, whether marked as the will of the enslaved in line with that of the master, or as the enslaved acting inevitably in fear of the will of the master. While scholars such as Angela Davis, Rebecca Hall, and many others have demonstrated that black women struggled together in solidarity with black men against their common enslavement, this story portrays black women's resistance to slavery as an imposition against the will and well being of the black community.

The spectacle of the community of slaves lynching the enslaved black woman further displaces the violence of slave-owning white men and the racist and sexist law inasmuch as this image makes lynching something that enslaved black people do, rather than some-thing that whites, particularly white men do. Even after slavery, white men killed black people with impunity, and carried out thousands of lynchings, mostly of black men, in the late nineteenth and early twentieth century United States. Black men who were lynched were typically falsely accused of raping white women or otherwise degrading white womanhood. In Myrtles discourse it is the black woman, Chloe, who threatens white womanhood and childhood, and it is a mob of black slaves who lynch her in response. Myrtles effaces white men's violence against black women by making violence appear to be something originating with black people.

Interestingly, Judge Woodruff appears untouched by the violence of this narrative. His ghost is not called up in this tale. Myrtles preserves the position of mastery for this white man who owns slaves. The uneven relationships between each of these haunted figures—Woodruff and Sarah Matilda, this couple's children, and the enslaved Chloe— suggest the racialized and gendered terms through which tourists are to be interpellated into the time and space of the Antebellum grandeur. Tourists are called to be a part of the scene of plantation life, in the same time as these figures, no less. These ostensibly historical personages are supposed to lurk about the grounds in spectral form. As such, tourists might find themselves reflected in one of these figures, or they might simply find themselves next to, in conflict or alliance with, these ghosts who populate the plantation alongside them. If Woodruff's ghost is not there, perhaps tourists are to view the planta-tion through the eyes of the absent master-enslaver.

In this example, ghostly entertainment, aesthetic appreciation, and nostalgia are vehi-cles conveying ongoing relations of force derived from slavery. The tourist spectacle aligns with and rehabilitates nineteenth century cultural beliefs that imagined black women as seductresses who brought about the downfall of white families. Black revolt is seen as criminality, a threat to tranquility. The white family trope laments and disavows the loss of slave relations. White men's violence against white and black women is blamed on black women, while the white man and the law are posed to protect, directly or through proxies, white family plantation life from the enslaved. The tourist is invited to occupy the posi-tion of the white family in tranquility, as either master or master's family, cared for (and possibly threatened) by the enslaved. This haunted tourism brings the white family and black slave back in ghost form, subject positions suspended in time, structured through forms of exclusive white kinship and black social death. By proposing that the plantation is in Antebellum time, wandered by ghostly masters and slaves, and that tourists enjoy engaging in this temporal-spatial arrangement of white subjectivity and black objecthood, haunted tourism mobilizes slavery's ongoing antagonism.

DESTREHAN PLANTATION, DESTREHAN, LOUISIANA:
ANTAGONISM BETWEEN WHITE GENEALOGY AND THE SLAVE REVOLT

At one point, over two hundred enslaved people were held in captivity at Destrehan Plantation. Its mansion, today refurbished and preserved, was first constructed in the 1780s. The River Road Historical Society, which has run Destrehan since 1971, insists that history is the main objective in Destrehan preservation and heritage work, and denies ever propagating ghost stories. Still, scenes from *Interview with a Vampire*—a haunted though not ghost story—were filmed at Destrehan. Additionally, guidebooks and the *New Orleans Times-Picayune* newspaper have printed stories about tourist and employee experiences with haunting.[16] *The Ghostly Register*, a guidebook from 1986, notes, "the current proprietors of the mansion go so far as to issue a flyer telling of recent sightings of apparitions, titled, *Ghost Sightings at Destrehan Plantation? You Be the Judge.*" Expressing skepticism, for "anecdotes seem, however, to be of recent origin, after major restorations had been undertaken and tours were instituted on a systemic basis," this guidebook nonetheless avers, "the sheer number of apparent witnesses—many of them employees of the place but many others tourists—does give pause even to the hardened skeptic" (135).

The lengthiest published account of Destrehan Plantation haunting is the 1991 book, *Past Masters*, written by Madeline Levatino, who had been a Destrehan tour guide in the 1980s, and illustrated by Phyllis Barraco, who had been the gift shop manager in the 1980s.[17] The text can be treated as a template for haunted tourism discourse at Destrehan, as several guidebooks cite *Past Masters* as authoritative. The epigraph demonstrates the book's reverie for the house, views on kinship, and high esteem for enslavers: "The house has stood on the east bank of the Mississippi River for more than 200 years. It has endured time, the elements, abandonment and desecration. Within its walls, dreams were nourished and tragedies sheltered, for it was home to some of the noblest families in Louisiana." The "noble" families in question—white families, for the slave is not allowed the possibility of kinship—are subjects of admiration and empathy. In the first half of the book, framed as the more historical section, each chapter is titled with the name of a different male proprietor of the plantation, all members of the Destrehan family. Events are narrated through these slave-owning white men's lives. Chapters focus on these men's business interactions, notable accomplishments, estate improvements, marriages, relationships, personal virtues, and emotional dispositions. *Past Masters* bemoans several events in these men's lives, including deaths of wives and children and various financial losses, and valorizes the "masters."

White enslavers are the protagonists of Destrehan Plantation ghost lore, which treats enslaved people as typically unimportant, but periodically threatening. The "history" section of *Past Masters* occasionally mentions purchases or ownership transfers of slaves, or tasks slaves were ordered to carry out. Anything slaves built is discussed as a feat that the master achieved. One chapter, "1811, A Major Slave Uprising," however, details "the largest slave uprising in United States history," or the German Coast Uprising.[18] The uprising did not begin at Destrehan, but ended there with a trial and mass execution of twenty-one black people. The trial's jurists consisted of local white men who owned both plantations and slaves. One was Jean Noel Destrehan, who has a whole chapter dedicated to him, in which the reader learns of his agricultural innovations and home expansions, his fondness for the plantation and sadness at the death of his wife, his "noble" upbringing and "non-extravagance." In contrast, Levatino refers to people revolting against their own enslavement as a "murderous group [...] looting and burning" (20). One slave-holding plantation owner is depicted as taking a last stand: "After sending his wife and children to safety, Trepagnier armed himself and defiantly awaited the insurrectionaries, determined to protect his property" (20). The story gives consideration to the well being of white families; individual whites killed are noted by name; white people's emotions such as defiance, or even "fear and panic" as they "hastily packed trunks and fled" are all noted in some detail.

In contrast, the experiences and emotions of black people struggling against slavery are not explored; black community or family concerns are not allowed for; their revolt is decontextualized—they are simply "murderous." The only relation the black slave has is to the white master, and that relation is summed up as either loyalty or murderous betrayal. In one passage, Levatino makes fleeting reference to the emotion of a slave: "Trepagnier was shot to death, reportedly by one of his own slaves who had become angered because of a failed promise of freedom" (20). It seems by this account that anger could only arise from some specific offense within enslavement—as if slavery in and of itself were not enough to merit revolt or even anger. In another instance, "Whites living on plantations in the vicinity were warned of the uprising by loyal house servants" (20). Apparently, when the enslaved are "loyal" they deserve the euphemism "servant." The very notion of "loyalty"—like the discourse of "romance"—is an effacement of slavery's complete domination and terms of utterly violent subjection, in which the slave is to have no agency that is not always already folded into the sovereign will of the master. Levatino can give no explanation of what rebellion could possibly mean to the enslaved, to black people in revolt. It is as if all that could possibly matter for the interested tourist or for history as such is the meaning of the uprising from the perspective of whites invested in maintaining slavery. As with Myrtles, any instance of enslaved people's rebellion against their oppression appears first and foremost as a disruption of plantation "tranquility" and as a matter resolved finally with the force of law:

> All 21 leaders were found guilty of murder and rebellion and condemned to death, with the sentences to be carried out immediately. They were taken to their own plantations and shot. Once executed, each was decapitated and their heads were put on poles placed along the levee road—as an example to all who would disturb the public tranquility. (22)

In stories offered as historical background explaining haunting, Destrehan tourist discourse places itself on the side of slavery law. Destrehan tourist discourse is marked by slavery's alliances and hostilities, with factions mobilized through alleged contemporary interactions between living persons and ghosts.

Contemporary anti-blackness and white kinship organize the affect circulating in haunted plantation tourism. Ghosts of the white family, enthroned as the rightful proprietors to the preserved plantation, are posed as basically benevolent ghosts, with which tourists can interact on friendly, educational, or empathetic terms. In Levatino, ghost children roll out a ball to tourists. Another ghost mourns the death of his wife. Another reminisces of raising his granddaughter. Levatino fondly remembers being a tour guide, witnessing hauntings, documenting sightings, and working to discover the identities of Destrehan family spirits. Connecting the Destrehan family and the Historical Society with employees who curate, maintain, and guide tourists through the house, Levatino expresses a sense of generationality and lineage. This heritage is racially selective, as a reported encounter between a guest and Jean Noel Destrehan's ghost makes clear:

> The woman continued, "We began talking and he asked me—in a thick French accent—why had I come to Destrehan? I told him that my research of a past family member had led me to believe that possibly he may have lived here as a slave, and that maybe there was documented evidence filed here to clarify this. The woman explained that she then told the gentleman the slave's name, to which he replied, "There was no one by that name who lived or worked here." (58; first quotation unclosed in original)

In Levatino's account, the ghost of the white master refuses a traceable lineage to the descendent of the slave, thus bringing to bear what Orlando Patterson terms, "natal alienation," wherein the enslaved is denied familial and kinship connections, left without forbears or contemporaries. Here, it is the contemporary black tourist who is confronted with this natal alienation.

Destrehan curatorial, historical preservation, and docent practices have prioritized the extension, into the present, of the interests, legacy, and even kinship of the white enslaving class. It is as if recent plantation administrators and staff have acted as "surrogates" (to call on Joseph Roach's term) for the Destrehans, by acting in their place. For example, in *Louisiana's Haunted Plantations*, Pascoe claims that the ghost of one of the Destrehans smiled with approval upon looking over the River Road Historical Society's restoration of the grounds and mansion. Barbara Sillery's *The Haunting of Louisiana*, published in 2001, similarly constructs a continuity of white kinship amidst which the enslaved black is constituted as a nonentity, if still a commodity. In Sillery, one tour guide recounts and relates to Destrehan kinship in this way:

> Marion is dressed in character as one of the Destrehan wives who lost her husband at a young age. [...] When pressed to identify a few of these entities, Marion confesses, 'I am drawn to Nicholas. That's the simplest way I can put it. There's something about him that touches my heart and saddens me. I read a lot about Nicholas. He married at the age of twenty-one to a girl named Victoire Fortier. He loved her dearly. They were married for eleven years when she died. Nicholas mourned her for the rest of his life.' [...] A deep sigh escapes from Marion. 'Sometimes it's almost like I can feel Nicholas, his presence, his sadness.' (53)

Performing as a wife of a Destrehan man, the docent Marion also affectively occupies this subject position, as she "feels" and is "drawn to" this "entity," who lived from 1793-1848. Marion mourns this family and their tragedies. At times, Marion acts "[l]ike a mother of a wayward child [...] indulgent when it comes to Nicholas" (52).

In another instance couched in familial affect, this same docent argues that the ghost of the pirate Jean Lafitte, which can be spotted at the plantation, is no indication that any Destrehan consorted with bayou pirates, avoiding paying taxes on stolen "'Black Ivory' (slaves)" (51). Contrary to such accusations, writes Sillery, "Destrehan docent Marion

Herbert is positive the honorable patriarch, Jean Noel Destrehan, would never have stooped to dealing in such illicit trade. 'Here's a man who's putting together the state constitution and believes in the laws that he's writing'" (51). Business with pirate Jean Lafitte is disreputable not because that entailed participation in the enslavement of black people, but because that meant breaking laws put in place to keep the system of slavery robust. Most important to this heritage tourism is the maintenance of the good name of the slave-holding class of whites. This is the only mention of slavery in this particular guidebook's entry on Destrehan. In this discourse, enslaved blacks are positioned as non-entities, adjuncts to the main story, or props in the life dramas of white men. Black people are at issue only as property, and the status of and allegiances between white men remain based on this fundamental antagonistic relation of enslavement.

To further defend the Destrehan family from challenges to its estate, this same docent characterizes any encroachment on slavery-derived wealth as a form of sexual violation. Sillery's guidebook reports that the ghost of pirate Jean Lafitte was seen "pointing to a secret cache of buried treasure," inciting "looters" to go "on a rampage, nearly annihilating the historic structure in their quest for gold. Ascending the staircase, the fiercely protective docent denounces the grave impact on Destrehan as 'rape'" (47). McPherson points out that plantations are often described as women, and challenges to plantation property are often discussed in tourist and other popular white culture as paralleling sexual violence against white women. As an excuse for anti-black laws, lynching, and other repressive measures undertaken to reverse trends toward redistributing some power and wealth to black populations in the wake of the Civil War, whites regularly falsely accused black men of raping white women. While here treasure-hunters are the issue, the notion of "looters" "raping" the house subtly references portrayals of Union soldiers and black people confiscating Southern whites' property. Plantation tourism frequently mentions plantation owners burying their wealthy belongings in caches about their properties, in hopes that it would not be taken by the Union. In more than one text, Destrehan Plantation tourism narratives express a tone of tragedy when discussing the period after the Civil War during which the Destrehan Plantation mansion was turned into a Freedman's Bureau, followed by a tone of relief when recounting that the house was eventually returned to the control and ownership of a Destrehan family member, Pierre Adolph Rost—or "the last master," as Levatino calls him.

Due to broad criticisms of plantation tourism and local efforts by black historians and museum curators to include more representations of slavery from African American viewpoints, in 2011 Destrehan participated in a commemoration of the historic 1811 revolt that shook the foundations of the slave system all along the River Road and that eliminated several enslavers before the people were re-captured and executed. The River Road Historical Society cooperated with the New Orleans African American Museum in Treme and Tulane University in several events throughout the course of the year.[19] Despite recognition of the importance of a dramatic event that both crystallized and challenged the fundamental antagonism that makes plantation tours possible today, this commemoration remains supplemental to Destrehan. The slave revolt is but a temporary interruption to the Destrehan schedule. Despite its participation in several days of revolt commemoration events in 2011, including a couple of days at the Destrehan Plantation, Destrehan under River Road Society administration continues its valorization of white kinship, evidenced by "The Legacy" section of the website, where the Destrehan family line—a white line, exclusive of any enslaved black biological relatives, of course—is narrated through brief biographies for each cherished member. Plantation life ways continue to be celebrated in "historic demonstrations" on the site now, where employee-actors perform various tasks that people on the plantation might have carried out. Whites demonstrate open hearth cooking, bousillage construction (a method for making insulated walls), indigo dying and candle making. It is questionable of course to what extent slave-holding whites would have done any of these activities rather than force the work upon enslaved black people. Demonstrations also now include "African American herbal remedies," described on the website in the following terms: "Just as Africans brought their customs, traditions and religious beliefs with them from Africa, they also brought their medicinal remedies and cures. They also developed cures and remedies themselves. These remedies were highly valued by the white population of the plantation." Apparently these remedies are still valuable to white members of the population, as the methods of production are again commodified and easily appropriated for tourist educational entertainment. This accumulation of surplus value and surplus pleasure is just part of the idyllic scene that Destrehan continues to create. This instantiation of Destrehan tourism, more than haunted-themed versions, aptly fits Hartman's observation that "[t]he restored plantations of the South reek with the false grandeur of the good old days, and the cabins don't appear horrible enough" (Hartman 2002, 774). Haunted tourism revels in horror, as part of the grandeur. This does not mean that Destrehan's revised staging, sans haunting, is so different from haunted plantation tourism. The seemingly contradictory tourist mise-en-scene, wherein slave revolt commemoration participation sits right alongside the happy re-enactment of the white family tree and celebratory demonstrations of plantation daily life (minus demonstrations of whipping, rape, murder, and other specific modes of discipline), can be understood as a form of narrative, spatial, and affective containment.

Tracking Destrehan haunted fare alongside recent onsite curatorial shifts, the contradictions of plantation tourism—both that tourism explicitly claiming to be haunted, as well as that claiming to be historical at the exclusion of haunting—become clear. If ghost tourism revels in stories of killing, it only brings to the surface particular signs of violence. For the entire institution of slavery is violence—black captivity and social death. Whether in haunted Destrehan tourism, today confined to guidebooks and reports from employees and ghost hunting enthusiasts, or in official tours that favor "historic demonstrations" over ghost stories, Destrehan discourse celebrates and reconstructs white familial genealogy and kinship. Whether construing black revolt against slavery as a scary ghost spectacle or humoring a brief commemoration alongside typical tourist fare, Destrehan promotes identification with white enslavers and containment of black revolt. White master and black slave positions are antagonistic. As such, the perspectives of white masters and black slaves cannot happily co-exist side by side.[20] Were people invited to participate in revolt rather than to simply commemorate revolt, the entire contemporary social structure that stages such a pairing would be thrown into question.[21]

RECURRING VIOLENCE: TOURIST ROUTES AND BLACK SOCIAL DEATH

Although texts and curatorial practices across Loyd Hall, Myrtles, and Destrehan vary somewhat and shift over time, long-standing is a mode of address that figures contemporary whites and to a lesser extent other nonblack people as the subjects of this tourism, and treats contemporary black people variously as non-tourists, as potential tourists to whom no consideration need be extended, or as tourists who become significant only in afterthoughts. This racially organized address to the potential tourist has ramifications for haunted plantation tourism's rendition of time and space. If, as Holland observes, white people are granted the capacity to move through time, while black people are fixed in space (2012, 18), then haunted plantation tourism enacts this by granting generationality to whites and potentially other nonblack tourists, through the invitation to join in kinship and solidarity with past white enslavers—a position antithetical to black freedom, let alone tourist mobility. Blackness is a subject position that emerged with captivity, so that blackness has been defined through and stuck to, as Wilderson puts it, "slaveness," and as Holland argues, white culture still cannot imagine a shift from black slave to free subject. But clearly, haunted plantation tourism does not overtly invite black people today to identify as slaves. For this tourism, only white identification travels across time, while black ghosts remain captive in plantation spaces without making the leap into kinship with contemporary black people.

At first, it might seem as if the denial of black movement across time challenges haunted plantation tourism's dramatic proposition of a temporal folding, wherein nineteenth century ghosts and violent domination act in the present. However, the prescription of black spatial fixity and temporal stillness are extensions of slavery's modes of domination. Like the ghosted nineteenth century slave, the contemporary black potential tourist too is fixed in space, in that tourist routes are narrowly circumscribed when destinations threaten anti-black violence. Moreover, as extensive scholarship in black studies has demonstrated, there seems to be nowhere black people are not vulnerable to gratuitous violence. Thus, the denial of a black genealogy further enables the logic of black fungibility. For the commonality of a refused kinship is one more sign of the objectifying exchangeability allotted to the ghostly black slave and contemporary black people. It is no wonder that Judith Jackson Fossett, having conducted participant-observation research on plantation tourism, reports being treated "like a ghost," such that, "as a black woman [...] the role of tourist within these spaces always seemed like an ill-fitting garment."

Notes

1. Pascoe's author biography indicates that she has worked at several reputedly haunted historic houses.
2. See Wilderson, *Red, White, & Black*. Wilderson also considers how American Indians are positioned within antagonisms constitutive of U.S. antagonisms.
3. Tara McPherson argues that plantation tourism and Southern tourism more generally operate within a "lenticular logic," in which nostalgic appreciation of the Southern past appear alongside representations of racism's history, but the two are held apart as if unrelated. Contrary to McPherson's assertion, what is at hand here is perhaps better gleaned not as a repression or sidelining of violent realities inconvenient to fantasies of a glorious South, but instead as violence immediately noticeable in plantation tourism. Slavery, in its material and spectral manifestations, are precisely the spectacle on offer.
4. While certainly the majority of haunted plantation tour-goers are white, this is not to say that no black people ever go on such tours. In fact, black scholars who have researched and gone on plantation tours and other slavery-related tours have provided important critiques that centrally inform my study here. However, my article is focused on the dominant discourse of these tours, especially as it forms a template across a range of texts.

5. Examples of scholarship employing or discussing this method of analysis include: Dann and Seaton's *Slavery, Contested Heritage, and Thanatourism*; Mercedes J. Quintos' "Museum Presentations of Slavery: The Problems of Evidence and the Challenge of Representation"; Alderman and Campbell's "Symbolic Excavation and the Artifact Politics of Remembering Slavery in the American South"; and Buzinde and Santos' "Interpreting Slavery Tourism."

6. "Master enslavers" is Eichstedt and Small's term emphasizing whites' active perpetration of enslavement of black people. Eichstedt and Small refer to "enslaved black people" rather than simply saying "slaves" in order to emphasize that people were enslaved, even if the law and white culture did not recognize the personhood or humanity of enslaved black people. While I have chosen to follow Eichstedt and Small's lead in this terminology, I do not intend to efface the radical exclusion of blackness from the human. For more on anti-blackness as constitutive of the ontology of the human, see work by Franz Fanon, Sylvia Wynter, Hortense Spillers, Saidiya Hartman, Frank Wilderson, and Jared Sexton.

7. "Antiblackness" is a term that Frank Wilderson, Jared Sexton, and many other scholars in black studies use to distinguish racial domination exercised over black people from racism more generally.

8. For scholarly work on haunting in popular culture, see Blanco and Peeren's edited volume, *Popular Ghosts*. My essay in that volume on haunted prison tourism considers slavery's legacy, to some extent. Other scholarly work on kitschy popular cultural enactments of haunting (though not by ghosts) in the wake of slavery includes Deborah Christie and Sarah Juliet Lauro's edited volume, *Better off Dead*.

9. Again, this is not necessarily a commentary on what emotions actual tourists feel. Although I would suggest that many tourists do embody the affect foregrounded in this tourism's discourse, my article does not offer an empirical study of reception.

10. There are hundreds of guidebooks on haunting in the United States. In the book I am writing, *Haunted Guidebooks: Siting Violence and Tourism in American Culture*, I offer theoretical consideration of the guidebook as a figure to think through haunted tourism. For more on the national politics of guidebooks, see Grewal.

11. However, Myrtles operators did not always officially promote or endorse ghost tourism. According to a local newspaper, for a brief period in the late 1980s, house operators discontinued ghost tours, weekend murder mystery events, and Halloween tours (Hamilton, 1989).

12. The official Myrtles website boasts its extensive media coverage: "The Myrtles has been featured in *New York Times, Forbes, Gourmet, Veranda, Travel and Leisure, Country Inns, Colonial Homes, Delta SKY* and on the Oprah Show, A&E, the History Channel, The Travel Channel, The Learning Channel, National Geographic Explorer, and *GOOD MORNING AMERICA*. It was also featured in *The haunting of Louisiana*." [caps in original]. (http://www.myrtlesplantation.com/history.html), accessed Sept 2013

13. Though details may vary slightly across iterations, the tale of Chloe and the poisoned family members has a recurring template, repeated in a number of texts. When I went in person on a tour at Myrtles in 2009, the tour included this story with roughly the same basic details, and showed photographs supposedly capturing Chloe on film.

14. Hartman explains: "[T]he law's selective recognition of slave humanity nullified the captive's ability to give consent or act as agent, and at the same time acknowledged the intentionality and agency of the slave but only as it assumed the form of criminality. The recognition and/or stipulation of agency as criminality served to identify personhood with punishment. Within the terms of the law, the enslaved was either a will-less object or a chastened agent." (80)

15. Following Hartman, Wilderson and Sexton see the position of the black female slave as paradigmatic of the most extreme violence to which black subjects are exposed and through which the black is subjected.

16. Guidebooks that discuss Destrehan include: Buxton's *Haunted Plantations*; Dickinson's *Haunted City*; Hauck's *Haunted Places: The National Directory*; Myers' *The Ghostly Register*; Norman's *Haunted Historic America*; Pascoe's *Louisiana's Haunted Plantations*; Sillery's *The Haunting of Louisiana*; Smith's *Journey Into Darkness...Ghosts and Vampires of New Orleans*.

17. This biographical information is from *Past Masters*, guidebooks discussing *Past Masters*, and from reporting in *The New Orleans Times-Picayune*.

18. For a scholarly historical account of this rebellion, see Rasmussen, *American Uprising: The Untold Story of America's Largest Slave Revolt*.

19. For news coverage of exhibit opening and schedule of events, see Thompson, "1811 slave revolt leaves mark on U.S. history—Opening Exhibit set at plantation."

20. A *Times-Picayune* news article reported that one exhibit attendee "related to slave owners affected by the revolt" claimed to "want to talk about this without judgment, to try to understand it from both sides."

The article's title, "New exhibit helps some find pieces of their past," begs the question as to whose past the exhibit will retrieve. Significantly, the article only interviews people identified as descendants of "slave owners." See Urbaszewski.

21. News coverage in the *Times-Picayune* tended to follow the lead of the River Road Society's placement of the revolt in the past. See, for example, Littice Bacon's "Fight for Freedom." As part of the commemoration, Tulane University, with significant participation from the History Department, put together a conference called "Black Resistance in an Age of Revolution," the title of which suggests the temporal placement of the revolt in the past. For conference schedule, see: http://blackresistance.wordpress.com/about/ (accessed Feb 24, 2014). Predictably, the conference and news coverage would focus on present historiographical questions. Significant for the sake of my argument, however, is that Destrehan tourism would not invite people to be a part of revolt, as haunted plantation tourism invites (white) people to take up the place of the master.

Works Cited

Alderman, Derek H. and Rachel M. Campbell. "Symbolic Excavation and the Artifact Politics of Remembering Slavery in the American South." *Southeastern Geographer* 48.3 (2008): 338-355.

Bacon, Littice. "FIGHT FOR FREEDOM: 200 years ago, a makeshift army stormed the River Parishes in the largest slave revolt in U.S. history." *Times-Picayune* 4 Jan. 2011: A01.

Baucom, Ian. *Specters of the Atlantic: Finance Capital, Slavery, and the Philosophy of History.* Durham, NC: Duke University Press, 2005.

Bissell, Walter. "Myrtles Plantation." *Angels and Ghosts.* N.p., 2004-2007. Web. Accessed 26 March 2011.

"Black Resistance in an Age of Revolution." *Black Resistance in an Age of Revolution.* N.p., n.d. Web. Accessed 24 Feb. 2014.

Buxton, Geordie. *Haunted Plantations: Ghosts of Slavery and Legends of the Cotton Kingdoms.* Chicago, IL: Arcadia Pubising: 2007.

Buzinde, Christine and Carla Almeida Santos. "Interpreting Slavery Tourism." *Annals of Tourism Research* 36.3 (2009): 439-458.

Christie, Deborah and Sarah Juliet Lauro. *Better Off Dead: The Evolution of the Zombie as Post-Human.* Fordham University Press, 2011.

Dann, Graham M.S. and A.V. Seaton, eds. *Slavery, Contested Heritage, and Thanatourism.* Binghamtpon, NY: The Haworth Hospitality Press, Haworth Press, Inc., 2001.

Davis, Angela. "Reflections on the Black Woman's Role in the Community of Slaves." *The Massachusetts Review* 13.1-2 (1972): 81-10.

Dickinson, Joy. *Haunted City: An Unauthorized Guide to the Magical, Magnificent New Orleans of Anne Rice.* New York, NY: Citadel Press, 2004.

Dwyer, Jeff. *Ghost Hunter's Guide to New Orleans.* Gretna, LA: Pelican Publishing Company, 2007.

Fossett, Judith Jackson. "Slavery's Ephemera: The Contemporary Life of the Antebellum Plantation." *Vectors* 2.1 (2006). Online multimedia article. Accessed 30 November 2014.

Gordon, Avery. *Ghostly Matters: Haunting and the Sociological Imagination.* Minneapolis, MN: University of Minnesota Press, 1997.

Grewal, Inderpal. *Home and Harem: Nation, Gender, Empire, and the Cultures of Travel.* Durham, NC: Duke University Press, 1996.

Hamilton, Anne Butler. "THE MYRTLES *** Come to dinner—no ghosts invited." *Baton Rouge Morning Advocate.* October 5, 1989. 1G.

Hartman, Saidiya. "The Time of Slavery." *The South Atlantic Quarterly* 101.4 (2002): 757-777.

Hartman, Saidiya. *Scenes of Subjection: Terror, Slavery, and Self-Making in Nineteenth Century America.* New York, NY: Oxford University Press, 1997.

Hauck, Dennis William. *Haunted Places: the National Directory.* New York, NY: Penguin Books, 2002.

"History." *Myrtles Plantation.* Myrtles Plantation, n.d. Web. Accessed March 2011.

Holland, Sharon Patricia. *The Erotic Life of Racism.* Durham, NC: Duke University Press, 2012.

Holland, Sharon Patricia. *Raising the Dead: Readings of Death and (Black) Subjectivity.* Durham, NC: Duke University Press, 2000.

Holland, Sharon. "The Question of Normal." *GLQ: A Journal of Lesbian and Gay Studies* 10.1 (2003): 128-131.

"Home." *Myrtles Plantation.* Myrtles Plantation, n.d. Web. Accessed 25 May 2011.

Kermeen, Frances. *The Myrtles Plantation: The True Story of America's Most Haunted House.* New York, NY: Warner Books, 2005.

Laughlin, Clarence John. *Ghosts Along the Mississippi: The Magic of the Old Houses of Louisiana.* New York, NY: Bonanza Books, 1948.

Levatino, Madeline. *Past Masters: The History & Hauntings of Destrehan Plantation.* New Orleans, LA: Dinstuhl Printing and Publishing, 1991.

Louisiana Department of Commerce and Industry. *Louisiana Plantation Homes.* LA: Louisiana Department of Commerce and Industry, circa 1960.

Marriott, David. *Haunted Life: Visual Culture and Black Modernity.* New Brunswick, NJ: Rutgers University Press, 2007.

McPherson, Tara. *Reconstructing Dixie: Race, Gender, and Nostalgia in the Imagined South.* Durham, NC: Duke University Press, 2003.

Montz, Larry and Daena Smoller. *ISPR Investigates the Ghosts of New Orleans.* Atglen, PA: Whitford Press, Schiffer Publishing, 2000.

Myers, Arthur. *The Ghostly Register: Haunted Dwellings—Active Spirits A Journey to America's Strangest Landmarks.* Chicago, IL: Contemporary Books, Inc., 1986.

Norman, Michael and Beth Scott. *Haunted Historic America.* New York, NY: Tom Doherty Associates, 1995.

Pascoe, Jill. *Louisiana's Haunted Plantations.* Baton Rouge, LA: Irongate Press, 2004.

Peterson, Christopher. *Kindred Specters: Death Mourning, and American Affinity.* Minneapolis, MN: University of Minnesota Press, 2007.

Quintos, Mercedes J. "Museum Presentations of Slavery: The Problems of Evidence and the Challenge of Representation." George Washington University, 1999. Web. Accessed March 20, 2011.

Rasmussen, Daniel. *American Uprising: The Untold Story of America's Largest Slave Revolt.* New York, NY: Harper Perennial, 2012.

Roach, Joseph. *Cities of the Dead: Circum-Atlantic Performance.* New York, NY: Columbia University Press, 1996.

Scheets, Gary. "Plantation Haunting Described by Many." *nola.com: Everything New Orleans.* nola.com, 2008. Web. Accessed 26 March 2011.

Sexton, Jared. "'The Curtain of the Sky': An Introduction." *Critical Sociology* 36.1 (2010): 11-24.

Sexton, Jared. "People-of-Color-Blindness: Notes on the Afterlife of Slavery." *Social Text* 28.2 (2010): 31-56.

Sharpe, Jenny. *Ghosts of Slavery: A Literary Archaelogy of Black Women's Lives.* Minneapolis, MN: University of Minnesota Press, 2003.

Sillery, Barbara. *The Haunting of Louisiana.* Gretna, LA: Pelican Publishing Company, 2001.

Smith, Katherine Kalila. *Journey Into Darkness…Ghosts and Vampires of New Orleans.* New Orleans, LA: De Simonin Publications, 1998.

Spillers, Hortense. *Black, White, and in Color: Essays on American Literature and Culture.* Chicago, IL: University Chicago Press, 2003.

Sturken, Marita. *Tourists of History: Memory, Kitsch, and Consumerism from Oklahoma City to Ground Zero.* Durham, NC: Duke University Press, 2007.

Thompson, Angel. "1811 slave revolt leaves mark on U.S. history—Opening of exhibit set at plantation." *Times-Picayune* [New Orleans, LA] 6 Jan. 2011: I02.

Titone, Connie. "Tell whole story of plantations." *Baton Rouge Advocate.* January 13, 2000. 8B.

Urbaszewski, Katie. "New exhibit helps some find pieces of their past—Slave revolt observance kicks off in Destrehan." *Times-Picayune* [New Orleans, LA] 9 Jan. 2011, Metro sec.: B01.

Wilderson III, Frank. *Red, White, and Black: Cinema and the Structure of U.S. Antagonisms.* Durham, NC: Duke University Press, 2010.

Young, Hershini Bhana. *Haunting Capital: Memory, Text, and the Black Diasporic Body.* Lebanon, NH: Dartmouth College Press, University Press of New England: 2006.

Specters of Slavery and the Corporeal Materiality of Resurrection in George Washington Cable's *The Grandissimes* and Octavia Butler's *Kindred*

by Sarah Hirsch

The opening line of Octavia Butler's novel *Kindred* (1979) details the story of Dana, a black woman living in 1970s Los Angeles who is mysteriously transported back to the antebellum South in order to save the white man who will eventually father her ancestor: "I lost my arm on my last trip home. My left arm" (Butler 1988, 9). Introduced in Butler's sci-fi, neo-slave narrative's provocative prologue, Dana is reminiscent of another literary figure that appears—a century prior—in George Washington Cable's historical melodrama *The Grandissimes* (1880). The legendary tale of Bras-Coupé, the insurrectionary one-armed slave turned maroon, interrupts Cable's gothic tale. The diversion away from the travails of the first families of Louisiana to invoke the story of a character that links their fates illustrates Cable's preoccupation with race and slavery which shadows the text. The story of Bras-Coupé is said to be based on a true story that was widely reported in the newspapers of New Orleans at the time of Cable's writing, but one has to wonder if Bras-Coupé is based on another one-armed slave who led a rebellion: his Saint Domingue counterpart, François Mackandal.[1] Mackandal is famous for conspiring to poison the white masters of the colony. Though he was betrayed and captured, his significance in the fight for Haitian independence is evident as his image is embossed on Haiti's currency. All of these stories—some true, some fictional, and some indistinguishable with regards to their mythic status—point to an interesting phenomenon regarding the corporeal interpolation of slavery. A social death that is played out upon the body, and ultimately upon the landscape of the South itself in a psychosomatic rendering of abjection.

This essay aims to investigate a trending occurrence in the stories of slavery that invoke the haunting of the South through the phantom limbs of black revolutionary figures. The phenomenon of the phantom limb is a complex one as it unites both physiological and psychological factors. Medical research acknowledges that "[a]mputees invariably continue to perceive a ghost of their amputated limb as a phantom" (Giummara et al. 2010, 791). This ghosting often corresponds with physical pain, but also initiates a cognitive perception of the "bodily aspects of the phantom [limb]," including size, shape and length (791). Essentially, the concept of the phantom limb merges the "non-spatial 'psychic facts' (e.g., the body-for-itself)—such as volitions to refuse or accept the injury, emotions linked to trauma, and fixations which impede memory of the injury—with the material 'physiological facts' (e.g., the body-in-itself) of nervous influxes" (Felder, Robbins 2011, 361). The phantom limb is a shifting concept, "as much a function of the subject's psychology and sociohistorical context as of anatomy" (Grosz 1994, 79).[2]

The figures of Bras-Coupé, Mackandal, and Dana take on aspects of both the psychic and the material. Bras-Coupé's story takes up just two chapters, but it resonates throughout Cable's entire novel. He continues to haunt the text as he repeatedly returns as a specter of slavery and insurrection. Like Macakandal, Bras-Coupé is said to be a voudou priest, and is rumored to have bewitched and poisoned the white master's plantation with his "grigis" (translated by Cable as "spells").[3] Dana too, in her capacity to traverse time, is perceived as a spectral entity engaging in aspects of the paranormal. Though separated by time and space the stories correlate with one another as each invokes the history of slavery and its damage into the lives of its characters and onto their bodies. Like the fear that permeated the South in the wake of the Haitian Revolution, the missing limb serves as the mark and reminder of the undead past and the possibility of insurrection through resurrection—a ghostly remnant of something gone, but still eerily there.

Although there are many temporal shifts and disjunctions that take place in the texts themselves, this article moves in chronological order. The first part starts with the story of Mackandal and its connection to the legend of Bras-Coupé. This portion discusses the legacy of the Haitian Revolution and its effect upon the U.S. South as well as how marronage played a major part in both Mackandal's large-scale plot and Bras-Coupé's subversion of the slave system in New Orleans. Marroange refers to the concepts of flight and survival that arise within the act of escape. Many escaped slaves, or maroons, fled into the mountains of Saint Domingue, finding refuge in the elevated terrain of the island. This act of marroange, or abandoning of the plantations, was the first act of rebellion against slavery and its condition. In the corresponding colony of New Orleans, the swamp became the place of the clandestine fugitive.

The revolutionary act of absconding, leads into the second section which takes on the importance of voudou and compares the popular use of poison by slaves on the island colony and the curse, or "grigis," Bras-Coupé unleashes on the Grandissime plantation. It explores how voudou in connection with herbal medicines and talismans became an organizing feature of rebellion and instigated fear and hysteria among the white population in both the Caribbean and Louisiana.

The final section returns to *Kindred* and investigates the temporal shifts that come to mark Dana psychologically, and how this psychic toll manifests itself on the body. As the novel progresses the distinctions between time periods as well as who she is become muddled and fragmented. The antebellum South and twentieth century Los Angeles begin to cross over, causing an uncanny rendering of belonging and alienation.

THE MAROON AND THE REBEL: THE SHADOW OF HAITI IN THE STORIES OF MACKANDAL AND BRAS-COUPÉ

The story of Mackandal and his plot to overthrow white supremacist power in asserting black ownership of the French colony is a varied one. It is complicated as much by its legendary status as it is by its historical account. Much of the documentation of the attempted poisoning is based on white colonial official reports and suppositions. Diana Paton explains that "[m]uch of the evidence about [Mackandal's] activities and those of his followers was acquired through interrogation under torture and is overlaid with centuries of myth, making it impossible to establish precisely their actions or intentions" (2012, 253). Yet Saint Domingue's power structure, its dependency on slave labor for its economic sustainability and the racial hierarchies put into place and violently enforced to maintain this system in which the slave population and free people of color significantly outnumbered the white contingency, produced the elements that allowed for Mackandal's revolutionary plan, though unfulfilled, to take shape.[4] As Carolyn Fick asserts, "The component elements comprising [the plan's] general framework were those found within the material and historical parameters of mid-eighteenth-century slave society in Saint Domingue: poison, voudou, marronage" (1990, 71). These core aspects of slave life incorporated both for resistive and survival purposes are significant in that they are articulated overtly in the story of Bras-Coupé and more tacitly in Dana's narrative of temporal crossover.

The stories of Mackandal and Bras-Coupé echo one another, though Bras-Coupé's individualized insurrection occurs in 1803, in the wake of the Haitian victory—46 years after Mackandal's failed attempt in 1757. Mackandal's specific origins in Africa are hard to pinpoint. It is speculated that he was from Guinea, born into a prominent family and well educated. He was fluent in Arabic, showed interest in the arts, such as painting, music and sculpture, and was highly knowledgeable about tropical herbs and their medicinal qualities (Fick 1990, 60). Captured as a prisoner of war he was sold into slavery and arrived in Saint Domingue where he later took to the woods and become a maroon leader.[5] Bras-Coupé was also a captive from Africa and like Mackandal came from illustrious origins: "Bras-Coupé, they said, had been, in Africa and under another name, a prince among his people. In a certain war of conquest, to which he had been driven by *ennui*, he was captured, stripped of his royalty, marched down upon the beach of the Atlantic, and attired as a true son of Adam, with two goodly arms intact, became a commodity" (Cable 1988, 169). The circumstances regarding Mackandal's and Bras-Coupé's capture and subsequent enslavement are in close correlation. But Bras-Coupé's name is also significant to the story as Cable acknowledges that the prince-turned-slave has, in the process of being transformed into a commodity, undergone a name change:

> His name, he replied to an inquiry touching that subject, was ——, something into the Jaloff tongue, which he by and by condescended to render in Congo: Miko-Koanga, in French Bras-Coupé, the Arm Cut Off. Truly it would have been easy to admit, had this been his meaning, that his tribe, in losing him, had lost its strong right arm close off the shoulder; not so easy for his high-paying purchaser to allow, if this other was his intent; that the arm which might no longer shake the spear or swing the wooden sword, was no better than a useless stump never to be lifted for aught else. But whether easy to allow or not, that was his meaning. He made himself a type of all Slavery, turning into flesh and blood the truth that all Slavery is maiming. (171)

Bras-Coupé's metaphorical name is a point of subversion. He takes on a name that interpolates his lack of agency placing it onto the body, rendering the body useless or insufficient for the purposes of slave holders. This material representation of his social condition also invokes the image of his colonial double. The rebel Mackandal also hosts a corporeal injury; he lost his right hand when it was caught in the grinding machinery used in sugar mills (Fick 1990, 60). Sugar was the colony's most precious resource and export. The processing of it was especially grueling. An average workday on a sugar plantation ranged from eighteen to twenty hours (Fick 1990, 28). Many slaves died from overwork or accidents caused by the means of production. The most dangerous of these was the grinding process: "one could easily lose a finger, a hand, or one's whole arm in the mill wheel, and all the more dangerous since it was part of the night work" (Fick 1990, 29). This is how Mackandal's hand came to be amputated, as his accident occurred during a night shift.

It is unknown whether Cable, writing in the 1880s, was aware of Mackandal's planned attack on the town of Le Cap in 1757, but the trajectory of Bras-Coupé's story and Mackandal's is strikingly similar in that Bras-Coupé also becomes a maroon, taking refuge in the swamp after attacking his master. Cable describes the Louisiana swamp as a land of "reptiles, silence, shadow, decay" (1988, 9). It is an eerie, dank and desolate place. He describes in detail the abject landscape that Bras-Coupé must descend into in his quest for freedom and survival:

> And what surroundings! Endless colonnades of cypresses; long, motionless drapings of gray moss, broad sheets of noisome waters, pitchy black, resting on bottomless ooze...serpents great and small, of wonderful colorings, and the dull and loathsome moccasin sliding warily off the dead tree; in dimmer recesses the cow alligator, with her nest hard by; turtles a century old; owls and bats, raccoons, opossums, rats, centipedes and creatures of like vileness...a solemn stillness and stifled air only now and then disturbed by the call or whir of the summer duck, the dismal ventriloquous note of the rain-crow, or the splash of a dead branch falling into the clear but lifeless bayou. (182)

As a place of austere beauty, mystery and potential danger, the swamp is a place that conceals. Its lurking hazards deter those searching for a runaway slave, while providing protection for the fugitive. As the narrator in Cable's text informs us, the story of Bras-Coupé is "the story of a man who chose rather to be hunted like a wild beast among those awful labyrinths, than to be yoked and beaten like a tame one" (10).

Like the seemingly uninviting uninhabitable swamp, the maroons of Saint Domingue also retreated into treacherous terrain. They set up camp in the mountain ranges along the violent and contested border between the French portion of the island and the Spanish side, Santo Domingo. The taking to marronage and abandonment was notorious in Saint Domingue. It provided a means of escape as well as a means of fighting back. Though they tended to operate in different factions, many maroons banded together to form intricate networks, often working clandestinely with free blacks or slaves in raiding plantations for provisions, weapons for protection and in the acquisition and distribution of poisons. They were societies with governing entities, including political and spiritual leaders, of which Mackandal was one. C.L.R. James notes how maroons had a long history of endangering the colony, disturbing its hierarchal boundaries and undermining the power of the minority white population:

> In 1720, 1,000 slaves fled to the mountains. In 1751 there were at least 3,000 of them. Usually they formed separate bands, but periodically they found a chief who was strong enough to unite the different sections. Many of these rebel leaders struck terror into the hearts of the colonists by their raids on the plantations and the strength and determination of the resistance they oganised against the attempts to exterminate them. The greatest chief was Mackandal. (1989, 20)

It is interesting that James refers to Mackandal as a "chief," which then makes the maroons a type of tribe. Again this marks a point of connection between him and Bras-Coupé, who as a royal prince was a person of high standing in his own tribal society. Marronage was significant to the organization of Mackandal's plot. It allowed Mackandal to recruit the followers of his movement. Many of these followers operated as *pacotileurs*, mobile slaves and free blacks who sold small European items to those living in the slave quarters. Marronage also supplies Bras-Coupé with a notorious reputation for resistance and subterfuge, which makes him a feared entity. He subverts the slave system in New Orleans and the overreaching power of the Grandissime family's patriarch Agricola Fusilier.[6]

It is not surprising to find these similarities between Mackandal's narrative and that of Bras-Coupé. Haiti looms large in Cable's text as the narrative takes place in 1803, the same year that the Haitian Revolution culminated in a victory for the Haitian rebels and black liberation. The fact that Mackandal's plan never came to fruition as he was betrayed by a fellow conspirator, subsequently captured, tried and burned at the stake, did not mean that the threat of revolt was eliminated as it sowed the seeds for the revolt of 1791 when hundreds of slaves coordinated a mass abandonment of numerous Saint Domingue plantations to form a united revolutionary front (Fick 1990, 75). The eventual triumph of the Haitian Revolution in 1803 and the first ever successful slave revolt provoked an extreme fear of slave rebellion and paranoia that permeated throughout the U.S. South. Bras-Coupé the rebellious slave who refuses to work due to his royal African lineage, challenges his master's authority by looking him in the eye, and deserts the plantation defying detection in the swamp (thus eluding punishment for his violent transgression of the *Code noir*) becomes the Mackandal of Nouvelle Orleans.[7]

As the ghostly remnant of Mackandal, Bras-Coupé invokes the consequences of Haiti upon its colonial French counterpart, New Orleans, which is negotiating a transformation of its own as it undergoes Americanization in the wake of the Louisiana Purchase. New Orleans's relationship to the Caribbean and to Haiti in particular, is what drives up the stakes with regards to Bras-Coupé "practically declaring his independence" and eluding capture after his offense (Cable 1988, 181). As in the case of Mackandal's failed poisoning attempt, "[w]hat [the masters] thought the slaves could and would do, was equally as important as that which the slaves actually did or did not bring about through poison" (Fick 1990, 67). The increasing comparison between Caribbean society and New Orleans's society in 1803 is what puts the more conservative members of the Grandissime family, like the planter class in Saint Domingue, on edge.

The New Orleans of 1803 experienced a vast amount of changes in a short period of time. The onslaught and culmination of the Haitian Revolution in 1803 led to the ultimate migration of Afro-Creoles, white Creoles, slaves, and free people of color who resettled in New Orleans by way of Cuba. As the proud protector of the Grandissime family name, Agricola Fusilier fears the loss of his family's influence, wealth, and power as the region undergoes its American transformation at the same time that Haiti gains its independence as a result of its successful slave revolt and subsequent revolution. Furthermore, the articles of the original *Code noir* or Black Code of 1685, along with the Jean Baptiste Colbert's "One Blood" philosophy which promoted interracial connections, were being employed throughout Louisiana. The original *Code noir*, aside from instruction on slave punishment, stipulated three important things: the self manumission of slaves, the formation of a free black population, and the allowance of intermarriage between slaves and slave holders, black or white (Roach 1996, 57). While France briefly held the American continental colony in 1803, the French government attempted to curtail these practices. But "the intimate liaisons once legitimated by Colbert's One Blood and the *Code noir* of 1685 continued to enjoy a degree of popularity in custom long after they had been stigmatized by law" (57). In order to push back against this Agricola insists upon the privileging of a Creole identification; an identification that unequivocally establishes itself as white, Louisianan, and French. He is overheard exclaiming, "The Louisiana Creole is the noblest variety of enlightened man!" (Cable, 1988 50). Agricola uses this Creole exceptionalism to reassert his family's Anglo roots and to reify the privileged status of his family's settlement and close connections to European colonial governments.

The carefully distinguished racial and caste systems of Louisiana risk being upended by the new U.S. administration. As one French Creole says to another, "You know, everybody in Louisiana is to be a citizen, except the negroes and mules; that is the kind of liberty they give us—all eat out of one trough" (Cable 1988, 238). This critical take on U.S. democracy exemplifies the Creole exceptionalism that Agricola so staunchly tries to establish, preserve and protect. This is why his nationalist language takes on racial rhetoric. When the hostility between the American new-comers and the native white population, Creole and otherwise, reaches a breaking point, Agricola utilizes racial fears heightened by the slave revolt in Haiti to strike up fear of the American government as well as to heighten the threat of Bras-Coupé's transgression of the *Code noir*. Thus, couching U.S. rule with that of slave anarchy:

> [He said] that by trickery Louisianans had been sold, like cattle, to a nation of parvenues, to be dragged before juries for asserting the human right of free trade or ridding the earth of sneaks in the pay of the government; that laws, so called, had been forged into thumb-screws, and a Congress which had bound itself to give them all the rights of American citizens—sorry boon!—was preparing to slip their birthright acres from under their feet, and leave them hanging, a bait to the vultures of the Américain immigration....Its apostles, he said, were even then at work among their fellow-citizens, warping, distorting, blasting, corrupting, poisoning the noble, unsuspecting, confiding Creole mind...The smell of white blood comes on the south breeze...Virginia too, trembles for the safety of her fair mothers and daughters. We know not what is being plotted in the cane-breaks of Louisiana. But we know that in the face of these things the prelates of trickery are sitting in Washington allowing throats to go unthrottled that talked tenderly about the "negro-slave;" (283)

Fusilier's speech to the mob invokes the rhetoric of slavery, casting the early colonial Creole (white) population as the ones stripped of their human dignity and natural rights; "sold, like cattle." But it also utilizes the paranoia of slave revolt, of a foreign government cast to set that revolt into motion or to idly sit by, of how the transference of Louisiana into the hands of the United States is also a transference of blood—a contamination, a threat to or loss of Louisiana purity. The discursive modes of the speech—race baiting, nationalism, paranoia, violence—work to conflate miscegenation and interracial mixing with international mixing.

Amidst all this lurks the legacy of Bras-Coupé. His mythical status in New Orleans is intricately connected to that of the Grandissime family, and his demise after his eventual capture continues to have implications on the family long after his death. Within the story of Bras-Coupé the history of the Grandissimes as beneficiaries of the system of slavery and participants in doling out the punishments associated with draconian colonial practices, such as the *Code noir*, are revealed. It is at the height of the Grandissime's reign when Bras-Coupé arrives in New Orleans and is promptly bought by Agricola Fusilier and sold to his sister's fiancé Don José Martinez to work on the plantation then known as "La Renaissance." This is just the beginning of their ominous relationship. The name of the plantation takes on special significance as this is the place where Bras-Coupé commits his crime, thus resulting in his transformation or rebirth into the revolutionary maroon figure who haunts the Louisiana swamps. The taking on of Bras-Coupé turns out to be disastrous for all involved, but the inclusion of the story is Cable's not so tacit critique of slavery as the most significant of New Orleans's social ills and inadequacies.

The crux of the story is this: Bras-Coupé is betrothed to Palmyre. She is the servant and former companion of Aurora De Grapion. The Nancanou-De Grapion family and the Fusilier-Grandissime clan have been embroiled in a bitter feud that dates back to the seventeenth century. Though Palmyre admires Bras-Coupé for his militant stance against his condition and "untamable spirit," she does not love him and instead longs for the son of the great family and nephew of Agricola Fusilier, Honoré Grandissime,—a man she can never have due to her mixed racial status (Cable 1988, 175). Nonetheless, upon Arigcola's insistence she is forced to take Bras-Coupé's hand. Ultimately Bras-Coupé finds out that his love is unrequited. Don José, in keeping with Agricola's order, promises Bras-Coupé that in exchange for the slave's labor he will deliver Palmrye's hand in marriage. Palmrye's rejection, in essence, forces Don José to break his promise. Bras-Coupé thus compromises his identity forged in his initial refusal to work—a stance which distinguished him apart from the other slaves on the plantation—for nothing in return. The weakening of his resistance against the system that renders him a commodity drives his rage against Don José. The psychic aspect of the phantom limb, which Bras-Coupé's name embodies (the body-for-itself) takes over. His attack on Don José "reflect[s] a desire to retain even an illusory sense of power and integrity by resisting submission to an exclusionary cultural-symbolic system" (Felder, Robbins 2011, 366). Wild with drink and despair Bras-Coupé strikes his master, an offense punishable by death under the Black Code, and flees into the swamp. Months later he is captured on the Congo Square and it is Agricola who interprets the *Code noir* and determines the punishment in all its brutality:

> "The runaway slave," said the old French code, continued in force by the Spaniards, "the runaway slave who shall continue to be so for one month from the day of his being denounced to the officers of justice, shall have his ears cut off and shall be branded with the flower de luce on the shoulder; and on a second offense of the same nature, persisted in during one month of his being denounced, he shall be hamstrung, and be marked with the flower de luce on the other shoulder. On the third offense he shall die." Bras-Coupé had run away only twice.

"But," said Agricola, "these 'bossals' must be taught their place. Besides, there is Article 27 of the same code: 'The slave who, having struck his master, shall have produced a bruise, shall suffer capital punishment'—a very necessary law!" (191)

The *Code noir* of Saint Domingue endures. It is adopted by Louisiana and applied to Bras-Coupé, illustrating the reach of the island's colonial history as it is embedded into Louisiana's system of slavery and corresponding legislative practices. Thus in death, Bras-Coupé gets marked for a second time, but it is more than metaphorical; it is physically administered as he is branded not just as a slave but as a fugitive. As Joseph Roach contends in his discussion of the significance of the *fleur de lys* stamp, "The body so marked becomes an effigy by way of example, performing the law, so to speak, enacting the body politic in the materiality of the natural body, wearing on his or her persona the ineffaceable insignia of national memory" (1996, 56). The materiality of a social death is demarcated by the mutilated body, which represents the antebellum South's ultimate rejection as well as fear of the black revolutionary figure.

Despite this rejection and casting off, the legend of Bras-Coupé is incapable of being erased as his imprint is embossed in New Orleans's memory as well as its landscape. Bras-Coupé ultimately becomes associated with and inscribed on the subterranean swamp that harbored him:

The pack of Cuban hounds that howl from Don José's kennels cannot snuff the trail of the stolen canoe that glides through the somber vapors of the African's fastnesses. His arrows send no tell-tale reverberations to the distant clearing. Many a wretch in his native wilderness has Bras-Coupé himself, in palmier days, driven to just such an existence, to escape the chains and horrors of the barracoons; therefore not a whit broods he over man's inhumanity, but, taking the affair as a matter of course, casts about him for a future. (Cable 1988, 182)

The mystery applied to the place of marronage, adds to the spectral everlasting legacy of Bras-Coupé. The past in New Orleans reverberates among its present. As a part of that past, Bras-Coupé is automatically indoctrinated into the city's present, and therefore its future.

THE RESURRECTION OF VOUDOU: POISON AND "GRIGIS"

Bras-Coupé's spectral presence continues to haunt the text as his story is articulated numerous times by many of the characters throughout. He remains a ghostly palimpsest, just beneath the surface of the many tensions that strain the narrative with regards to race, caste, slavery, betrayal and illicit secrets. The voudou belief that "those who have died can reenter the world of the living" informs the narrative of return and resurrection that again links Bras-Coupé's story with Mackandal's (Squint 2007, 176). After his execution many of Mackandal's followers were certain that he was not really dead and believed that he would return to "fulfill his prophecies" (Fick 1990, 63). As a practitioner of voudou, Mackandal himself believed that his spirit would return to the world of the living in the form of a mosquito: "Having convinced his followers that he was immortal, Mackandal had once declared that if ever the whites captured him, it would be impossible for them to kill him, for upon breathing his final breath, he would escape in the form of a mosquito, only to return one day more terrifying than ever" (Fick 1990, 292n.87). The fact that Mackandal chooses the mosquito is quite telling in that he picks an insect that can carry disease and like a poison infect people and cause a devastating epidemic.

Bras-Coupé is also a practicing voudou priest and like Mackandal his story holds messianic undertones as he communes with not just the dead, but with zombis. As Sarah Juliet Lauro and Karen Embry state in their article "A Zombie Manifesto," "There is the Haitian *zombi*, a body raised from the dead to labor in the fields, but with a deep association of having played a role in the Haitian Revolution (thus, [the zombi is] simultaneously resonant with the categories slave and slave rebellion)" (2008, 87). Lauro and Embry also go on to state that the American zombie with the "ie", serves as a metaphor that, like the Haitian *zombi,* signifies not only the slave but slave rebellion: "While the human is incarcerated in the mortal flesh, the zombie presents a grotesque image that resists this confinement—animating the body even beyond death" (2008, 90). Zombies enact a type of terror that is different from the specter.[8] Bras-Coupé exists as a zombi/ie type figure. In dying his revolutionary spirit is resurrected, which makes his narrative of rebellion and its enduring legacy all the more real and thus all the more threatening: "Its immorality is a defining attribute of the zombie that both terrifies and tantalizes" (Lauro, Embry 2008, 88). This is why Bras-Coupé's story is told again and again with fear, reverence and delight by the various characters in Cable's text. Bras-Coupé returns, becoming part of the living dead that can traverse between the spiritual world and the land of the living. As long as his myth remains, his threat lives forever.

As a voudou priestess Palmyre routinely resurrects Bras-Coupé's revolutionary spirit in her commitment to avenge his death and to curse Agricola for not only bringing the brutality of the *Code noir* down upon Bras-Coupé, but by further enacting it by fortifying the racial lines that forbid her from pursuing Honoré Grandisimme[9]:

> She had heard of San Domingo, and for months the fierce heart within her silent bosom had been leaping and shouting and seeing visions of fire and blood, and when she brooded over the nearness of Agricola and the remoteness of Honoré these visions got from her a sort of mad consent. The lesson she would have taught the giant [Bras-Coupé] was Insurrection...A wild aggressiveness that had formerly characterized her glance in moments of anger...now came back intensified and blazed in her eye perpetually. Whatever her secret love may have been in kind, its sinking beyond hope below the horizon had left her fifty times the mutineer she had been before—the mutineer who has nothing to lose. (Cable 1988, 184).

The resurrection of Bras-Coupé reorients the insurrection Palmyre intended to nurture within him while he was alive, and instead she channels it into herself. Bras-Coupé's revolutionary intentions are thus embodied by Palmyre, altering her significantly by transforming her from the occasional mutineer into the steadfast rebel.

The character of Palmyre is speculated to have been modeled on the figure of Marie Laveau,[10] "queen of New Orleans voudou" (Benfey 1997, 204). Within the story of

Bras-Coupé, Palmyre's history is also told, and her significance to the plot of the novel is divulged. Through Palmyre's threats, Bras-Coupé haunts Agricola specifically, as he was the one to dole out the final punishment. But what this haunting also reveals is that despite Agricola's resistance to the "cultural creolization"[11] in New Orleans, he nevertheless defers to the power of voudou. Though he does not practice it, his fear of its potential to do harm indicates a belief in its efficacy.

Agricola is warned that Bras-Coupé "is a voudou" before the onset of his marriage to Palmyre (Cable 1988, 177). He purposely keeps this information from Don José in order to rid himself of Palmyre and to keep the Don from backing out of the deal. Furthermore, he is cognizant of the religion's influential sway and its effect upon those of the La Renaissance plantation after the matrimonial fracas. In the wake of Bras-Coupé's sorrow, despair, and ultimate abandonment of the agricultural estate, Don José begins to believe he has been cursed by the runaway slave and blames Agricola for his misfortune:

> [H]is heart conceived and brought forth its first-born fear, sired by superstition—the fear that he was bewitched. The negroes said that Bras-Coupé had cursed the land. Morning after morning the master looked out with apprehension toward his fields, until one night the worm came upon the indigo and between sunset and sunrise every green leaf had been eaten up, and there was nothing left for either insect or apprehension, to feed upon.
>
> And then he said—that the very culpability of this thing rested on the Grandissimes, and specifically on their fugleman Agricola, through his putting the hellish African upon him. Moreover, fever and death, to a degree unknown before, fell upon his slaves. Those to whom life was spared—but to whom strength did not return—wandered about the place like scarecrows, looking for shelter, and made the air dismal with the reiteration, "*No' ouanga* (we are bewitched), *Bras-Coupé fe moi des grigis* (the voudou's spells are on me)." (185)

Bras-Coupé's "grigis" acts like the poisons used by slaves in Saint Domingue to inflict fear and terror into the white population. Poison was used to economically cripple the plantations by applying it to crops and livestock, but slaves also used it as a means of resistance. They employed it on the master and other slaves who could not be trusted with secrets. The curse, like the poison, is wielded as a weapon, and the land as well as those who work upon it take on a psychosomatic sickness representative of slavery's subjugation. The plantation becomes an "invalid camp," a barren and desolate landscape full of weeds and thorns. It is populated by wandering sickly herds with "staring bones and shrunken sides" (187).

This psychosomatic rendering was not limited to the materiality of the land and body, but also manifested itself psychologically. The scene at the plantation serves to cement Agricola's fears as to what the power of voudou can do. Palmyre is just as powerful as Bras-Coupé if not more. She becomes known in New Orleans as Palmyre Philosophe, "noted for her taste and skill as a hair-dresser, for the efficacy of her spells and the sagacity of her divinations, but most of all for the chaste austerity with which she practised the less baleful rites of the voudous" (Cable 1988, 60). Palmyre's reputation precedes her and Agricola does not doubt nor wish to challenge her capacities. His paranoia regarding

Palmyre causes him to partake in rituals to ward off potential bad spirits, and thus implicates himself as a participant in the cultural creolization he is so vehemently against. He is adamantly "anti-voudou" (226) but when he awakes to find four charms at the corners of his pillow, his fear provokes him to make amends to the harbingers of death:

> Did Agricola believe in the supernatural potency of these gimcracks? No and yes. Not to be foolhardy, he quietly slipped every day to the levee, had a slave-boy row him across the river in a skiff, landed, re-embarked, and in the middle of the stream surreptitiously cast a picayune over his shoulder into the river. Monsieur D'Embarras, the imp of death thus placated, must have been a sort of spiritual Cheap John. (308)

Agricola, just like Don José, harbors powerful superstitions that prompt him to take action to ward off the powers of the talismans which consist of: "an acorn drilled through with two holes at right angles to each other, a small feather run through each hole; a joint of cornstalk with a cavity scooped in the middle...and the space filled with parings from that small callous spot near the knee of the horse, called the 'nail;' [and] a bunch of particolored feathers" (307). Beyond these voudou charms, a small cloth bag is found on the Grandissime grounds containing a "quantity of dogs' and cats' hair, cut fine and mixed with salt and pepper" (306). Agricola's initial reaction to these amulets is to go over to Palmyre's house and shoot her, but he does not as he is too afraid to approach her and instead puts her house under nightly surveillance. Agricola's reaction illustrates the irrationality and fear that was characteristic of the hysteria prompted by the rash of poisonings that happened in Saint Domingue less than a century earlier.[12]

The talismans present a crucial link between Bras-Coupé's grigis, Palmyre's charms and Mackandal's plan to poison the water of Le Cap. In the wake of the foiled rebellion, Mackandal's name became associated with poison. Voudou talismans were referred to as "mackandals" as well as voudou priests and anyone who engaged in voudou practices (Fick 1990, 63). The making and ownership of a "mackandal" was forbidden by colonial officials. Poison and "mackandals" thus became culturally linked through a sense of spirituality. This phenomenon not only points to the psychological significance of the use of poison and grigis, but also to an interesting aspect of cultural exchange and connection that occurred in Louisiana as a result of the slave trade. As Diane Paton explains, "Poison was relative: its effect was not a simple physiological matter but one intimately related to the spiritual world...Africans who were brought to the Americas as slaves, shared with Europeans the sense that harm could be done to people through spiritual or occult means and that physical substances (poisons) could be involved in such attacks" (2012, 248). This is why Agricola is so fearful, yet at the same time engages in occult practices of his own. The "mackandals" point to both the psychological and material effect African and Caribbean cultures had on the racially stratified city of New Orleans. Turning to *Kindred*, Dana's small gym bag which is tied to her waist and filled with 20th century provisions, becomes her own version of the "mackandal;" except that the bag contains aspirin, a pocketknife and a map—items that become crucial to keeping her alive in antebellum Maryland.

TEMPORAL DISPLACEMENTS AND ABJECT GHOSTS

Butler describes her novel *Kindred* as a "grim fantasy" (Crossly 1998, xii). Indeed Butler's "own history-writing occurs as a collaboration between the archive and her imagination" (Schiff 2009, 127). *Kindred* follows the story of Dana, a young black woman living in 1976 Los Angeles, who is repeatedly called back to the nineteenth century to save the life of her white slave owning relative, Rufus Weylin, the father of her matriarchal ancestor. Navigating this time warp, Dana is forced to confront her slave lineage, which is not left behind when she travels back to 1976, but marks her and inserts itself into her twentieth century moment. Whenever she returns to her present she still bears the scars of slavery's psychological and physical violence. As critic Lisa Long posits in her analysis of the novel: "History is always inside us, and it works its damage from the inside out" (2002, 462). Like Mackandal and Bras-Coupé, Dana too is physically marked by her experience with slavery. In the Prologue she is left to contemplate her missing limb, stating, "I was almost comfortable except for the strange throbbing of my arm. Of where my arm had been. I moved my head, tried to look at the empty place…the stump…I felt as though I could have lifted my other hand…I felt as though I had another hand" (Butler 1988, 10). Similar to the limb that haunts her with its physically seeming presence, her experience on the Weylin plantation in 1819 haunts her. Dana is first called back in time by her white ancestor Rufus, then a young boy who summons her to save him from drowning. When she returns to Los Angeles she cannot shake the images that make up the bizarre scene she is a part of: the struggling boy gasping for breath, the hysterical shrieking of his mother, and the sickening feeling of looking down the barrel of his father's gun. These figures take on a spectral essence for Dana, possessing her: "They stayed with me, shadowy and threatening. They made their own limbo and held me in it" (18). The Weylins remain a lurking presence for Dana, inhabiting and disrupting her temporal framework. Furthermore, the time travel they represent renders Dana's presence in the nineteenth century correspondingly spectral. Dana does not just leave and return, she disappears and reappears instantly like an apparition. Rufus's father does not believe in ghosts but after witnessing her vanishing twice he grants her a supernatural quality demanding of her, "Who are you? *What* are you?" (130; emphasis mine).

As ghostly figures to one another, the Weylins and Dana share a material presence of haunting, as ghosts are more opaque than transparent. They are physical in nature. This physicality and material affect is evidenced in Dana's interaction with the customs of nineteenth century slavery. When Dana is transported back in time she becomes a physical part of Rufus's time frame. The corporal violence she experiences—the beating she receives from a patroller who mistakes her for a runaway slave and the whipping she endures for teaching a young slave how to read—remain on her body, as does the pain, when she returns to 1976. As a flesh-in-blood ghost, she "imports a charged strangeness into the place or sphere [the slave holding South] she is haunting, thus unsettling the propriety and property lines that delimit a zone of activity or knowledge" (Gordon 1997, 63). Dana's spectral presence disturbs the system of slavery on the Weylin plantation as well as challenges Rufus's social standing as the master and owner. Disappearance in connection with apparition is characterized by certainty and doubt (74). Dana's physicality redoubles this dialectic and puts all social identifications based on the system of slavery into question.

Butler at the beginning of the novel situates us firmly in the present, only to traverse the temporal and spatial boundaries of the story. Dana begins her narration saying, "The trouble began long before June 9, 1976, when I became aware of it, but June 9 is the day I remember. It was my twenty-sixth birthday. It was also the day I met Rufus—the day he called me to him for the first time" (Butler 1988, 11). The specificity of the date is interesting as the duration of Dana's disappearances into the nineteenth century do not sync up with her temporal present. When she reappears after her first trip back in time she tells her husband, Kevin, that she was gone for only a few minutes, but according to him she was only gone for ten or fifteen seconds. The day of June 9, 1976 becomes the starting point in which the time away is compared and measured. The trips back in time last for hours, days and months. Upon return, months turn into days, days turn into hours and hours turn into minutes. Gone for two months in the nineteenth century Dana returns to find that she has only missed two days in the twentieth: "I learned that it was Friday, June, 11, 1976. I'd gone away for nearly two months and come back yesterday the same day I left home. Nothing was real" (116). This temporal dissonance causes the two time frames to converge together, which results in reality collapsing in upon itself. As the time traveler, Dana inhabits the liminal space between both worlds; pushed out of a linear time line,[13] Dana's days don't "mesh" (115). 1819 and 1976 rub up against one other, with Dana as the conduit that links the two temporal planes.

Butler's novel features an "embedding" of the early nineteenth century into 1976, which causes an even more jarring temporal disjunction as the novel is set during the year of the United States Bicentennial celebration (LaCroix 2007, 116). By inserting the space of the slave owning South into 1976, Butler disrupts the linear timeline necessary to nation building.[14] She reveals the absurdity of the U.S. narrative of freedom indoctrinated in the Declaration of Independence, the document that led to the American Revolution and served to establish the United States as a sovereign nation. The histories of slavery are made to coalesce with the histories of nation making. As Sarah Eden Schiff explains, "[B]y exposing the haunting enduring legacies of discrimination, *Kindred* narrows the divide between the past and the present and so bares the inadequacies of America's origin stories that depend on a progressive chronology as well as strategic forgetting" (2009, 112). The incursion of the antebellum era into the bicentennial moment serves to integrate the historical forgetting and erasures that occur in narratives of national myth making. Interestingly enough the last day Rufus calls Dana back is the Fourth of July. Dana will secure her freedom that day, but it will come with a temporal hangover and an enduring corporeal alteration; an incomplete break, as Rufus's grip traps her between the two time frames. The place where Rufus grabs Dana's arm is ultimately where the arm is amputated; yet as a phantom limb she can still feel its psychic and physical effects. The arms still feels attached, an attempt to make the corporeal body whole, yet the throbbing that resonates from its severing serves to mark the body and re-inscribe the injury both psychologically and physically—the body simultaneously in-itself and for-itself.

The temporal limbo Dana finds herself in renders her presence in the antebellum South as abject. Julia Kristeva explains how abjection threatens systems of order, time being among them. She states, "It is thus not lack of cleanliness or health that causes abjection but what disturbs identity, system, order. What does not respect borders, positions, rules. The in-between, the ambiguous, the composite" (1982, 4). Rufus continually resurrects Dana out of time, thus Dana is out of order. This time rupture ultimately has corporeal consequences for Dana as she figures out that the only way she can return to the present is to put herself in physical danger—she can only transfer back to 1976 when she fears for her life. Because this happens numerous times, and because Dana adjusts to the varying forms of physical violence released upon her, it ups the stakes with regards to what levels of violence she can and cannot endure. At these times of bodily crises, when the body can take no more, when it begins to release itself, she is resurrected back into the present.[15] As a subject rendered into an object and back again, Dana's "[a]bjection is a resurrection that has gone through death (of the ego). It is an alchemy that transforms the death drive into a start of life, of a new significance" (Kristeva 1982, 15).

As an anachronistic figure Dana also threatens the order to Rufus's time frame. As a white male brought up in the slave holding South, Rufus has trouble making sense of Dana's twentieth century subjectivity as a free black woman. Their relationship in some ways mirrors what Orlando Patterson refers to as "parasitism" in which a master disguised his dependence on the slave by ascribing to an ideology that the slave was naturally parasitic and dependent upon the master. Eric Sundquist in discussing "parasitism" argues that slaves in response "camouflaged, or masked, their resistance to slavery—and hence the nature of their freedom through consciousness—only on occasion removing the mask and exposing the parasitic relationship of slavery as an 'ideological inversion of reality'" (1993, 42). Aware that time is out of order, Dana knows that is she is a composite made up of two worlds. In order to ward off the identity crisis that abjection triggers, she plays the role of a slave in front of people who are unaware of her predicament; yet with Rufus she removes the camouflage. This is what makes Rufus both confused and scared of her.

In reclaiming her identity as a twentieth-century subject, Dana reveals Rufus's abjection: his parasitic dependence on her. Rufus is deathly afraid of Dana leaving him. In a revealing conversation he tells Dana that he used to have nightmares about her:

> "I'd dream about you and wake up in a cold sweat."
> "Dream…about me killing you?"
> "Not exactly." He paused, gave me a long unreadable look. "I'd dream about you leaving me."
> I frowned. That was close to the thing Kevin had heard him say—the thing that had awakened Kevin's suspicions. "I leave," I said carefully. "I have to. I don't belong here."
> "Yes you do! As far as I'm concerned, you do. But that's not what I mean. You leave, and sooner or later you come back. But in my nightmares, you leave without helping me. You walk away and leave me in trouble, hurting, maybe dying." (Butler 1988, 254-55)

This exchange illustrates Rufus's dependence on Dana. His assertion that Dana indeed belongs to his time period is a way of possessing her, keeping her in an abject position. If she acquiesces to his desperate need for her he then gets to displace his abjection onto her and reclaim his position as subject. Thus, Rufus's subjectivity is dependent on Dana's abjection, which is why Rufus equates Dana's leaving him with death.

Yet, ultimately it is death that brings the two together. Through her various cross-overs into the antebellum South, Dana figures out that the fear of dying is what triggers her travel. She tells Kevin, "Rufus's fear of death calls me to him, and my own fear of death sends me home" (Butler 1988, 50). Dana soon finds that her fears play out among slavery's trauma. Her returns home follow a life and death struggle with a white patroller who takes her for a fugitive slave and a ruthless whipping and beating by Rufus's father for teaching one of the slave children how to read. Rufus's summonings require Dana to engage with and participate in her abject past—to confront the "deep well of memory that is unapproachable and intimate" (Kristeva 1982, 6). She is locked in the abject past by Rufus who routinely calls upon her to save his life, which she must do in order to ensure her own in the future. But the result of saving his life ensures that Rufus can grow up to enslave and repeatedly rape Alice, who will later give birth to Hagar, Dana's great-great-grandmother. Engaged in this past, Dana comes to know that she can only escape through the threat of death. She comes face to face with the subjugation of slavery as it is played out physically upon her body.

One reason why the time travel is so jarring, why the liminal limb is so frightening is because the physical ramifications of it are real. Violence invokes the time switch. It is the material mark of slavery on the body but it also symbolizes the violence of a social death. In order to hold on to her subjectivity Dana acts out the role of a slave, but as her time in the nineteenth century increases she feels her handle on identity slipping away from her. It is the coffle of slaves for sale and the selling of the slaves on the Weylin plantation that prompt her to enact her own agency upon her own body. In trying to transport herself back to the twentieth century, to avoid a social death, Dana has to undergo a self mutilation and slits her wrists. What is interesting is that she undertakes this drastic act after Rufus hits her for vehemently protesting against the perverse transaction: "He hit me…It was a first, and so unexpected that I stumbled backward and fell…And it was a mistake. It was the breaking if an unspoken agreement between us—a very basic agreement—and he knew it" (Butler 1998, 239). This betrayal by Rufus breaks the fragile veil of trust that exists in their complex relationship, which is a result of their negotiation and engagement with a past that is out of order. Up until this moment, Rufus's dependence on Dana instilled his protection of her to some extent. But his violent act against her reveals to Dana that she and Rufus cannot exist in the same temporal plane for much longer. Though they need each other in order to survive, they have now become threats to one another's existence. In this moment Rufus displays the violence of abjection. In striking her, Rufus embodies the abjection of the slave owner; the "immoral, sinister, scheming and shady: a terror that dissembles, a hatred that smiles, a passion that uses the body for barter instead of inflaming it, a debtor who sells you up, a friend who stabs you" (Kristeva 1982, 15). Within this act of violence Dana recognizes Rufus as the abject body and it redoubles her efforts to get back to her present in order for her to figure out if his abjection—if his ontological "*want*" or need is mutual—the thing that ties them together.[16] She worries that if she severs that tie that she won't be able to return home; she worries that her power to traverse time is connected to Rufus being alive. She states, "Is the power mine, or do I tap some power in him? All this started with him after all. I don't know whether I need him or not. And I won't know until he is not around" (Butler 1988, 247). Dana's attempt on her life is meant to enact a slow death, one that will give her enough time to get back to 1976 without ultimately killing her. She explains this desperate act stating, "He [Rufus] has to leave me enough control of my own life to make living look better to me than killing and dying" (246).

To escape the past Dana must traverse not only the liminal borders of time and space but also life and death. In order to navigate and survive her time travel she must merge the "visible and the invisible, the dead and the living, the past and the present" (Gordon 1997, 24). Dana must die long enough to live, to transport herself home, but she is only one part of the equation. Rufus as the one who calls her instigates the temporal opening, and in order to close it Rufus has to die. As Lisa Long notes, "Dana's ontological crisis involves a lessening (she literally kills her past)" (2002, 470). Rufus's death is a result of his attempt to make Dana the object of his sexual pleasure as he sees this as the only way of owning her. This last act of betrayal prompts the break and Dana's resolve to kill Rufus: "I could feel the knife in my hand, still slippery with perspiration. A slave was a slave. Anything could be done to her. And Rufus was Rufus—erratic, alternately generous and vicious. I could accept him as my ancestor, my younger brother, my friend, but not as my master, and not as my lover" (Butler 1988, 260). In reclaiming her subjectivity, and the will to do with her own body what she wants, Dana's life is returned to her in the death of Rufus and his ego. As Rufus dies the time portal closes, but it is not a clean break. Dana's transfer back to the twentieth century results in her being literally caught in the closing wall:

> I was back at home—in my own house, in my own time. But I was still caught somehow, joined to the wall as though my arm were growing out of it—or growing into it. From the elbow to the ends of my fingers, my left arm had become part of the wall. I looked at the spot where flesh joined plaster, stared as it uncomprehending. It was the exact spot Rufus's fingers had grasped. (261)

In the twentieth century enactment of the Code *noir* Dana loses her arm as punishment for killing her master, connecting her act of resurrection to that of Bras-Coupé and Mackandal. Rufus and the nineteenth century still have a hold on Dana, which makes the amputation of the arm necessary, but the limb as the phantom still remains; a remnant of Rufus, the past and the trauma of slavery.

"[E]ndings that are not over is what haunting is all about" (Gordon 1997, 139). The resurrection of Mackandal in the legend of Bras-Coupé in the nineteenth century and Dana's story of temporal transfer in the twentieth century speaks to this sentiment. The immortality of the story, the limb, the phantom, leaves an uneasy feeling, the sense that something invisible is being felt in order to be seen. But in order to see that which isn't there requires an uncomfortable confrontation with the "stump," the figure that haunts. The maroon, the rebel and the abject mutilated body are relegated to the grave but not subjected to the blight of the zombie. Instead it is a reunification of the soul with the body, the living dead who walk among us and tap us on the shoulder and whisper in our ear, "Look over there."

Notes

1. The spelling of Mackandal's name varies. It is sometimes spelled as Macandal with a *c* or as Makandal with a *k*. I chose to use the spelling C.L.R. James uses in his book *The Black Jacobins*, but in references the reader might find the different spellings mentioned here.

2. For more on the phantom limb and its duality with regards to its psychological and physiological attributes see Maurice Merleau-Ponty *The Phenomenology of Perception* (1962); *The Visible and Invisible* (1968); Andrew Felder and Brent Dean Robbins "A Cultural-Existential Approach to Therapy" in *Theory and Psychology* (2011). On phantom limbs and culture see Catherine Irwin "Phantasmatic Reconstructions" *Journal of Literary and Cultural Disability Studies* 6.1 (2012) and Susan Crutchfeld and Marc Epstein eds. *Points of Contact: Disability, Arts and Culture*. On notions of the body and the psychoanalytic see Elizabeth Grosz *Volatile Bodies* (1994). With regards to the body and the abject also see Judith Butler *Bodies that Matter* (1993) and Julia Kristeva *Powers of Horror*.

3. I am using the New Orleans Creole and Haitian Creole spelling of "voudou" in keeping with George Washington Cable's spelling of the term. The spelling of the term varies according to location and language. "Voodoo" is the anglicized spelling of the term and "vaudou" is the French translation. The various spellings in English, Haitian Creole, and French invoke the creolized history of the religion which combines the practices of Roman Catholicism with that of the African Dahomean, Kongo and Yoruba religious beliefs.

4. In 1789 the slave population numbered 465, 429 compared to the white population numbered at 30, 826. These statics come from Kirsten Squint's article "Voudou and Revolt in Literature of the Haitian Revolution," *The College Language Association* (2007): 170.

5. Also see C.L.R. James, *The Black Jacobins* (New York: Vintage Books, 1989), 20-22.

6. Agricola's significance to Bras-Coupé's narrative will be discussed later in this section.

7. The Black Code or *Code noir* was legislation introduced to curtail slave assembly and desertion: "A fugitive slave in flight up to one month from the date of his reported escape would have his ears cut off and the *fleur de lys* branded on one shoulder. If his flight should span another month, he would be hamstrung, in addition, and the *fleur de lys* stamped on the other shoulder. After that the punishment was death," (Fick 1990, 53). This exact language is utilized in *The Grandissimes* with regards to Bras-Coupé's punishment after his capture.

8. Here I am treating the zombie as an "ontic/hauntic" object as posited by Lauro and Embry in their article "A Zombie Manifesto" *Boundary 2* 35.1 (2008). In regards to the ontic/hauntic they theorize: "In part, we are claiming that there is such a thing as a materially real zombie; thus an ontic object, for our interest is not just a zombie as an epistemic thing. However, we are also, following Derrida, taking up the paradoxical nature of the zombie as neither being nor nonbeing; but of course, the zombie is more substantial than a ghost" (86n.6). Bras-Coupé's haunting is more "substantial" as he represents the threat of revolt.

9. According to Haitian folklore, voudou priests were the ones who raised the zombis from the dead, see Lauro and Embry 90.

10. The fact that Cable gives Palmyre so much prominence in the novel and models her after Marie Laveau is not surprising given that he wrote the novel during the height of Marie Laveau's fame. Roach notes in *Cities of the Dead*, "Revived (or at least more intensely publicized) in the 1880s, voudou in nineteenth-century New Orleans is popularly associated with the successful practices of the Voudou Queens, a mother and daughter, both bearing the name Marie Laveau. Operating through the intervention of spirits, or *loas*, the Voudou Queens, caretakers of memory, resisted the segregation of the dead. The ethos of spirit-world possession pointedly focuses attention on the autonomy and ownership of living bodies, an attention most unwelcome to slaveholders in antebellum times," (1996, 208). This explains why Agricola is so fearful of the voudou practice.

11. Nicholas Spitzer defines cultural creolization in the following way: "Cultural creolization in its fullest sense describes the development of new traditions, aesthetics, and group identities out of combinations of formerly separate people and cultures—usually where at least one has been deterritorialized by emigration, enslavement, or exile—and we can add exploration, though that usually is accompanied by a quest for territory or colonial control" (2003, 58).

12. Palmyre does induce spells on Agricola from afar and survives, while Agricola dies from a knife wound received by Honoré Grandissime the "f.m.c." (free man of color) as he is referred to in the novel, who is in-love with Palmyre; he is the half-brother of the white Honoré Grandissime. It is unclear if he stabs Agricola in an act of revenge in the name of Palmrye or due to the insults Agricola hurls at him.

13. This non-linear format classifies *Kindred* as a new slave narrative as the non-linear time frame is a convention of the slave narrative genre.

14. See Benedict Anderson's *Imagined Communities*. (London: Verso, 1993), 22-36.

15. Long comments on this stipulation of Dana's time travel. She notes: "Dana is pulled into the past by a threat to Rufus's life, but can only return to the present via a threat to her own. Thus, it is Rufus's claim upon Dana's body—his ability to call her to him—that enslaves and endangers her in both her present and her past. For her part, Dana sees her existence as reliant upon her ability to endure the tortures of

slavery and keep Rufus alive so that he can father the children who will be her ancestors. That Rufus and Alice's children are the product of rape makes Dana complicit in Alice's sexual slavery as well. Dana's dark skin may make her a slave like Alice, but Rufus, not Alice, is Dana's true kindred spirit. Thus, the loss of her arm—cut off where Rufus grasped her in his death throes—symbolizes the drag of family history, the complicated nature of Dana's relationship to her white and African ancestry, and the permanent, disabling wound that slavery leaves on individuals today. There is no ontological refuge, Butler tells us; the supernatural means of garnering any knowledge about one's origins do not stabilize the subject, but rather unmoors his or her sense of self, making selfhood as we understand it in Western culture ultimately uncertain" (2002, 469-70).

16. Kristeva explains how abjection is based on want. She writes, "There is nothing like the abjection of self to show that all abjection is in fact recognition of the *want* on which being, meaning, language, or desire is founded" (1982, 5).

References

Benfey, Christopher. 1997. *Degas in New Orleans: Encounters in the Creole World of Kate Chopin and George Washington Cable*. Berkeley: University of California Press.

Butler, Octavia E. *Kindred*. 1988. Boston: Beacon Press.

Cable, George Washington. *The Grandissimes*. 1988. New York: Penguin.

Crossley, Robert. 1988. "Introduction." In Butler (1979) 1988, ix-xxvii.

Felder, Andrew J. and Brent Dean Robbins. 2011. "A Cultural-Existential Approach to Therapy: Merleau-Ponty's Phenomenology of Embodiment and its Implications for Practice." *Theory & Psychology*. 21.3: 355-376.

Fick, Carolyn E. 1990. *The Making of Haiti: The Saint Domingue Revolution from Below*. Knoxville: University of Tennessee Press.

Giummarra, Melita J., Nellie Georgiou-Karistianis. Michael E.R. Nicholls, Stephen J. Gibson, Michael Chou and John L. Bradshaw. 2010. "Corporeal Awareness and Proprioceptive Sense of the Phantom." *British Journal of Psychology*. 101: 791-808.

Gordon, Avery F. 1997. *Ghostly Matters: Haunting and the Sociological Imagination*. Minneapolis: University of Minnesota Press.

Grosz, Elizabeth. 1994. *Volatile Bodies: Toward a Corporeal Feminism*. Bloomington and Indianapolis: Indiana University Press.

Irwin, Catherine. 2012. "Phantasmatic Reconstructions: Visualizing Phantom Limbs in the Works of Alex Wright and Frank Bidart." *Journal of Literacy & Cultural Disability Studies*. 6.1: 69-84.

James, C. L.R. 1989. *The Black Jacobins: Toussaint L'Ouverture and the San Domingo Revolution*. New York: Vintage.

Kristeva, Julia. 1982. *Powers of Horror: An Essay on Abjection*. New York: Columbia University Press.

La Croix, David. 2007. "To Touch Solid Evidence: The Implicity of Past and Present in Octavia E. Butler's *Kindred*." *Midwest Modern Language Association*. 40.1 (Spring): 109-119.

Lauro, Sarah Juliet and Karen Embry. 2008. "A Zombie Manifesto: The Nonhuman Condition in the Era of Advanced Capitalism." *Boundary 2*. 35.1: 85-108.

Long, Lisa. 2002. "A Relative Pain: The Rape of History in Octavia Butler's *Kindred* and Phyllis Alesia Perry's *Stigmata*." *College English*. 64.2 (March): 459-483.

Paton, Diana. 2012. "Witchcraft, Poison, Law, and Atlantic Slavery." *The William and Mary Quarterly*. 69.2 (April): 235-264.

Roach, Joseph. 1996. *Cities of the Dead: Circum-Atlantic Performance*. New York: Columbia University Press.

Schiff, Sarah Eden. 2009. "Recovering (from) the Double: Fiction as Historical Revision in Octavia E. Butler's *Kindred. Arizona Quarterly*. 65.1 (Spring): 107-136.

Spitzer, Nicholas. 2003. "Monde Créole: The Cutlural World of French Louisiana Creoles and the Creolization of World Cultures." *Journal of American Folklore* 116 (Winter): 57-72.

Squint, Kirsten L. 2007. "Voudou and the Revolt in Literature of the Haitian Revolution." *The College Language Association* 51.2 (December): 170-185.

Sundquist, Eric J. 1993. *To Wake the Nations: Race in the Making of American Literature*. Cambridge: Harvard University Press.

E S S A Y

I WANT TO DO BAD THINGS WITH YOU: HBO's *TRUE BLOOD*'s RACIAL ALLEGORIES IN A POST-RACIAL SOUTH

by Lisa Woolfork

Although HBO's *True Blood* has ascended the heights of mainstream vampiric popularity, students of African American literature will also infer additional meanings from its title. Understatedly described as "some farmer" by the hapless protagonist of Ralph Ellison's classic novel *Invisible Man*, Jim Trueblood is a blues-singing sharecropper who claims to have impregnated his wife and daughter. His incestuous acts change not only the lives of his family, but also ultimately lead to the narrator's expulsion from college and displacement into the cold urban North.

The story of Ralph Ellison's Trueblood fosters a better understanding of the transgressive properties embedded in sexual transactions and vampiric identity in HBO's *True Blood*. The distance between Trueblood (the instigator of taboo sex acts) and Tru-Blood (the synthetic human blood substitute meant to assist the integration of vampires into dominant culture) reveals larger allegories of anti-black prejudice and miscegenation. Just as Jim Trueblood's name allegorizes (if not justifies) incest as an inversion of miscegenation (redirecting anxiety about inter-racial sexual mixing toward its opposite taboo, intra-familial sex), *True Blood* uses the vampire body as an allegory for historical concerns about the social consequences of racial desegregation and consensual black-white sex. From the first episode ("Strange Love"), *True Blood* explicitly deploys civil rights narratives and assimilation stories of racial passing. In fact, *True Blood*'s fictional setting, Bon Temps, Louisiana, is largely evacuated of black-white racial tensions. Instead, it discusses these issues through the lens of vampirism. *True Blood*'s vampires (both within their own community and in the public sphere of Bon Temps) allegorize the simultaneous invisibility and hypervisibility of black bodies, especially over-sexualized black masculinity. These vampires illuminate anti-black prejudice and miscegenation anxiety while also obfuscating the black struggles for civil rights equity on which they are based.

The southern locale is vital to the success of this allegorical project. The south permits a reinscription and an interrogation of the anxiety surrounding white women's vulnerability to sexual attack from (or consensual sex with) black men. In *True Blood*, this once-common fear and defense of racial segregation (as illustrated by former President Harry Truman's rhetorical question "Would you want your daughter to marry a Negro?"[1]) emerges in the form and degree of attention paid to white women. The first season emphasizes the dire consequences that befall white women who "mix" with vampires. Most of the plot revolves around the protagonist, Sookie Stackhouse, and her contemplation of a relationship with a vampire, Bill Compton who was made a vampire in the aftermath of a Civil War skirmish. At the same time, five other white women— three of whom have had sex with vampires, another who is addicted to vampire blood, and another who believed in vampire social equity—are murdered and posthumously reviled as "fang bangers" and "women who had tainted themselves and their race." If the stigma surrounding social and sexual contact with vampires in *True Blood* feels familiar, that is because it is: the southern context illuminates and animates well known anxieties about racial mixing and desegregation.[2]

The vampires in *True Blood* provide an allegorical connection to black bodies, black cultural mythologies and the social history of black struggles for civil rights in a southern context. To link blackness and vampirism does not produce a singular or stable allegory; instead, it illustrates, as Eric Lott does with blackface minstrelsy, "a subtler account of acts of representation. Where representation once unproblematically seemed to image forth its referent, we must now think of, say, the blackface mask as less a repetition of power relations than a signifier for them—a distorted mirror, reflecting displacements and condensations and discontinuities between which and the social field there exist lags, unevennesses, multiple determinations" (Lott 8).

This essay seeks to unearth the black referent beneath HBO's Louisiana, which has been thoroughly scrubbed of any trace of its historically documented anti-black prejudice and legal codes. Once Louisiana's history of "blood truths" has been established, it is easier to see Bill Compton's character and Bon Temps' vampire anxiety as an elaborate process of signification at work. Bill Compton's character oscillates between white privilege and black social vulnerability. Bill's shifting social place (fluctuating between white power and black abjection) can be considered to reflect the allegorical aspects of vampire sex. The representation of human-vampire sex uncannily reproduces anxiety, censure, and violence similar to the white supremacist response to black male-white female sex in the post-Reconstruction era and beyond. Bill Compton's character, like the vampires in the series, is a distorted mirror that reflects not just surface appearance, but looks backward and laterally to a variety of anti-black social anxieties and discrimination.

The slings and arrows of outrageous fortune that afflict Bill Compton are intelligible because they are comprised of the same materials as the injustices once experienced by blacks in the historic south. To perceive Bill Compton with DuBoisian pity and contempt is to peer through him and toward the black historical referents on which his social standing in Bon Temps is based. The depiction of vampires in *True Blood* signifies on many of the circumstances that blacks confronted during the Jim Crow era. Frequently in season one, Bill is placed in compromising or threatening situations similar to those that black men faced in a climate of changing civil rights. It is, as Henry Louis Gates says of signification, "repetition with a difference." The differences are myriad and rely on an absence of black-white conflict. Charlaine Harris's novels—the basis for the HBO series—are largely devoid of black characters (Lafayette, the novel's only black character, is killed in the second book). While Charlaine Harris's books neglect black characters and only obliquely refer to racism, HBO's *True Blood* is decidedly post-racial rather than non-racial (i.e., predominately white). The television series took a radical step by elevating a minor character to a major role, and changing her race. Charlaine Harris's Tara Thornton is a young white woman who owns a used clothing store, Tara's Togs. She is Sookie's supportive friend, but does not play a large role in the narrative. HBO's Tara Thornton practically doubles the number of black characters from the source material. However, rather than increasing the visibility of blackness or black concerns in Bon Temps, HBO's Tara serves to underscore the lack of anti-black prejudice. As one scholar observes, "Tara often uses the race card in the series and this functions as both a reminder of Southern racism as well as a character trait revealing her vulnerabilities and her knowing humour" (Amador in Cherry 128).

Although Tara is vulnerable and may provide a grim comic relief, I disagree that Tara's "reminders" of Southern racism are a meaningful contribution to the series. I suggest that the story gains its traction, in part, from a vision of the South that is largely free of racial conflict. In fact, the only way that Tara can provide "reminders" to white characters is if racism itself has been forgotten. The absence of credible instances of anti-black racism in *True Blood*'s Louisiana paves the way for vampires to fill that void as the suspect racial other. In this way, Tara, as one of only two significant black characters in the series, is largely responsible for carrying themes of anti-black racism. In Bon Temps, anti-black racism occurs in situations where Tara is involved. Tara is introduced as the stereotypical angry black woman who provokes a confrontation with her white boss, then slaps him and quits her job. This prompts one of the show's few moments of inter-racial conflict. In this scene, Tara's hostility is presented as a character flaw, as is her deployment of anti-black stereotypes to make white interlocutors uncomfortable and apologetic. She refuses to assist the white customer who asks for help (sitting sullenly, then begrudgingly replying to her inquiries), then offers a story of a violent imprisoned boyfriend who she hopes will kill her, relieving her misery. In this way, Tara performs a surfeit of racist stereotypes, offering her white listeners a vision of black laziness, pent-up rage, violence, broken relationships, and imprisonment. Such displays erase (or worse, discount) the anti-black racism that informed every aspect of life in the South, and for which it is still known, in a more modulated form, today.

The use of Bill Compton as an allegory for Blackness is not as sharp as "racial ventriloquism," but it is similar. Susan Gubar's exploration of "white skin, black face" considers the many forms that white writers, musicians, and artists craft white figures to amplify (even as they supplant) black presences and figures in their work for a variety of reasons.[3] *True Blood* deploys a similar strategy, offering a strange refractory visual arrangement whereby the show establishes interconnectedness between blood, race, sex and piety, and revels in the grotesquery that results when boundaries are crossed.

Anne Rice, a progenitor of the Southern vampire genre, understands her depictions as one congruent with marginalization: "The vampire is an outsider. He's the perfect metaphor for those things. He's someone who looks human and sounds human, but is not human, so he's always on the margins" (Stern, digital file). Bill's "outsider" status, his life as a liminal figure, particularly since he straddles the boundaries between human and monster, dovetails neatly with an already established set of anti-black racist beliefs, and concomitant practices to manage the resulting anxiety.

LOUISIANA'S BLOOD TRUTHS

Scholars and critics have identified Louisiana as a particularly useful location for *True Blood*. As one reviewer observed, "Sultry and otherworldly Louisiana, with its complex history of slavery, prejudice and discrimination, is the perfect setting for a vampire mystery" (Treble, Digital file). Appropriately, the fictional Louisiana town of Bon Temps owes its name to the Creole Mardi Gras slogan "Laissez le bon temps rouler" ("Let the good times roll") suggesting a festive, even bacchanalian, aspect to the carnival celebration. Yet while the "bon temps" may roll, that process has always been marked by racial barriers. Consider something as innocuous as the music that accompanies most good times. Mid-twentieth-century propaganda posters written by the Greater Louisiana Citizens Council, for example, warned business owners and residents of the dangers to be found in African American music. The "savage music of these records" would lead to the moral decline of its white citizenry: "Don't let your children buy or listen to these negro records!" Such warnings expose an invidious white fear of even sonic blackness, suggesting the degree to which the racial landscape was segregated by white hostility. This racial landscape (a form of social geography) while not visible in the same ways as the physical locations of Louisiana in which *True Blood* is set remains relevant to HBO's overall project. As Anne-Marie Paquet Deyris notes, Louisiana's social and physical geographies are both relevant to the series, "the sense of belonging to a specific region but also to one big extended family, of being impacted by it as much as by "the racial nightmare" (Baldwin, *The Fire Next Time*) and by class, gender and species issues stems from the peculiar status of the southern soil and 'manners'" (Paquet Deyris 193).

The power of southern soil is first established in the opening credits of *True Blood*, which have been examined and acclaimed for the degree to which they address the specificities of the town of Bon Temps. Reviewing the opening credits, Joshua Alston describes them as "the perfect *amuse-bouche* [offering] a flip book of Deep South postcards: images of hungry gators and modest homes, neon crosses and dirt roads. In the final shot, a woman is dunked for a river baptism and appears to emerge in hysterics. Either she's in rapture, or just a hairbreadth from drowning. This is the world of 'True Blood,' where quaint, romantic notions of the South are recast with dread." What simmers just beneath the surface is the notion of consumption: to bite, to eat, to penetrate, masticate, and digest. The opening credits establish some of the racial and sexual codes used to generate sympathy for Bill Compton, and also create credibility for the vampire's larger quest for public social equity. To call the opening scene an "amuse-bouche" is to reveal the ways in which it whets the appetite for the main course ahead. The credits draw on documented historical aspects of Southern discrimination (the Ku Klux Klan appears twice), and supplement that with a revision of anti-gay church slogans ("God Hates Fangs" is posted on a church marquee, in a play on a religious slur "God Hates Fags"). By setting the show's parameters and context, including religious piety and sexual play, the opening montage endeavors to promote notions about the interconnectedness of a rural Louisiana landscape, its institutions and people with anti-black and homophobic practices. The credits lay the groundwork for the spectral south of Alan Ball's Louisiana.

The Louisiana of the credits is a lush and historical ecological backdrop. "Beneath the murky surface of a Louisiana swamp. A weird-looking fish loiters as the camera booms up and out of the mire like a sinister creature rising from its watery lair. The camera then floats past rows of stately but dilapidated homes, drawing closer to civilization. Flashframes of naked bodies writhing on a floor segue into scenes of religious fervor, civil unrest and roadkill" (Stasukevich 12). In addition to the animals and plant life, a little white boy chomps away (in two scenes) on strawberries, turning his smiling mouth a dull blood red.

Featured prominently in the opening sequence, and for a longer period than the red-mouthed boy, is a Black church service. It was not filmed on location; nor was it comprised of historic footage, like the attacks on civil rights workers and photos of a Klan cross-burning. These Black church scenes include both the general Protestant Black church practices of clapping while singing and the particular Pentecostal worship styles of "laying of hands" (a prayer style involving physical touch), women "catching" the Holy Spirit, and a preacher jumping up from the ground. The church scenes have been transposed from

VHS footage of black Pentecostal services in Chicago. The footage underwent a layering process to make it look rough and congruent with the overall visual style. This Black cultural element (a mixture of the sensational, solemn, and the strange) undergirds and authorizes something genuine about this Louisiana. This Black element was likely deemed necessary to round out the perception of the setting as valid. In the minds of many, Black blood is needed to bind the Southern context, to make it "authentic."

Louisiana is unique in the South because a high percentage of its population is racially mixed. In the nineteenth and for most of the twentieth century, Louisiana's social and legal codes determined the racial particularities of its citizenry.[4] In its antebellum days, the attitudes about racial and cultural admixture were fluid, if at times fetishized. Octoroon Balls of the nineteenth century were convened for white men to socialize and meet women who were one-eighth black. The system of *plaçage* was an informal marriage arrangement between mixed race women and white men. Though Louisiana's frequent sexual mixing produced many gradations of blackness (mulatto, quadroons and octoroons, etc.), which implied lenient standards for interracial sexual congress, it is important to recall that the state was also the site of the single most decisive decision to inaugurate the Jim Crow era. The landmark case Plessy v Ferguson, which ultimately legalized segregation and "separate but equal," was first adjudicated in Louisiana, before appeals led it to the US Supreme Court. Plessy v Ferguson established racial segregation as the law of the land, making "separate but equal" conform to the American constitution.

In the twentieth century, Louisiana state legislatures and local officials adopted practices to calculate blood ratios and determine racial place based on those calculations. Anti-miscegenation codes preventing marriage between people of different races had been enforced since post-Reconstruction days. But in 1970, the state legislature went a step further to calculate and manage the blood of its citizenry. Act 46, "Designation of race by public officials," maintained: "In signifying race, a person having one thirty second or less of Negro blood shall not be deemed, described or designated by an public official in the state of Louisiana as 'colored,' a 'mulatto,' a 'black,' a 'negro,' a 'griffe,' an 'Afro-American,' a 'quadroon,' a 'mestizo,' a 'colored person' or a 'person of color'" (Davis 200). The state developed a mathematical formula to determine the percentage of black blood: "½ of the father's fraction of negro blood (FNB) was added to the ½ of the mother's fraction of negro blood (MNB) to equal the child's fraction of negro blood (CNB). In formula: ½ of (FNB) + ½ of (MNB) = CNB" (Davis 202, note 22). This statute was maintained—with dire consequences for those on both sides of the color line—until the mid-1980s.

Given the region's historical preoccupation with calculating and classifying blood, it is worth considering the ways in which HBO's Louisiana is evacuated of racial prejudice. While other bigotries persist, including classism and homophobia (which is relegated to the lower classes),[5] anti-black racism—a structuring cultural staple throughout the South's recent and distant past—is conspicuously absent from Bon Temps. Vampires operate on a range of allegorical frequencies in *True Blood*. The process of vampires coming "out of the coffin" references the language of gay and lesbian identities struggling for recognition and acceptance in a heteronormative context. Later in the series, hate groups (both Louisiana state agencies and informal citizen watches) terrorize vampires with curfews and biological weapons. This evokes the ways in which African Americans, gays, and lesbians have found themselves the target of violence as a means of social control. Later seasons of the series feature both internment camps (vampires are imprisoned without due process) and concentration camps (where vampires are tortured and killed in the name of science and social control), bringing to mind the aspects of World War II Japanese internment and Hitler's anti-Semitic genocide. The complexity of the vampire's racial and cultural allegory serve as a useful foundation for the black racial lens through which one can unearth important aspects of _True Blood_'s spectral southern landscape.

The shifting allegorical measures of Bill Compton and his vampire race parallel the spectral dimension of HBO's Louisiana. In the context of joining the American "mainstream," _True Blood_'s vampires can be seen as screens through which to see the tale of Black struggle for civil rights in a white America hostile to their interests. Blacks used many strategies to confront the thorny problems of white supremacy: assimilation, agitation, radicalism, and behavior modification to demonstrate that blacks were "a credit to their race." However, the show's allegorical connection between vampires and blackness is not directly referential, nor does it need to be. This instability opens up a useful space in which to consider the meanings, limitations, and possibilities for post-racial sensibility in the twenty-first century.

BILL AS "OPTIC WHITE"

"If it's Optic White, it's the Right White" the protagonist of _Invisible Man_ is told while working for Liberty Paints, a company with the slogan, Keep America Pure (Ellison 217). The paint color Optic White is so effective that it can turn a piece of coal white. The optic of whiteness informs the visual presentation of Bill Compton. Like most (white) vampires, Bill is very pale, whiter than the other white people around him. But his spectral whiteness, amplified by an absence of blood flow, oxygenation, and sun exposure, is more than just skin deep. Bill Compton also benefits from the social and cultural privileges of white men in the Deep South. Bill Compton's whiteness is congruent with the universalizing tendency of whiteness in American culture, which results in whiteness lacking visible racial particularity. One scholar describes racial categorization this way: "Black people are Black, Asian people are Asian, while White people are simply people" (Kirkland 93).[6]

Bill Compton's whiteness is more complicated than that of other white men in Bon Temps, but it still benefits from a set of established white privileges that Bill wields and benefits from. Unlike early representations of white vampires that were demonized, ostracized, and placed firmly on the margins of society, Kirkland argues that contemporary vampires such as Bill Compton (e.g., _Twilight_'s Edward Cullen) represent significant advances toward white cultural assimilation. "Firmly embedded in mainstream society, the vampires of recent film and television might also be associated with racial Whiteness rather than racial marginality through the considerable privilege and power they enjoy" (Kirkland 104). _True Blood_'s Louisiana, in its current moment, is purged of the anti-black racism that produced formulas for determining fractions of "negro blood" among its citizens until 1983. Bill Compton benefits from a post-racial context that erases blackness as a meaningful category of experience or source of conflict. At the same time, the displacement of black struggles for social justice does not diminish the white privilege Bill acquired as a young man in the 1850s, and continued to capitalize upon throughout the last century. Kirkland explains, "the White privilege vampires enjoy is accrued through means largely associated with White operations of power. As a result of their longevity, vampires manage to maintain and build upon original family capital, inherited wealth and status being a significant preserve of the White upper class" (Kirkland 104).

Rather than displacing the effect of white privilege by rendering racial differences moot, *True Blood*'s racially vacant Louisiana and its long-lived white vampires reify the quotidian mechanics of white supremacy, such as inheritance. "If the power vampires exercise is analogous to White power and that power derives from the vampire's innate superhumanity, such narratives in their largely uncritical disposition towards their vampire protagonists represent a tacit justification for the operation of White privilege, suggesting that the superior lifestyles enjoyed by White people derive from White human's superiority over non-White" (Kirkland 104). The optics of Bill's whiteness exceeds what Ralph Ellison's *Invisible Man* described as "the peculiar disposition of the eyes of those with whom I come in contact" (Ellison 1). Bill's whiteness is visible, yet other non-visible elements, aspects of his character, including inherited wealth and the extra-ordinary powers of his vampirism, also fortify his character.

Bill's antebellum life provides the early basis of his privileged whiteness. During that time Bon Temps was not a racially neutered landscape. Bill lived through the Civil War, fighting for the Confederacy and a states' rights doctrine that included slaveholding, a de facto system of racial ranking with whites on top and any fractional iterations of blackness below them. Speaking with Sookie about his war experiences, he recognizes that the soldier pool was unevenly class-based, with causalities skewed toward the poor rather than the landowners. Rather than describe the Civil War in large terms as the War Between the States or, even, The War of Northern Aggression, Bill remembers his place among a "bunch of starving, freezing boys, killing each other so the rich people can stay rich." However, during his visit with Sookie, Jason, Adele and Tara bring up what is framed in the scene as a taboo subject:

> **Tara**: Did you own slaves?
> Sookie (shoots her a reprimanding glare): Tara!
> **Bill** (nonplussed): I did not, but my father did.
> Tara: Hmmph.
> **Bill**: A house slave, a middle-aged woman whose name I cannot recall, and…And a yard slave. A young, strong man named Minus.
> **Adele**: This is just the sort of thing my club will be so interested in hearing about.
> **Tara** (glares): About slaves?
> *Sookie visually chastises Tara.*
> **Adele**: Well, about anything to do with that time. ("The First Taste")

Tara, in her role here as stereotypical angry black woman, raises an issue that in Sookie's mind is as impolite as it is unsuitable for civil conversation. Jason and Adele are oblivious to Tara's discomfort, which is clearly coded by her (unjustified) rage. Sookie is embarrassed by Tara's inappropriate line of questioning. The post-racial Louisiana is the perfect setting to contextualize Tara's inquiry about Bill's role in slavery. The current-day Bon Temps has done what so many racists want all black people to do (that is "get over it" when it comes to the historical realities of anti-black racism, slavery, Jim Crow, and any other injustices black people can't seem to forget), and move forward to a racially neutralized future. Under conditions of anti-black erasures in Bon Temps, the antebellum South is idealized through the gaze of nostalgia. Adele's club, Descendants of the Glorious Dead, is devoted to remembering the Civil War era, recording local genealogies and celebrating their nineteenth-century ancestors.[7] The selective memories are crucial to the understanding of Bon Temps as a place free of anti-black bigotry: as such, the Civil War era can be discussed, even celebrated, in polite company, but slavery cannot. Tara's reference to slavery is in poor taste, in this context free of anti-black prejudice. Bill's antebellum life bolsters his whiteness. His antebellum past combined with his vampiric longevity allows him to claim the old Compton homestead as its last remaining heir. This inheritance, in part, is another benefit of his position as a white landowning male.

Bill accepts Adele's invitation to speak at the local library about his life in antebellum Bon Temps. As a man in the rare position of being able to speak firsthand about the distant past, Bill is uniquely qualified to address the Descendants of the Glorious Dead. This is also the town's first opportunity to see the Vampire Bill in the flesh. The spectacular quality of Bill's presence is seen in his whiteness, so spectral, that his pallor nears translucence. A child, impressed by the optical paleness of Bill's whiteness, makes a remark that usefully allows a transition to the other side of Bill's characterization. As earlier shown, Bill oscillates between whiteness and blackness as allegorical aspects of his social status. In this scene, this becomes explicit. Peering at Bill as he prepares to address the assembly, Arlene's young son whispers to her:

Cody: Momma, he's so white.
Arlene: No, darling. We're white. He's dead. ("Sparks Fly Out")

Kirkland views this comic passage as "indicative of the manner in which the vampire throws racial Whiteness into relief, forcing Whiteness to acknowledge its particularity through its proximity to an identity that is white but which is not human" (Kirkland 106). I concur with this assessment, particularly insofar as Cody, as a child, recognizes whiteness as a single optical level: Bill has pale skin like his own therefore he must be white. In fact, Cody's description of Bill as "so" white, implies that Bill's whiteness is whiter than white. Arlene's correction—"We're white. He's dead"—teaches her child that all whiteness is not created equal. In addition to indicating the marginal aspects of Bill's whiteness, this scene also usefully illuminates another (an Other) aspect of Bill's character.

BILL'S BLACKNESS, OR WHEN BLACK THINGS HAPPEN TO WHITE PEOPLE

The perception of Bill Compton as a romantic "dark" antihero with glimmers of heroism is animated by a broader social and cultural Southern context. Historically, in the south blacks were treated with thorough, overt and subtle brutality. In this way, Bill Compton's allegorical blackness allows for sympathy through displacement similar to that of John Howard Griffin's work *Black Like Me* (1958).[8] In this social experiment cum expose of Southern racism, John Howard Griffin darkens his skin (with pills and excessive light treatments) and travels throughout the South for six weeks, living as a black man. The book was immensely popular for its insights into black life under the tyrannies of Jim Crow, insights that were trustworthy (and slights more injurious) because their purveyor was white. Nearly ten years after its original publication, Griffin's book was in its thirty-first paperback printing. A 1968 review of the text reports that although *Black Like Me* has "severe limitations because it has been written by a white man," the narrative "gains a great deal because of the white narrator who has less of a gap to bridge between himself and his audience. For part of this white audience, the book may also be more credible and less likely to be accused of exaggeration, special pleading, or self-pity" (Rank 814). Griffin's six weeks disguised as a black man has granted him greater authority on the "Negro problem" than black people who had been writing about their lives and this issue for more than a century.

Bill Compton is no John Howard Griffin. He does not imitate blackness, nor does he deliberately engage in the subtle yet deliberate acts of recessed cultural blackface.[9] Instead, Bill's blackness is context driven. At several junctures in the early part of the series, Bill's character and actions are informed by circumstances that reflect common experiences of blacks in the desegregating South. In this way, Bill's contextual and allegorical blackness reflect a process similar to the sympathy that John Howard Griffin was able to generate because of his whiteness. Merlotte's is a popular bar and restaurant in Bon Temps. It is the setting for many scenes, perhaps because Sookie is employed there, and most of *True Blood*'s characters circulate through that lively social venue. Because of its status as a hub of activity in the small town, Merlotte's is also a useful setting in which to gauge the response to vampire integration as a concept. I suggest that Bill's treatment by customers and employees of Merlotte's signifies on the reactions that black civil rights activists received during the days of restaurant desegregation. Given the shifting nature of *True Blood*'s allegories and the intricacies of signification (repetition with a difference), the reactions to a vampire in a Bon Temps bar are not the same as those of blacks at a segregated Woolworth's lunch counter, nor need they be. The suspicion, fetishization, disdain, and anxiety prompted by Bill's presence are similar to the response of whites that resented, and protested against, blacks sharing the same lunch counter.

Bill's first appearance in the series takes place at Merlotte's. Though Sookie suspects that "Merlotte's just got its first vampire," he looks like any other pale patron of the restaurant. Sookie, correctly guessing that Bill is more than he appears to be, enthuses to Sam: "Can you believe it? Right here, in Bon Temps! I've been waiting for this to happen since they came out of the coffin two years ago!" ("Strange Love"). Even before Bill has identified himself as a vampire, Sookie has expressed an anticipatory interest. Sookie's enthusiasm can also be seen as a form of fetishization. Directly opposed to the many people in the town who instantly dislike Bill's vampirism, Sookie takes an almost instant liking to him. The suspicion that Bill generates is based on irrational fears, but Sookie's ready fondness for him is similarly based. As the instructor of a course blog titled "Monstrous Discourse, Modern Culture" asks: "doesn't her fascination with Bill seem *itself* like a kind of exotifying gesture? While most of the bar sees him as automatically bad, is the urge to see him as automatically good not just another form of fetishizing his difference?"[10] Sookie goes out of her way to make Bill feel more comfortable, less isolated. Even though Sam has been uncomfortable about vampire integration, Sookie tries to cast him as more welcoming than he actually is: "Oh, don't worry about Sam. He's cool. I know for a fact he supports the Vampire Rights Amendment" ("Strange Love"). In laying out the welcome mat for Bill, Sookie must revise Sam's actual opinion and transform his hostility—which is clearly proven later in the series—into tolerance.

Sookie is depicted as a kind-hearted, yet naïve innocent.[11] And it is the contrast between her pure, virginal nature that produces such outrage among those who disapprove of her socializing with Bill. Though no one in Bon Temps knows Bill, most people fearfully perceive him as a bloodthirsty monster intent on harming any human, especially the wholesome Sookie that crosses his path. Sookie's choice to connect with Bill on a personal level leaves her open to scrutiny and condemnation. This is seen when Bill visits Merlotte's a second time and Sookie takes a moment to talk with him. Sookie is a telepath. This extraordinary ability has also been a disability, since her capacity to read people's thoughts prevents her from bonding with her parents (who she could tell feared her ability) or dating (she can tell when men have sexually objectified her) as an adult. The judging thoughts of her friends and unknown restaurant patrons flood through her mind:

> **Sam** (thinking): He's got her in his sights. I need to protect her.
> **Woman** (thinking): That's that vampire she saved last night.
> **Man** (thinking): Sookie, please do not…
> **Man** (thinking): It ain't right, him being here with normal people. I hope she…
> **Woman** (thinking): I always thought she was nice, but I just wonder what kind of a good Christian girl would even look at a vampire…
> **Man** (thinking): I don't think he looks that scary to me.
> **Lafayette** (thinking): Looks like she likes them tall, dark, and dead…
> **Dawn** (thinking): Who is that? And why isn't he talking to me?
> **Man** (thinking): Stackhouse family ain't nothing but trash. ("Strange Love")

The scrutiny that trickles through Sookie's consciousness is more than just a question of the conflict between an outsider and an insider. Bill is indeed an unknown stranger, while Sookie is a hometown sweetheart, a little odd, but still embraced as a member of the community. A Greek chorus of curiosity, suspicion, concern and hostility is at play in Sookie's mind as she sits down with Bill. The perceptions of Sookie as not "nice" or a "good Christian girl" and "nothing but trash" seem directly related to the aspersions cast upon white women known to sexually associate with black men in the nineteenth century. Though some of these views persisted throughout the twentieth century, Martha Hodes's study of illicit sex in the nineteenth century reveals that white women who were known to have sex with black men were often seen as having a "poor" or "low" character. "Voluntary association with a black man immediately implied depravity for a white woman" (Hodes 162). Many of these assessments deem Sookie to be deeply flawed for associating with a vampire, much as white women who had sexual contact or relationships with black men were viewed. Bill's hypervisibility as a racial other is also amplified in this scene.[12] Bill asks Sookie, "Do you realize that every person in this establishment is staring at us?" Sookie hears him, but disagrees, explaining that the crowd is staring at her because of her brother's legal problems. Bill contradicts her, however, "They are staring because I am a vampire and you are mortal" ("Strange Love"). Bill recognizes that his vampire identity renders him suspect in the social context. Holding Sookie's hand reveals an intimacy of which many in Merlotte's disapprove.

Later, Sookie and Sam (whom she believed to be in favor of vampire equity) have a conversation that explicitly references anti-black codes. Sookie tells Sam that she's going to Fangtasia, a vampire bar to help clear her brother's name. Sam warns her not to go, fearing for her safety with so many vampires present:

> **Sookie:** And frankly, Sam, I'm surprised at you. I thought you were for the Vampire Rights Amendment.
> **Sam:** Well, I think they should have their own bars. I just don't think people ought to go there.
> **Sookie:** So you want to return to the days of "separate but equal"?
> **Sam:** I don't give a fuck about equal. We can give them more than we got. Just so long as everything's separate. ("Escape from Dragon House")

Sookie's reference to "separate but equal" is one of the few times that *True Blood* deliberately connects vampirism to blackness. Sam's response takes this legal precedent further saying that vampires can have "more than we got," as long as vampires remain segregated from the human community.[13]

Bill's allegorical blackness is not only apparent when he is the only vampire among humans, but is also made clear when he spends time with other vampires. In the first season of *True Blood*, Bill Compton is seen as an exception within his community: a vegetarian vampire hoping to (re)join the American mainstream. In this regard, Bill's assimilationist attitude and synthesized diet conform to the agenda publicized by the vampire governing body, the American Vampire League (AVL). In several moments throughout the first two episodes, Nan Flanagan, the league's president, appears on cable news and talk shows to promote the vampire's "mainstreaming" agenda. Flanagan and the AVL proclaim that the synthetic blood substitute TruBlood is the answer to centuries of vampire-human predation. For this reason, vampires can unveil their once secret presence and become a visible part of human society.

Bill and Sookie's friendship can thrive only if Bill proves himself to be better than commonly held stereotypes about his race. He must not conform to preconceived notions about vampires. His actions must be forthright and superior to those of other vampires. He must especially distance himself from those vampires who choose to revel in their difference and their power. Bill must act as a "credit to his race," a back-handed compliment used by whites to describe blacks who both conformed to their ideas of white standard and rejected those blacks who refused that standard. As a phrase, a "credit" to one's race implies that in the tally of public opinion the race in question is beset by deficits.

We see Bill engage with such socially deficient vampires early in season one. A trio of aggressive, almost feral, vampires (and two human companions) is visiting Bill when Sookie arrives. The vampires try to scare and "glamour" Sookie, but neither option works.[14] Later, after Sookie refuses to talk with Bill because Liàm, Diane, and Malcolm have frightened her, Bill stops by their "nest" in an effort to convince them of the error of their monstrous ways. These three vampires are not vegetarians: they keep humans, most likely by the power of glamour, for feeding and sex. On the occasion of Bill's visit, they have killed and disposed of one of the two humans. The second human, whose throat is slit, hangs upside down, bleeding to death into a waiting bucket. Liam drinks some of this blood from a large glass, offering some to Bill, who declines.

In the grim light of vampire violence against humans, Bill's special quality as an ambassador shines forth. He is hopeful about the possibility of easy assimilation with humans, longing to fit in, even if it means controlling his innate nature. He longs to connect with humans and to do so requires crafting a positive image:

> **Bill:** You know, you're doing nothing to help our cause.
> **Diane:** Not everyone wants to dress up and play human, Bill.
> **Liam:** Yeah. Not everybody wants to live off that Japanese shit they call blood, either—as if we could.
> **Bill:** We have to moderate our behavior now that we are out in the open.
> **Malcolm:** Not everybody thinks it was such a great idea. And not everybody intends to toe the party line. Honey, if we can't kill people, what's the point of being a vampire? ("Mine")

Bill's advocacy for behavior modification and a moderate, rather than radical, approach to attaining civil rights and public acceptance reflects a similar conflict that took place within African American community organizations. Some groups were known for passive resistance, such as the NAACP and SNCC; while others, like the Black Panther Party or The Nation of Islam, were more radical in their approach. Bill claims that public visibility requires vampires to behave in ways that contradict the stereotypes that humans came to believe over the years.[15]

Bill's discussion with the three feral vampires (who are ultimately killed by white racists when their nest is burned to the ground) is part of the larger project of proving that vampires can earn a place at the table of humanity. Bill's strong advocacy for an assimilationist approach to human-vampire relations is another component of the show's racial allegory. The final example of Bill's allegorical blackness is a visual scene from episode 8, "Fourth Man in the Fire." At the start of this episode, Sookie believes that Bill has been trapped in the fire that killed the three feral vampires. Sookie grieves deeply for Bill and in the dead of night walks to the nearby cemetery to deposit flowers on his grave. Sookie turns to leave but is stopped when a hand, protruding from the ground, grabs her ankle and pulls her to the ground. Sookie struggles to escape the naked man crawling from the grave until Bill calls her name. Recognizing his voice, Sookie kisses him and they have sex in the graveyard. As strange as this description may sound, the dissonance is greatly enhanced by Bill's physical appearance. His naked body is covered in black dirt from the grave. The spectacle of Sookie's white skin contrasted with Bill's artificially blackened skin is a rare glimpse beneath the layers that comprise the show's racial allegory. The image of a black(-ened) male lying atop and penetrating the body of a white female operates on the same register as anti-miscegenation sexual anxiety.

"FANG BANGERS" AND FEAR OF VAMPIRE SEX

The aforementioned graveyard scene reveals another significant counterpoint to the black dimensions of Bill's characterization. Vampire sex is a tantalizing yet deeply feared possibility in *True Blood*. The vampire bar, Fangtasia, is shown to play on the balance of desire and revulsion: the fantasy of fangs. The preoccupation with vampire sex draws upon the hostile white response to black struggles for civil rights. As Martha Hodes notes of post-Emancipation equity, "black men's hopes for and insistence on equality brought public expressions of fear from white Southerners, and those fears included direct references to white women and sex" (Hodes 143). It is useful to recall that the American Vampire League is frequently shown on television advocating for vampire equity. This engagement with civil rights discourses is made clear in the early scenes of the first episode. Nan Flanagan, speaking with Bill Maher, exemplifies the polished talking points of a well-oiled organization:

> **Nan Flanagan**: We're citizens. We pay taxes. We deserve basic civil rights, just like everyone else.
> **Bill Maher:** Yeah but, come on. Doesn't your race have a rather sordid history of exploiting and feeding off innocent people? For centuries?
> **Nan Flanagan**: Three points. Number one: show me documentation. It doesn't exist. Number two: doesn't your race have a history of exploitation? We never owned slaves, Bill, or detonated nuclear weapons. And most importantly, point number three: now that the Japanese have perfected synthetic blood which satisfies all of our nutritional needs, there is no reason for anyone to fear us. [...] I can assure you that every member of our community is now drinking synthetic blood. That's why we decided to make our existence known. We just want to be part of mainstream society. (Enthusiastic audience applause) ("Strange Love")

The use of Bill Maher, an actual political commenter for HBO, adds a layer of verisimilitude to the interview. Maher's presence allows for the possibility that this fictional scene might, if it were real, look like this. In addition, Flanagan's talking points reflect actual reasoning used to justify black civil rights, as she rebuts objections and fears with facts. An additional layer of reality comes from the historical connection of vampire rights and vampire sex anxiety to black civil rights and interracial sex anxiety in the antebellum era. While the system of slavery[16] was still in effect, sexual contact between black men and white women was largely tolerated or addressed in local communities. During and after the Civil War, however, "White Southerners now began to alter their strategies in responding, not only to such liaisons, but also to the idea of such liaisons. Under slavery, sex between black men and white women violated the rules of patriarchy and racial hierarchy, and yet had never overwhelmingly threatened either system. With the demise of slavery, however, evolving—or devolving—white ideas about the dangers of black male sexuality would become intimately intertwined in the violent politics of the Reconstruction South" (Hodes 146). I suggest that the "intertwined" nature of black freedom and fear of black male sexuality (unfettered by the social controls of slavery) forms the basis for *True Blood*'s representation of vampire sex anxiety. Just as segregationists (from the nineteenth century to the 1950s) feared that increased social proximity of blacks and whites would result in black male-white female sexual contact, human-vampire sexuality is both feared and fetishized in HBO's Louisiana.

The term "fang banger" is used to describe women (and men, but it is more punitively applied to women) who have sex with vampires. I suggest that the term "fang banger" gets its punitive charge from the anti-black slur "nigger lover." "Fang banger" and "nigger lover" as derogatory phrases depend upon the negative charge of their root words, "fanger" and "nigger." In *True Blood*, the term "fanger" operates on the same register as "nigger," as some insults to vampires take the form of "fucking fanger" similar to "fucking nigger." "Nigger lover" describes a white person deemed to have transgressed the racial barrier to love or care for a black person (or black community).[17] To be a "nigger lover" is to betray the white race. Similarly, to be a "fang banger" is to step outside the human family. White men are largely responsible for policing these sexual boundaries. "Fang bangers," like "nigger lovers," violate the racial integrity code that declares white women to be the property of white men. In this way, it is fitting that *True Blood* features a white man who struggles mightily with vampire sex anxiety.

Jason Stackhouse's first appearance in the series is highly sexualized, establishing an important feature of his character. Jason's introduction is framed by the close-up torso shot of a sweating woman watching a reality TV dating show. The camera pans back, revealing the woman to be naked; her hands clutch a man's head buried between her thighs, engaged in cunnilingus. Viewers hear the results of his sexual labors before we see him, as the woman laughs and writhes in delight. Jason comes up for air, noticing two red pin-sized pricks in Maudette Pickens' thigh:

> **Jason:** What the fuck is this?
> **Maudette:** Oh…it's…just a…mosquito bite.
> **Jason:** You had sex with a vampire!
> **Maudette**: OK…once! I went to that vampire bar down in Shreveport. Look. I was broke and he paid me a lot of money. [...] He offered me a thousand dollars to bite me. What was I gonna do? Say no to a thousand bucks? ("Strange Love")

A voracious sexual appetite frames Jason's character, starting with this introduction and continuing throughout the first season. His indiscriminate sexual behavior is well known in Bon Temps; even his own sister, defending him, calls him a "horn-dog." Despite his frequent and arbitrary couplings, Jason still reserves the right to scrutinize and reprimand the sexual choices of others. It is also worth considering the bites as physical evidence that remains on Maudette's body. This is an example of the ways in which *True Blood*'s post-racial vampirism engages and exceeds the limits of a clear-cut racial allegory. There are no discernable marks left upon a white woman's body to indicate that she has had sex with a black man. Racists and white supremacists might well consider such a woman "tainted" by her black sexual contact; however, such a taint would not be apparent on her flesh. Vampire sex, as depicted in *True Blood*, signifies on the prevalent racist anxiety about black male-white female sex. Vampire-human sex is cast as unusual, "strange love" (the title of the episode), predatory, and dangerously beyond the pale of normal human sexual intercourse. Vampires are hyper-sexualized, moving at speeds imperceptible to the human eye (When moving at vampire speed, they are always filmed at a blurred and accelerated pace, often accompanied by a squealing soundtrack, whether dancing, walking, or having sex. This is meant to suggest that vampire pace is undetectable by the human eye). By rendering vampire sex visible on the white female body, as marked by the two puncture marks, *True Blood* emphasizes a minimally dual penetration of the women who have sex with vampires: sexual orifice penetration and arterial penetration to extract blood. These puncture wounds mark the white women who have been sexually involved with vampires; their skin announces that transgressive action to the broader community. Maudette explains that she only had vampire sex once. Maudette is not proud of her actions nor was this step prompted by curiosity or desire. Her financial need outweighs her reluctance. She justifies this sexual act as a financial transaction, nothing more. It is also clear that Maudette has not been converted to the belief that vampires are more sexually skilled than humans.

> **Jason**: What was it like?
> **Maudette:** Scary.
> **Jason**: You know, I read in *Hustler*, everybody should have sex with a vampire at least once before they die.
> **Maudette:** Once was enough for me. He was way too rough. I mean, I like to be rough…sometimes. But…("Strange Love")

Hustler, a pornographic magazine, participates in the fetishization of vampire sex. The idea that "everybody should have sex with a vampire at least once before they die" suggests a hyper-sexualized view of vampire sexual capacity. In this way, it is easy to peer beneath this and see the similar sexualization of black masculinity. The heavy symbolic burden normally placed on black male sex organs and sexual performance is displaced onto vampires. Offended by Maudette's confession, Jason prepares to leave, but Maudette convinces him to stay, saying that she taped her vampire sexual escapade. Jason watches the footage, captivated. In the video, Maudette is naked and bound by the wrists with a chain suspended from a hook in the ceiling. A large white bald vampire—covered with tattoos, including one down his spine articulating his vertebrae—stands at Maudette's back, tightly gripping her hips while penetrating her from behind. As Jason watches, the vampire (who will later be identified as Liam) thrusts into Maudette at lightning-fast pace. In sexual ecstasy, his head swivels around quickly, eyes roll back into his head, and his tongue flashes in and out of his mouth.

Linda Williams's work on inter-racial pornography is instructive on the visual logics of this scene. Discussing comparative interracial pornography scenes between black women-white men and white women-black men, Williams notes "The black woman does not articulate her pleasure in the 'whiteness' of the white man's cock, as the white woman articulated hers to the black man. Only the black man and the white women's sexual-racial differences are singled out" (Williams 276-77). The viewer is instructed to watch the vampire, to remain focused on his unusual body movements, the speed of his thrusts, the whites of his eyes, the terrifying sound of his grunts and roars. Maudette is merely incidental to the scene, her pleasure or pain matters little: the vampire is the center of attention. The scene horrifies, repulses, and attracts Jason, who is silently stunned while watching the video. Jason's next scene, however, suggests that witnessing a vampire-human sex act was impressive. Jason and Maudette re-enact the sex scene from the video with Jason shouting at Maudette. As he penetrates Maudette from behind, he loudly reprimands her for breaking the vampire-human sex taboo:

Jason: You like this?
Jason: Being punished?
Jason: You're a sick little vampire fucker!
Jason: You like that, Pickens?
Jason: You look at me.
Jason: You let a dead man fuck you?
Jason: You fucking disgust me!
Jason: It's too bad I don't have fangs, huh?
Jason: Rip your fucking throat out. ("Strange Love")

Jason continues to shout at Maudette, squeezing her throat while penetrating her. This scene is important in that it allows Jason to regain a sense of lost mastery over Maudette's body. As a white woman with whom he was having sex, Maudette's vagina represents Jason's exclusive, even if only temporarily so, piece of property. Jason was made anxious, some might say traumatized, by witnessing Liam's wild and explosive sex with Maudette. Jason, as a human man, is unable to replicate the power of Liam's sex acts, and thus suffers from performance anxiety.

The images from this vampire-human sex tape will linger in Jason's imagination throughout the season, and influence his opinions on vampire civil rights and their integration into human culture.[18] Jason's sex life remains haunted by Liam in ways that compromise his promiscuous heterosexuality. Jason finds a new sex partner in an old girlfriend, Dawn, who works with Sookie at Merlotte's. A sex scene is filmed from Jason's point of view. Dawn reclines on her back as Jason penetrates her from an upright kneeling position. This vantage point provides a clear view of Dawn's face and torso. Jason is penetrating Dawn, seemingly to their mutual satisfaction, when Dawn's face is instantly replaced with Liam's face, the vampire from Maudette's sex tape.

Liam (speaking with Dawn's voice): What's wrong? Jason, baby. What is it?
(Jason loses his erection, and withdraws from Dawn.)
Jason: I hate that you've been with vampires.
Dawn: And how exactly is that any of your business?
Jason: Well, they're fucked up, Dawn. They're freaks. They're fucking dead! What's wrong with you, letting something nasty like that even touch you?
Dawn: For your information, that was the best sex I ever had in my life. And who are you to judge? You fuck anything with a space between its legs.
Jason: You're lying, "that was the best sex you ever had!" You told me I was the best sex you ever had! ("Mine")

It is important to pause and consider the replacement of Dawn's face with Liam's. Jason remains troubled by the sex tape, even after re-enacting the sex act with Maudette. Though Jason blames his impotence on his disapproval of Dawn's previous sex with vampires, it is repulsion and attraction that are at work. Jason intensely hates and resents vampires, but the opposite of that feeling is also present. As Linda Williams writes of Fanon's theory of "negrophobia as a form of white sexual anxiety," "the deepest cause of this fear lies in the reduction of the black man to a penis, which ultimately constitutes a pathological projection on the part of the white man to his own repressed homosexuality" (Williams 277). Williams reads Fanon's claim as equating the white male obsession with black male sexuality as desire. It appears that this holds true for Jason, who does not see Liam in the room with him or in the mirror. Instead, Jason imagines Liam as his sexual partner, rather than as a usurper of sexual property that is exclusively his.

Jason's discomfort and disapproval could also result from a feeling that a vampire has been where he too has been, making them closer and more similar than different. The transformation of Jason and Dawn's sex act into Jason and Liam's sex act is a significant development that stresses the degree to which Jason's vampire sex preoccupation impacts him. He is distressed that Dawn is not only unashamed of her vampire sex, but she prizes it over all other sex she's had, including prior sex with Jason. Dawn and Jason continue to argue about her sexual choices, until she loses patience, "Ugh. God, just because you lost your hard-on doesn't mean you have to have a fucking meltdown. Believe it or not, Jason—the world does not revolve around your dick" ("Mine"). For Jason Stackhouse, however, the show suggests that indeed his world is centered on sex: the frequency and quality of sex comprise a significant component of his character.

At gunpoint (since Jason refuses to leave), Dawn claims her right to do as she pleases with her own body, "You do not own me, Jason Stackhouse. And if I want you out of my house, you better get your sorry ass out of here!" She continues to yell at Jason, referring to his sexual impotence and amplifying his anxiety: "That's right, you get the fuck out of my house! Limp dick motherfucker! Why don't you go try and fuck your grandmother with that limp dick!" Jason leaves Dawn's house and gets into his truck. Before driving away, he punches the steering wheel, blames those he believes responsible for this fight with Dawn, "Damn bloodsuckers! Fuck!" ("Mine"). In Jason's mind, vampires are responsible for the sexual difficulties he has experienced with Maudette and Dawn. Vampires have intruded upon what he believed to be his exclusive province: sexual access to white women in Bon Temps.

PROTECTING WHITE WOMANHOOD, NOT WHITE WOMEN

One might imagine that the racial line that vampires bifurcate is that drawn between the human race and vampire race. To call the vampires "undead," clarifies fundamental difference between the living and the dead. However, given its black racial allegories, vampirism in *True Blood* operates as a way to threaten the value of whiteness. Four of Bon Temps's white women are murdered in season one, the victims of a white male intent on punishing them for sexual and social congress with vampires. Three of these murders are considered to be less crimes than the self-induced consequence of violating a strict white racial code.

Jason Stackhouse is arrested for the murders of Maudette, Dawn, Amy, and Adele Stackhouse, his grandmother. Through the bars of his jail cell, he speaks with his friend Rene Lanier who, unbeknownst to everyone until the end of this season's finale episode, is actually Drew Marshall, a man who murdered his sister Cindy Marshall for being a "fang banger." Jason believes that he murdered these women and deserves to be incarcerated.

Jason: They ain't never letting me go, Rene. There's something inside of me that's just…it's wrong.

> **Rene:** Oh, come on, now. Ain't like you went and killed a bunch of inno-
> cent women.
> **Jason:** What?
> **Rene:** They were fang bangers. If you hadn't done it, it was just a matter of
> time.
> **Jason:** You calling my grandma a fang banger?
> **Rene:** No. Now, don't you get your back all up, you. I'm just saying you
> must have had your reasons, that's all. ("You'll Be the Death of Me")

In his efforts to console Jason, Rene justifies his own crimes as reasonable. Three murdered women were guilty and if Jason had not killed them, then someone else would have eventually. This impulse to punish transgressing women conforms to what historians have documented about nineteenth-century responses to interracial sex. The Ku Klux Klan made the protection of white women as part of its larger objective to maintain white supremacy. According to an early Klan document, "Females, friends, widows, and their households shall ever be special objects of our regard and protection" (Hodes 160). The protection white women garnered from these white supremacist men came at a price, however, "to earn the guardianship of white men against the presumed danger of black men, a white woman had to abide by certain rules" (Hodes 201). Lower class white women, "especially those who defied the rules of patriarchy," were vulnerable to censure from the Klan. Transgressing women "could not count on ideology about female purity to absolve them of alleged illicit sexual activity" (Hodes 161). Klansmen punished such women with whipping, sexual mutilation, public shaming, rape and other forms of violence, including murder.

Many Bon Temps residents believe that Maudette, Dawn, and Amy each earned their murder as just desserts for sexual contact with vampires. The atmosphere of Bon Temps pulsates with sexual energy and tension. Yet to be a "fang banger" is to be expelled from the human community and vulnerable to attack.[19] Sookie is exposed to this race-preserving ideology during her shift at Merlotte's after Dawn is killed. Sookie's telepathic ability gives her insights into those around her, but this time the thoughts of others are condemning. Sookie approaches a table and a woman across the restaurant thinks, "If you ask me, these whores had it coming, hanging out in vampire bars. That ain't natural and it ain't safe." Sookie serves a woman at her table and her thoughts echo in Sookie's mind, "You seem sad that girl is dead. I wonder if y'all were friends. And if you were, that means you're probably next. Fucking fang bangers" ("Escape from Dragon House"). These comments are not spoken aloud, but Sookie's ability renders them as a cacophony of disapproval. Arlene, who knows of Sookie's relationship with a vampire, asks Sookie directly, "Ain't there even a part of you thinks she had it coming?" Arlene and most of Merlotte's customers cling to a set of beliefs similar to those who endorsed violence against both black men and white women who engaged in interracial sex in the nineteenth century.

According to the racist logic of Bon Temps and HBO's Louisiana, vampire-human sex erodes the fabric of human society. Another layer of that decline, however, has to do with control over the behavior of white women. White patriarchy as an ideology requires pliant white women and exclusive access to their bodies. To maintain the system of control, white women who do not comply with its requirements can be eliminated, a gesture that only reinforces the benefits of staying in one's sexual place. The patriarchal aspect of this violence toward white women is apparent in the Fellowship of the Sun, an anti-vampire church that sends Orry Dawson, its representative, to Jason's jail cell.

> **Orry:** We are a religious organization dedicated to the preservation and salvation of the human race.
> **Jason:** Oh, good, because I thought you just hated vampires. And I used to, but then I got to know one and he was a pretty decent guy. Until I got him killed.
> **Orry:** You see, that's where you're wrong. What you did, it was a service to your race and to Jesus. And you should be proud of that.
> **Jason:** Yeah.
> **Orry:** You know, last year there were over 800 reported vampire-related attacks in Louisiana alone, and the law won't do nothing about it. They are too busy respecting those fiends and their civil rights. Well, what about our rights? Our rights to be safe on our own neighborhoods, our rights to our own blood.
> **Jason**: I don't know nothing about that.
> **Orry**: Look…officially the Church can't condone what you did. You took the lives of four women, women who had tainted themselves and their race but still, human women. Hey. But we do recognize that even though your methods may have been flawed, your intentions were pure. ("You'll Be the Death of Me")

The Fellowship of the Sun church promotes the salvation of the human race. To do this, however, requires the destruction and critique of anything (vampires) and anyone (transgressive white women) that interferes with this mission. As an institution, the Fellowship of the Sun (which will be shown in season two as a group that captures vampires to publicly execute them during special church services) is willing to tacitly endorse Jason's murders of white women—"who had tainted themselves and their race"—under the frame of "pure" intentions.

Orry Dawson, Jason Stackhouse, and Rene Lanier, represent a type of sexual and social discomfort produced by comparison to or contact with vampires. For them, white women who sexually transgress with vampires have crossed into a zone from which there is no return. Their mastery over these women has been compromised, prompting anxiety. Much of the sexual and social anxiety is a useful commentary on penetration anxiety and the results of that penetration. Though vampires do not reproduce sexually, the penetration of white human women by male vampires results in a permanent change, an alteration of the woman and her acceptability and value for human men. The anxiety demonstrated by Jason Stackhouse and Rene Lanier maps neatly onto the anxiety of white men when faced with the prospect of illicit sex between black men and white women post Civil War. The reappearance of these types of anxieties, so prevalent in Louisiana's distant and recent past, suggest that our post-racial America still has racial issues with which to contend.

This essay has considered the ways in which racial allegories of blackness underpin characterization and content of HBO's *True Blood*. Blood mixing, whether constructed through Louisiana's actual legal codes or visualized onscreen with a vampire's bite in an imagined Louisiana, is a central preoccupation for those who would preserve racial purity. The racial anxiety embedded in the term "miscegenation" is shown in *True Blood* to have a distinctive sexual counterpart. In this way, Bon Temps is part of a Louisiana that has evacuated the black-white racial axis and replaced it with that of human-vampire conflict. Given the operative racial codes (with vampires standing in as racial others), it is easy to understand the division as more than that that exists between human and vampire. HBO's *True Blood* has created a new Louisiana, one that resurrects the lush geography and gothic landscapes of the original. Yet the environment cannot escape the racial realities of the American South. Instead, it uses the same racial codes, images, hatreds, and ultimately violence and maps them onto different bodies.

Notes

1. In 1963, a reporter asked Truman if he thought interracial marriage would become popular. He replied, "I hope not. I don't believe in it. What's that word about ten feet long? Miscegenation? Would you want your daughter to marry a Negro?" (Sickels 32)

2. Recent scholarship engages a similar question, see Nicole Rabin's article, "*True Blood*: The Vampire as a Multiracial Critique on Post-Race Ideology," *Journal of Dracula Studies* 12 (2010): 17 pp.

3. Gubar describes a use of racial ventriloquism as a testament to "the acknowledged inability of white artists to represent the black Other and, by extension, the white self that longs to escape solipsism by knowing (or owning its own) Otherness" (Gubar 166).

4. Scholar Virginia Dominguez, describes Louisiana's blood "problem" as one based upon "the existence of widespread assumptions about the properties of blood—that identity is determined by blood; that blood ties, linearly and collaterally, carry social and economic rights and obligations; that both racial identity and class membership are determined by blood" (Dominguez 89).

5. One of the few instances of homophobia occurs in season one, episode five when a "redneck" refuses to eat the hamburger he ordered after Lafayette prepared it, claiming that it "has AIDS." Lafayette confronts the table:

    > Redneck: *Yeah, I'm an American and I got a say in who makes my food* Lafayette: *Well baby, it's too late for that. Faggots been breeding your cows, raising your chickens, even brewing your beer long before I walked my sexy ass up in this motherfucker. Everything on your goddamned table got AIDS.* ("Sparks Fly Out")

    This scene demonstrates the process through which anti-black prejudice is subsumed into an instance of homophobia. The men single out Lafayette's queerness as a site of bigotry and hostility. While black gay men indeed have been among those whose labor comprised the slave and serving classes, it is a historical fact that Black service (regardless of sexual orientation) both in slavery and beyond was a prevailing feature of life in the South. In this moment, Lafayette's blackness is understated (since Bon Temps lacks racism) and his gay identity is all that remains as an object of prejudice.

6. It is widely observed that whiteness occupies a dominant, yet invisible mode of racial identity. Given the myriad ways that whiteness structures American life and culture, it is not surprising that whiteness occupies what I like to call the "default" position. Shannon Winnubst describes the means through which white males diminish their bodies: "the white male heterosexual body erases its own corporeality—its own particularity and specificity—so that it can enter into the totalizing realm of the universal" (Winnubst 6). Here Winnubst refers to the result of a socialization process that allows white men to rarely consider the consequences of their race and gender. In the casual dimensions of American cultural expression, white men lack both race and gender. Gender expectations are something with which women and gay men must contend, much like race is something black people have.

7. The Descendants of the Glorious Dead is an allusion to an actual group, most likely, the United Daughters of the Confederacy: "the outgrowth of many local memorial, monument, and Confederate home associations and auxiliaries to camps of United Confederate Veterans that were organized after the War Between the States. It is the oldest patriotic organization in our country because of its connection with two state-wide organizations that came into existence as early as 1890—the Daughters of the Confederacy (DOC) in Missouri and the Ladies' Auxiliary of the Confederate Soldiers Home in Tennessee." Significantly, their emblem is a five-pointed star with an outsized cotton boll superimposed on it. See http://www.hqudc.org/about_udc/index.htm.

8. For an engaging analysis of this perennial act of black impersonation in American culture and letters, see Eric Lott's essay "White Like Me: Racial Cross Dressing and the Construction of American Whiteness."

9. Discussing the prevalence of black impersonation in the white imaginary, Lott writes, "Every time you hear an expansive white man drop into his version of black English, you are in the presence of blackface's unconscious return" (Lott, *Love and Theft*, 5).

10. From the course blog archive found here: http://monstrousdiscoursemodernculture.blogspot.com/2013/ 01/ blog-post-2-true-blood.html#comment-form. Posted February 1, 2013. Last accessed: September 23, 2013.

11. And while her interest in Bill has shades of fetish, she is the only person willing to help Bill when he is attacked by the Rattrays. This craven, drug-addled couple captures Bill outside Merlotte's, debilitating him with silver chains so they might exsanguinate him and sell his blood. Vampire blood is a powerful curative, hallucinogen, and aphrodisiac.

12. Bill's racial alterity is emphasized at many points throughout the first season. These moments include being stopped by police for driving while vampire (a nod to the condition Driving While Black that many black motorists experience) and receiving harsh "service" from bigoted waitresses like Arlene.

13. Sam's use of "we" here is ironic considering that he is revealed to be a shape-shifter, a human who can take on animal form at will. As the series evolves, shape-shifters join a large cast of "supes" or supernatural beings including vampires, fairies, werewolves, werepanthers, and maenads.

14. Both the books and HBO versions employ the vampire trope of glamour, a type of hypnosis/mental telepathy that vampires use to gain control of humans who are typically highly vulnerable to mental suggestion. The procedure involves the vampire staring directly into the eyes of the person they seek to influence. Significantly, black vampire fictions such as *The Gilda Stories* by Jewelle Gomez and Octavia Butler's *Fledging* use glamour not only to gain power over a human subject, but also to create a positive life outcome for the person under their influence. *True* Blood's vampires, however, often use glamour to turn people into tools of vampire convenience. As a telepath and, as will be revealed later, a fairy, Sookie is immune to glamour.

15. This strategy is congruent with black politics of respectability. At the end of the nineteenth century, this intra-racial conversation was designed to craft a positive image of black people in the eyes of whites who harbored largely negative views. Black civic organizations, like the National Urban League, used several strategies to promote the message of black compliance to a respectable standard. For instance, the 1915 Dress Well Club printed flyers to be distributed to black Southern migrants arriving, en masse, at Northern train stations after Reconstruction collapsed. These missives contained many helpful hints for the new arrivals, including firm advice on speaking quietly in public, not wearing overalls or house slippers to the park, and conducting oneself in a respectable manner.

16. In a review of Hodes's work, Steven Mintz explains, "Drawing on a remarkable range of legal testimony, personal diaries, and private correspondence, she persuasively argues that the late nineteenth century witnessed an abrupt shift in the South's treatment of such relationships. While antebellum white southern society did not condone such liaisons, it did exhibit a limited degree of toleration—a toleration that vanished following the Civil War, as southern white men saw their monopoly of political power challenged and the cotton economy collapse" (Mintz 1).

17. A "nigger lover" need not actually love, or even like, black people: as a slur, it was a potent tool to forestall any dissention among whites.

18. This will haunt Jason until he meets Amy, with whom he shares a vampire blood addiction. He and Amy will abduct a vampire. Eddie is a mild-mannered, shy vampire who likes nothing more than to watch TV and fool around with Lafayette with whom he has a sex-for-blood agreement. Amy and Jason hold Eddie captive, take his blood, then Amy murders him.

19. The reverse is also true in many minds. Arlene, for instance, asks Sam to escort her to her car after Dawn is killed. She says that because she hasn't socialized with vampires, she is an unlikely target but prefers Sam's company all the same. Arlene dislikes and distrusts vampires. She resents their presence in Bon Temps, believing them to be inherently evil and dangerous. Given her attitude toward vampires, she also believes that humans who associate with vampires deserve any negative consequences of that interaction.

Works Cited

Alston, Joshua. "Give HBO Some Credit." *Newsweek*. Sep 12, 2008. V152. P14, http://www.thedailybeast.com/ newsweek/2008/09/12/give-hbo-some-credit.html. Last accessed: September 18, 2013.

Amador, Victoria. "The Gothic Louisiana of Charlaine Harris and Anne Rice" in Mutch, Deborah, ed. *The Modern Vampire and Human Identity*. Palgrave McMillan: New York, 2013. 163-176.

——.In Cherry, Brigid. *True Blood: Investigating Vampires and Southern Gothic (Investigating Cult TV)*. I. B. Tauris. 2012.

Baldwin, Kate. "Black Like Who? Cross-Testing the "Real" Lines of John Howard Griffin's Black Like Me" *Cultural Critique*. 40 (1998): 103-143.

Brattain, Michelle. "Miscegenation and Competing Definitions of Race in Twentieth-Century Louisiana." *The Journal of Southern History*. 71.3 (2005): 621-658.

Cherry, Brigid. *True Blood: Investigating Vampires and Southern Gothic (Investigating Cult TV)*. I. B. Tauris. 2012.

Davis, Thomas J. *Plessy v. Ferguson (Landmarks of the American Mosaic)*. Greenwood: Westport, Connecticut, 2012.

Elison, Ralph. *Invisible Man*. Vintage: New York, 1953.

Gordon, Joan. and Veronica Hollinger. *Blood Read: The Vampire as Metaphor in Contemporary Culture*. Philadelphia: University of Pennsylvania Press, 1997.

Gubar, Susan. *Racechanges: White Skin, Black Face in American Culture*. New York: Oxford University Press, 1997.

Hodes, Martha. *White Women, Black Men: Illicit Sex in the nineteenth-Century South*. New Haven and London: Yale UP, 1997.

Kirkland, Ewan. "Whiteness, Vampires, and Humanity in Contemporary Film and Television" in Mutch, Deborah, ed. *The Modern Vampire and Human Identity*. Palgrave McMillan: New York, 2013. 93-110.

Lott, Eric. *Love & Theft: Blackface Minstrelsy and the American Working Class*. Oxford University Press, USA. 1993.

Mintz, Steven. Review of Hodes, *Martha, White Women, Black Men: Illicit Sex in the Nineteenth-Century South*. H-SHEAR, H-Net Reviews. September, 1998. URL: hŒp://www.h-net.org/reviews/showrev. php?id=2348. Last accessed: April 18, 2014.

Mutch, Deborah. Ed. *The Modern Vampire and Human Identity*. Palgrave McMillan: New York, 2013.

Nayar, Pramod. "How to Domesticate a Vampire: Gender, Blood Relations and Sexuality in Stephenie Meyer's *Twilight*" *Nebula*. 7.3 2010: 60-76.

Rank, Hugh. "The Rhetorical Effectiveness of "Black Like Me." *The English Journal* 57.6 (1968): 813-817.

Sickels, Robert J. *Race Marriage and the Law*. Albuquerque: University of New Mexico Press, 1972.

Stasukevich, Iain. "Short Takes. True Blood Titles Set Southern-Gothic Tone," *American Cinematographer*, 89.12 (Dec. 2008): 10-14.

Stern, Marlow. "Anne Rice on Sparkly Vampires, 'Twilight,' 'True Blood,' and Werewolves," *The Daily Beast*. November 23, 2011. http://www.thedailybeast.com/articles/2011/11/23/anne-rice-on-sparkly-vampires-twilight-true-blood-and-werewolves.html Last accessed: September 18, 2013.

Treble, Patricia. "It's Southern Gothic, with Fangs," Maclean's. http://www.macleans.ca/culture/entertainment/article.jsp?content=20080827_42265_42265&page=1. August 27, 2008. Last accessed. September 19, 2013.

Stasukevich, Iain. "Short Takes: True Blood Titles Set Southern-Gothic Tone," *American Cinematographer*. 89.12 (2008): 10, 12, 14. United Daughters of the Confederacy. "About the UDC" http://www.hqudc.org/about_udc/index.htm Last Accessed: April 18, 2014.

Williams, Linda. Ed. *Porn Studies*. Duke UP: Durham and London, 2004.

Winnubst, Sharon. "Vampires, Anxieties, and Dreams: Race and Sex in the Contemporary United States." *Hypatia*. 18.3 2003.

PHOTOGRAPHY

by Alrinthea F. Carter

Kudzu Welcome (Print in B&W): "Kudzu is an analogy for how we show love in the South; slowly, subtly, and before you know it, you're covered in it." Photo Location: West Union, SC."

Price of Gas (Print in B&W),
West Union, SC

IPA Southern Laminating I (B&W) Easley, SC

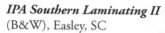
IPA Southern Laminating II
(B&W), Easley, SC

Kudzu House (B&W), Cleveland, SC. "After years of shooting abandoned houses and factories, I've become strangely comfortable with the smell of old wood, ghosts, squatters, and the occasional need to wade through a few feet of kudzu, and all that lies within. It's good to have a good pair of rubber boats."

Window Dressing (Color), Norris, SC

But you can never leave (B&W), Glendale, SC "There was an eerie calm when I visited the Glendale factory ruins, near Spartanburg. The whole town (or the remains of it) just carried this heavy sense of loss and despair. The towers of the factory seemed to be defiantly standing against the progress that was to be their ruin."

Guard (B&W), Glendale, SC

Textile King (B&W), Glendale, SC

Water of Glendale (Color), Glendale, SC

Julia Legare Burial Plot (B&W), Edisto Island, SC: "This is the site of the legend of young Julia Legare, a young addition to the ghost stories of the island. The legend tells us that Julia fell ill and succumbed while visiting her family. She was buried quickly, as they were in those days, and the masoleum containing her remains was undisturbed for several years. When the next family member died, the mausoleum was opened to reveal a horrible truth: Julia may not have been dead at her burial. Her bones lay out of her coffin, and crumpled at the door! Efforts to reseal the mausoleum were eerily thwarted, as it is believed that Julia was angry and refused to be contained in the building that witnessed her desperate death. It stands today without a door, and the spirit of Julia is at rest. For now."

WHAT THE LAND REVEALS:
A JOURNEY INTO A LOW COUNTRY RICE PLANTATION

by James O. Luken

T he ultimate 15 miles of the Waccamaw River in South Carolina include 40,000 acres of Coastal Plain wetlands known simply as the "rice fields." Locals that hunt, fish, or claim this tract do not readily offer much information about kills, catches or activities. There are valid reasons, some old and some new, for this reticence. A satellite view of the rice fields shows a patchwork of rectangles and squares, the stitching formed by dilapidated canals, ditches, and dikes. Although geometrically pleasing from the air, one gets a different feel when the view is close up, the abundance of "no trespassing" signs, makeshift barriers to boat traffic, and long-submerged watercraft giving a sense of very private property. The fish and wildlife biologists charged with protecting resident and migratory animals in this area stick to the notion that the rice fields are biologically rich and ecologically important, but on these matters data are sparse, leaving room for speculation and, in some cases, fictional assessments.

There are books, museum displays, internet sites, and even television shows providing virtual concepts of the rice culture and the rice fields that once thrived in the low country of South Carolina. However, making an honest journey into the rice fields is difficult due to limited physical access and a tendency of the historical record to glamorize. I was able to penetrate the rice fields from various access points. My business here was to understand how a single rice plantation and its associated fields were originally changed by people bought and sold for the task and how the land healed during the last century after the buying and selling stopped. I emerged from this journey much like someone long-afflicted with cataracts but suddenly given surgical clarity.

FIELDS FROM SWAMP

Historical rice fields are found throughout the coastal zones of many southern states and their origin is traced to the early 1700's. Plantation owners, known as planters, began growing rice as a cash crop in the 1600's, but it was during the early 1700's that the tidal system of rice cultivation gained prominence. Two factors spawned this agricultural revolution. Land grants from the King of England allowed planters to take "ownership" of the vast swamps along coastal rivers like the Waccamaw and the burgeoning commerce in slaves gave the planters the necessary human power to impose a new ecological order on these lands. This order came quickly in a region where slaves outnumbered freemen 10 to 1.

We know much about how rice was cultivated on the newly-cleared southern swamp lands, but the historical record is strangely silent on the process of clearing. Conversion of the swamp lands, done largely with hand tools and livestock, must have been a deadly and dangerous occupation considering the subtropical climate and the preponderance of reptiles and insect-borne diseases. Add these factors to the resistance of those ancient cypress and gum trees that had to be removed, roots and all. After the trees were grubbed out, the elaborate system of ditches and dikes was built by hand; this eventually allowed the planters to use the ebb and flood of the tides to either bring the water to the rice or take the water off the rice. In commerce and taxation, swamp land thus "improved" was valued three times higher than "unimproved" swamp land.

Once in place, the tidal system of rice cultivation was highly profitable due to relatively low production costs and relatively high commodity prices. The planters, feeling smug about their successful domination of humans and nature, built great monuments to themselves in the form of plantations modeled after the formal estates of England. The master's houses on these plantations often overlooked the rice fields, but the planters and their families quickly discovered that life on a coastal river was not all sweet tea and afternoon horse rides. It entailed perpetual hordes of mosquitoes, increased risk of disease, oppressive heat, and the round-the-clock task of personnel management. As such, planters and their families spent most of their time elsewhere and left the plantations in the often cruel hands of overseers. For proof of the idea that the rice culture lived and reproduced solely as a result of slave labor, one need only read the history books and discover how quickly it all ended after the Civil War.

ENTERING FROM THE LAND

In fall of 2006, I was granted an opportunity to explore and study one of the oldest rice plantations on the Waccamaw River. This site was unique in that very little disturbance had occurred since the plantation structures were razed and the land abandoned in the late 1800's. My work was guided by a previous archeological survey that had identified through artifacts the locations of various buildings: planter's house, overseer's house, rice mill, dairy, slave village. The only extant surface evidence for these structures was scatterings of bricks slowly making their way into the subsurface. The uplands of the plantation were now overgrown with loblolly pines and laurel oak, the forest that started when the plantation ended. The rice fields, on the other hand, resisted the return to normalcy and instead expressed a complex tangle of treeless marsh and shrub thicket with the occasional patches of stunted bald cypress.

My first reconnaissance showed the mingling of old and new. Hiking from the former location of the planter's house at the edge of the rice fields to the slave village located about a quarter mile inland, I encountered massive live oaks—some at least five feet in diameter—that once defined roads, walkways, and field borders. These squat and gnarled relics now stood in relative darkness beneath towering canopies of the pines that had colonized the site during the last century. To reach the slave village I had to climb over an earthen embankment, a wall of dirt about 20 feet wide and 10 feet high that stretched across the entire upper third of the plantation. The function of this earthwork was a matter of much speculation in the report produced by the consulting archeologist. It was likely intended as a physical or perhaps statutory separation between the personal lives of the slaves and the rest of the plantation.

Over the next several weeks I collected data that hopefully would show how various types of plantation land uses affected the ability of the land to support natural vegetation. The field work was relatively mundane, involving mostly the measuring and identifying of herbs, shrubs and trees, and the digging of soil pits. Even when working on the upland areas far from the river, I was constantly harassed by mosquitoes and deer flies.

One afternoon in late fall while digging in an area of the former slave village, my spade lifted a metal object that fell cleanly away from the sandy soil. It was a hoe and I immediately knew from historical photos it was the type of hoe used to cultivate the rice fields. I momentarily felt the excitement that comes from finding a unique, very old and perhaps valuable relic. But when I gave it a closer look, there was much more here than just an artifact. To describe the hoe as "worn" would be a great understatement. It was a weathered and rusted tool, reduced to a dull nub by innumerable chops at the ground. I carried the hoe out of the slave village because I was sure someone would want to put it on display and also because it had such a powerful effect on me. On my way through the woods, I realized for the first time I was on a path, not a deer trail or an old road, but a hard-parked depression shaped by the daily movements of slaves trudging from their modest cabins to the numbing and repetitive work of the rice fields.

By instinct, I followed the path and it took me more or less in a straight line right to the edge of a former rice field. Although this field was now grown up in gum saplings, alder and clumps of myrtle-leaved holly, I tried to imagine what it might have looked like when the swamp was cleared and the rice needed attention. The tangle of sapling and shrub floated firmly on the water below and the bare mud threatened to steal my boots, but there was an opportunity to explore the old field by jumping from hummock to hummock and using the woody stems as hand holds. By island hopping, I eventually came to a shallow stream that snaked though the thicket. There was a trickle of flow in the general direction of the river, but as if signaled by my arrival, the water hesitated and then reversed. It was not a wave or a flood, but still it was water, pushed by the rising tide, slowly working its way through hollows, depressions and roots. The front of the flow passed me and continued on its journey toward the shore.

My first urge was to get back to higher ground before being trapped by the rising water, but I was stopped by the unmistakable slurping sounds of feeding fish. There were bream—not big ones but large numbers of them—moving up the creek. They fed on insects, caterpillars, and other small creatures trapped by the water. The fish knew where the food was concentrated and they sped past me in an effort to stay near the productive hunting zone.

I worked my way out of the old rice field and eventually found the trail that brought me here. It was clear that this field was well on its way back to swamp and I constructed a mental hypothesis that trees and critters can come back to the rice fields where "normal" tidal fluctuation is reestablished. But as I gazed back at the swamp, I couldn't help but wonder what was buried in the mud of that place. I took my personal hoe and headed back to the car.

ENTERING FROM THE WATER

After successive failed attempts to travel by foot into the old rice fields, I decided to try a water entry. This required a boat and a suitable course that cut through a dike and joined with the canal system of a field. As I traveled down the Waccamaw from a landing near the resort town of Pawley's Island, the river widened considerably and the adjacent cypress swamps gave way to extensive marshes with tall stands of wild rice and southern cutgrass. These were the historical rice fields that for unknown reasons had not gone back to forested swamp. Some held to the view that years of rice farming had lowered the soil surface to the point that trees, even cypress, could not make it. Others, invoked the idea of salt water intrusion, something that happened in particularly dry years when less fresh water came down the river and strong tides pushed salt water up the river.

Regardless of the factors that keep out the trees, these lands—maybe not "lands" at all—are held in a kind of ownership purgatory. They were bought up by wealthy northerners after the Civil War and were managed primarily for the sport of duck hunting. Getting good numbers of ducks required similar management prescriptions as getting goods crops of rice: drain the fields and plant crops in the spring; flood the fields and harvest the crops in the fall. What made this all possible was a well-maintained dike and canal system with functional "trunks." The trunks were clever, wooden, valve-like structures built into the dikes. A trunk allowed the water to flow into the field on a rising tide. In contrast, a trunk could be closed thus impounding the water on a falling tide. This ingenious, water management system required no power; it did, however, require constant maintenance as the trunks and canals regularly clogged with sediment and detritus and the dikes tended to break.

In the heyday of the rice culture, any planter that did not direct his slaves to quickly patch up the dikes and repair the trunks was considered foolish and incompetent. However, when the modern landlords of the old rice fields attempted a similar type of maintenance using bulldozers, backhoes and draglines, they ran afoul of the federal government. There was the clear definition of public waters in the United States that included all matters aquatic up to the high tide mark. (This mark was of course shifted toward the river when the slaves built the dikes.) There was a wetland issue and an access issue, both linked to the fact that wetlands and public access are defined relative to the presence of navigable water. If the land owners patched the dikes they illegally cut off public access. If they didn't patch the dikes, channels formed and boats could "navigate" into the rice fields, thus making private land more or less public water. It was a conundrum that only a lawyer could love and it pitted the federal government against a bunch of highly motivated duck hunters. Apparently the nuances of "navigable" and "public waters" are still being sorted out. Unwisely, I ignored the consequences of this semantic debate.

I left the Waccamaw and steered up Jericho Creek, a relatively wide artery penetrating the heart of the rice fields. Both banks of the creek were lined by remnants of dikes. These windrows of soil offered rare raised ground and were colonized by trees, while the fields themselves remained generally treeless. The dikes were porous and the holes ranged from small cuts just big enough for a canoe to large gaps potentially accommodating a pontoon boat. Boat travel through the cuts was often discouraged by poles or stakes. In some of the larger cuts, people had constructed fences equipped with locking gates. In all cases, it was clear that maintaining structures to manage people was just as difficult as maintaining structures to manage water.

There was a strong incoming tide so I rode the water past a rusted water fence and into an old rice field. The canal, about three times as wide as my boat, had steep sloping banks and fiddler crabs scurried across the pockmarked mud. The water in the canal had the consistency of a chocolate milkshake. I leaned over the side of the boat to scoop up a sample in my hand but was startled by a gunshot close enough to make me drop and crouch on the floor of the boat. This shot was followed by another and then the wild rice on the near side of the canal erupted. Still taking cover on the bottom of the boat, I peered over the gunwale only to glimpse a huge, wild hog break out of the grass. It was a hairy, black and white beast with great upturned tusks. This animal immediately sensed my presence and quickly faded back into the cover; he was joined by what sounded like a sizable entourage. Somewhere out in that rice field I heard hunters laughing and talking in low voices. Public waters or not, I knew I was trespassing in a dangerous place, so I started up the engine and idled out of the field and into the relative safety of Jericho Creek.

A PROPER BURIAL

During the next week I showed my long-buried hoe to many people who I thought would find it interesting, moving, or at least worthy of conversation. Not much happened and no one picked up on the evidence of extreme use. Apparently the museums and schools had all the artifacts of the rice culture that they could handle, and, I was told that hoes like this were very common. It kept me company in my car for about a month and then one day while working on the old plantation, I knew it was time for a proper reburial. With shovel and hoe in hand I followed the path toward the area of the slave village. Although I'm not an archeologist, my intention was purely archeological: to put the artifact back in the ground with the hope that future research would interpret it properly. Unfortunately, I didn't mark the exact spot of my discovery so I started digging in the general vicinity. It wasn't long before once again new metal hit old metal. This time my discovery was a padlock attached to a short length of chain; the shackle on the other end of the chain seemed too small for restraining livestock. There wasn't anything else I could do but put the reminders of the past at the bottom of a hole and cover them with the loose, sandy soil.

LIVING ON THE PAST

The archeological report based on this plantation included a final section where the author—now deceased—pleaded for site preservation, interpretation, and more research. After spending a year sifting through sand and fragments of the past, he was convinced that a more thorough wide-ranging dig would reveal many unknown aspects of antebellum plantation life. His primary concern was that this plantation would go the way of most other old plantations and be transformed into a high-end housing development. When these long-abandoned sites are turned into bucolic enclaves of the wealthy and the recently retired, they lose their archeological value because the strata are destroyed by the churning of bulldozers and backhoes. And of course few people, once established in a mini-estate, are likely to appreciate or understand the occasional hoe, axe, or shackle that appears in the flowerbed.

My report on ecological change at the plantation was a poor representation of what I learned. As an ecologist I found that loblolly pines and laurel oaks quickly colonized the entire site regardless of the type of previous land use. The persistence of the massive live oaks, likely planted for dramatic effect by the planter, created a novel type of extant forest structure. But this was a relatively widespread occurrence in the area and was worthy of only a few descriptive sentences. The important discovery was not the type of thing that could be easily summarized in tables or figures or even presented as a statistical probability. It was instead a notion, a realization that time and gradual burial can take the hard, sharp edges of events and slowly make them soft and dull.

I frequently drive past the plantation on my way to Charleston; at least for now there is no evidence that a new housing development is in the offing. However, my sense of what is best for the site tends to shift with the weather. Should some cash-rich foundation mount a major research effort that would likely allow us to accurately interpret plantation life? On some days I go with this opinion but then realize that the results of the research, no matter how surprising or dramatic, would likely be presented to the public in venues that would ultimately miss the point. Indeed, there are plenty of extant publications derived from the very painful recollections of former slaves. Most people ignore them. On other days—usually when the sun is hidden by clouds—I hope to see orange survey flags, a sure sign that the real estate agents, developers and bulldozer operators are coming. Although generally held in low regard by conservationists and preservationists, these people do serve a useful function: they help in the process of forgetting.

ALLEN STEIN

JAMES WATSON, FORMER SLAVE

I heard that old Huck Finn had come back
from wherever out West,
worn out and sick,
to be buried in St. Pete.
Maybe knowing at the last
it was Missouri dirt would cover his coffin
satisfied him some.
I don't figure much else ever did,
'cause if all you want is to be let alone,
this world don't offer much in the way of satisfactions.
Tom Sawyer, who wanted 'most everything,
except to leave anyone be,
could've told him that years ago,
if he'd thought to take the time,
but Tom never had much thought nor time
for no one but Tom.
And, truth is, it wouldn't have changed Huck a whit.
That was a haunted boy, eager to be on the move,
like if he stayed in one place too long,
what-all hounded after him would catch hold—
it might have been the wind whisperings,
telling him that wherever he stopped
was the lonesomest place in the world,
or would be if he lingered awhile;
might have been his Pap,
lowest man ever to live on fatback and rotgut;
or it might have been some weepy-heart widow
just aching to make him fit
for what passed for civilization back there and then;
but most of all, clear as I could make it out,
it was the fear he carried close as his shadow
that he was no good and never would be.

I played the darky for him—
didn't have much choice, did I?
I knew what I wanted
(had that much in common with Tom),
and I needed Huck to get it.
Couldn't get nowheres being another Nat Turner,
whatever the gratifications,
so I widened my eyes,

trotted out the hairball and the horse-ass hocus pocus,
all that superstitious crap,
just to keep Huck running with me—
didn't even tell him his Pap was dead
as any doorknob in the house he lay in
floating downriver.
I'm not proud of one bit of that.
But I did try to help him understand some things.
Even if I could have, I wouldn't have cut his throat.

Tom was another story.
At Phelps Farm, I wanted that boy dead,
and I still do.
I was nothing but a dumb black toy to him,
same as my wife and child would have been.
Sure, he was just a kid,
but also the man he'd always be.

I got there just as they were putting Huck in the ground.
Stood off by myself in a stretch of shade,
no one looking my way.
There was just a few folks at the grave,
old-timers not saying much,
except for Tom, that is.
Looking down at the coffin in the hole,
he told them "Years back, Huck was always cheery,
dead eager for a harmless lark and a hearty laugh"
and that "nobody should be too hard on him
for ending up a worthless hobo,
because not everyone has the stuff
to make something of himself."
Someone said Tom was big in the railroad,
had come up from St. Louis in his private Pullman.
His coat was open, and I could see the watch chain
stretched across the tight vest at his swole belly.
The bullet they'd dug out of his leg at Phelps Farm
was hanging from it, just like he'd hung it back then—
the hero and his trophy.
I didn't go near him,
'cause I'd have split him with my blade
and stuck that slug into his open belly,
deep as a seed in a melon.

I knew I owed Huck some honesty.
So, after everybody was gone

and the diggers had done their work,
I went over to the small stone
and told Huck I was sorry
for pretending to be less than I was
and playing him like I did,
said I'd come a long way to tell him that,
all the way from Chicago.
Told him too that me and the wife
sell clothes in our little shop
down on the South Side,
doing all right using everything I learned
as a supply sergeant in Abe Lincoln's army

I knew he'd be pleased for me
and take my apology right off.
(Maybe he was too soft for this country
and sensed it from the first.)
Then I said, all choked, with tears in my eyes,
that I'm still so mad about so much,
and always will be,
but that the best moments of a bad time
were those I shared with him on the raft,
when, both of us on the run,
we watched the sun ease its way
soft through the mists over the river.

KATHLEEN HELLEN

APPARITIONS
FORT LINCOLN

A raccoon mounts its habitat.
A fox, a rabbit. Lest we forget,

herons pose in tops of dioramic loblolly and cedar.
A goose hangs freeze-dried from the ceiling

at the center where we set off for the Periwinkle Trail.
The long walk to Fort Lincoln. The bottom rails
on top, the soldier once had said, who penned

the prisoners. Confederate and Black. Contraband and rebel.
We call from kindling spirit smoke
as faces white and black ignite. Anonymous drones
that spark discomforted imaginations.

Fire as the sun sinks into causeway.
Fire as the darkness settles like a cloak.

AMERICAN HORROR

Take a cab from the foreclosure to a cut-rate habitation. The burnt sky floats
over interstates of fireworks and pecan logs and freak motels. The clouds drift,
impaled by trees, toward wasted fields of corn toward Armageddon.

The night clerk at the desk never asks, never looks up from her porn of
magazines. Pass

Elvis jock-strapped in black velvet. His eyes like Jesus' follow past new brochures
for sinking ships, tours to Mogadishu and Baghdad. Giveaways for Boeing on
the rack. Getaways for Green Berets and tourists from Japan who have traveled
in the past in humid months before the yen's collapse. The crippled nuclear reac-
tors. Pass

a vase shaped vaguely Grecian. On the neck, a band of running dogs appears
above the horns disturbing papers. On the handles, snakes. Around the body
of the vase, zombies in their armies forage flesh. Never touch the clay, however
tempted. Never point too closely at the canvas, a reproduction of the mansions
where they live. Cross the line of observation. A hand (or claw?) is reaching. Take

the stairs not the wings you have inherited. In the room where you undress, a faucet drips. A clock ticks. Things like keys go missing. From the black hole of a 50" tv, evil pops out genius in 3-D. Aliens and slashers. Devil-priests. The loved ones you dismissed when they were living.

Fast-forward to the demons in your Hyding. Is it envy? Is it sloth? You are seven. You are lost. Renfield's in the darkness right behind you.

RICHARD MICHELSON

PINECONE AND COMB

"Nowhere else in America—certainly not in the Antebellum North—had Jews been accorded such an opportunity to be complete equals as in the old South." Rabbi Bertrum Korn—*American Jewry and the Civil War*

My Bubbe,
blind with hindsight, claims the fight
for justice binds all Jews through generations.
She's whitewashed history. She's burnished reputations.
She's stacked the goods so I don't venture too far right,
or x the wrong box on my sixth grade civic ballot.
Lincoln, she whispers, was a *landsman* (hence his forename,
mythic beard and sad demeanor). Let anti-Semites blame
Reb Johnny Reb's discriminating palate;
Let kith-and-kin proclaim a level battlefield for all
while their personal Negroes set the Seder table.
Here today, in my descendants' distant past, I am unable,
still, to determine the Dixie line dividing ignorance from evil,
or my particular hoodwinks from my public boasts.
O, overeducated and overwhelmingly liberal 21st century
post-holocaust Jewish poets, how can we, dizzy with history,
condemn the colored preachers who hung pinecones from doorposts,
allowing only those a shade lighter to enter the Lord's home?
O, open-minded black poets of the American upper middle-class,
what kindness will you show your Maw-maws, trying only to pass
through their coarse and ironed hair, this fine toothed comb?

JESSE GRAVES

VESSEL

Morels sprout through leaf-murk under the dead
trunk of a hickory, where almost no one can find them,
shuttered among ferns and mosses and beetle-husks,
bitter delicacy sprung from the surging current of spring.

Bother yourself to know what it is you see, for you must
always look, there has never been any choice in that.
What choices have you had? You want to say none,
and the mountain will not talk you out of that.

Follow the salt-line back to your origins, the trail
grown thin as a single vessel of blood,
yet you may track it up the submerged river,
through the winding gap, and back across the ocean.

History will not hold you back, but will neither reveal
all the stories your people sent to the new world,
nor whisper their voices down through the corridors
of time, though something speaks out of the darkness.

Echoes in a language you don't understand,
vibrating through the lower chambers of your heart,
how certain you have been that the trail leads you here,
back through the circle you have already followed.

TENOR AT DAWN

Give your ear to the devil tonight, to whatever voice
his dry throat can muster, human or otherwise,
rasping his story of sickness across the mountain,

death keeping its white eye on those you love,
teasing them ever-closer with the whispery
fabric of his robes, the rustling silk of his veil.

All through the night clouds shift their weight,
restless to commence their falling, suspended
above the dry ground by his long curved finger,

and you watch how he withholds, how he punishes,
staying awake to hear what you imagine
he will pronounce upon the fates you pray for.

The tenor of dreams at dawn will lead you
up toward the crests, ice glistening the trails
that shape your narrow passage home,

where some lifelong dread awaits your arrival,
the devil having beaten the comfort of sunrise,
his voice ringing only a cold and silent warning.

SALT

Sarvis and redbud measure steep angles
with their pink and white scansion of color,
flourishing where soil barely clings to limestone,
where trunks curve upward like elbows,

up toward the monadnock where no trees
can hold against the wind's pressing knuckles.
The air around your body shudders with
cold breath, exhaled from opening blossoms,

root systems scrabbled over rocky ground,
salt of the ancient sea on your tongue,
and you try to imagine the mountain
underwater, submerged past the tree line,

fish the size of small canoes touring
through the canopy, their wide mouths
gaping high above your swiveled head.
The earth upside down, inverted time, now.

PITCH

The cabin you seek leans against a tulip poplar,
half-fallen and windowless, doorless, twice as old
as the tree, last lived in almost a century ago by a man
named Richard, who married your great-aunt,

for whom the entire tract of land has been called
your whole life—call it "The Richard Side"—
steep and runneled with floodwater wash-outs.

Someone cared enough for the cabin at one time
to haul it six miles on the back of a wagon,
protecting it from the river-becoming-lake
that would have swallowed it down like a pill,

salvaged because someone already long dead
had been born in one of its shallow rooms,
saving the birth-spirit from a final immersion.

Do you remember the screams of the panther
when you were a small boy, the woman-pitched
yowling that seemed to stir up from dreams,
except that your eyes were always open

when you heard them jarring through the night?
Do you remember how your brother raced home
from the woods after seeing the black streak?

Mother cat and her litter were what you imagined,
the last of something rare, alive in the hills
above your own house, so close to your window
you watched for her breath to steam the glass,

your arms locked frozen around your body,
muscles tensed against the mattress, waiting,
hoping to see her shadow, and hoping not.

One morning a blue and white pick-up truck
parked along the road bank, and two men
you had never seen before carried rifles
into the woods, strangers on The Richard Side,

and you knew what they had come for, so you
listened for their shots, but all morning standing
in the yard, you heard nothing, no guns, no cries.

After that, dogs barked in the night, the familiar
voices of the half-shepherd and the hound,
but the screaming never returned, even in dreams,
even when you tried to hear it your mind,

it was gone, when you lay with eyes pressed open,
envisioning cubs nursing her on the cabin floor,
praying to see it just once, that pitch made flesh.

CREEK SOURCE

Deer bolt from the creek, a herd of six
clashing through a cluster of small cedars.
They can smell their own destruction in the air,
simmering on your breath as it reaches them.

Your ancestors and theirs flanked these banks,
watching for some trace of the other, always
hungry, reading the ground, the air, for signs.

You might have slept under their skins,
filled your mouth with their roasted shanks,
stalking them with a different intensity
than now, hoping only for a closer look.

Run your fingers under the water's quick-
shifting surface, close to the mineral bed,
feel how the ages have passed, unchanging.

Cold unchanging through generations,
forests growing dense, and dying,
valley of fallen oaks, blighted hemlocks,
soil enlivened by the rotting interiors.

All of it feeding the creek, surging forward
like the most alive creature in the sphere,
breathing out the coldest breath, fiercest pulse.

R E V I E W S

PARADOX OF PHILOSOPHY

Eugene Thacker. *In the Dust of the Planet: Horror of Philosophy*, Vol. 1. UK: Zero Books, 2011. Pp 160. $15.28 paperback.

Reviewed by Sarah Juliet Lauro, Clemson University

If I called Eugene Thacker's *In the Dust of this Planet* (subtitled "Horror of Philosophy, Vol. 1,") a "hipster" text (making a comparison to that increasingly mainstream subculture of America's youth), I would not mean it in the disparaging sense that it is trying too hard to be alternative—(like a thrift-store cardigan, worn backwards, commodifying its alternative strategies to commodification)—or that it grows tiresome, continually eschewing its own affectation: "I genuinely prefer shaving with a straight razor." Instead, embracing what might be called "hipster" releases it from the category. This is just one of the delightful paradoxes that Thacker's sublime study of the "horror of philosophy" asks us to puzzle over.

But no doubt this is an odd way to begin. Except for a short treatment of black metal, Thacker is not concerned with the underground, but with the "unground," as posited in Jakob Böhme's theology as the *Ungrund,* "the divine…indifferent to the human" (141). And if we are going to reach for a (sub)cultural comparison oughtn't it be not to the hipsters of our era, but to the "angel-headed hipsters" of which Ginsberg wrote, with all the beatific resonances of the Beat generation? (The word "beatific," after all, appears at least three times in Thacker's work).

But, in fact, when I call Thacker's book both beatific and hip, I mean only that it is *extremely tidy*, and simultaneously, *productively punk*. For, example, in part, the book illustrates the ways in which horror is "a non-philosophical attempt to think about the world-without-us philosophically" (9), suggesting a philosophy might be made from analysis of satanic themes in heavy metal music, like putting two fingers up to stodgy, old-guard academics! And if it isn't *effortlessly* cool, (for the slim volume is precisely ordered, beautifully restrained), it is cool nonetheless, and I am jealous of it. This is a beautifully written, harrowing, hard little gem of a book, and I had to sit on my hands to keep from underlining every sentence that Thacker has penned.

Sandwiched between a preface, "The Clouds of Unknowing," and a prologue, "'The Subharmonic Murmur of Black Tentacular Voids," are three tightly focused sections consisting of "Three *Quaestio* on Demonology," "Six *Lectio* on Occult Philosophy," and "Nine *Disputatio* on the Horror of Theology." "Borrowing from thinkers such as Aquinas" (11), Thacker employs medieval scholastic forms (the inquiry, the lecture, and the debate or discussion), keeping each section tautly ordered. Each quaestio, for instance, contains within it three movements: *Articulus, Sed Contra,* and *Responsio.* The strict 3, 6, 9 mathematical balance lends to the book an architecture that might call to mind the significance of numbers in many branches of the occult, a central focus of his study. Overall, the rigidity of the form provides a comforting structure for Thacker's discussion of the formless, nameless, inchoate (im)material that is the subject of horror.

Thacker's book begins, "The world is increasingly unthinkable…" (1) and reading this book as I was in the weeks following the Sandy Hook massacre that claimed the lives of so many young school children, the sentiment of the book's opening line took on a particular valence. But although humanity is itself capable of unthinkable acts, Thacker's treatise is about the limits of thinkability in general, especially as relates to the nonhuman world: can we think "Life" apart from "living"? Can we think of the World apart from humanity? Is there truly a "world-in-itself" that is, neither the "world-for-us" or the "world-without-us"?

For Thacker, the world-in-itself "constitutes a horizon for thought" (5). For the moment we begin to think about the world in itself, it ceases actually to be the *world-in-itself*, as the very frame of our attempted comprehension of it includes the human in the picture. To think the "world-without-us" (as in apocalyptic or plague narratives, such as Mary Shelley's novel *The Last Man*, or in a variety of science fiction texts), Thacker says, is a speculative exercise, which allows us to conceive the "world-in-itself," but only insofar as it can be thought in the process of disintegration.

Thacker's book is about these "horizons for thought." The "horror of philosophy," says Thacker, delimits that zone where "philosophy reveals its own limitations and constraints, moments in which thinking enigmatically confronts the horizon of its own possibility—the thought of the unthinkable that philosophy cannot pronounce but via a non-philosophical language" (2). If the world cannot, as Thacker maintains, be articulated in philosophy, then where is this unthinkability made manifest? Thacker's answer is that "The genre of supernatural horror is a privileged site in which this paradoxical thought of the unthinkable takes place" (2).

Thacker's tour of the genre of supernatural horror is trans-historical and interdisciplinary, intrepid, and imaginative. Along the way, Thacker provides critical insight into Dante's Inferno, Sheridan Le Fanu's occult detective series, Aristotle's *De Anima*, Agrippa's *De Occulta Philosophia*, Marlowe and Goethe's versions of the Faust myth, and works by HP Lovecraft, JG Ballard, and Georges Bataille, among others. The reader is asked to consider the non-space of the occult's magic circle and the formless forms of speculative fiction and sci-fi: mists, oozes, blobs, and slime. It is in the guise of such paradoxes, Thacker suggests, that we can begin to think the unthinkability of the world, a world that does not include the human.

For example, in his discussion of black metal, Thacker explains that it "is not just a music genre, but also a subculture and a way of thinking about demons and the demonic in a world of religious extremes" (11). He reads a type of hard-core music with Satanic themes alongside Shopenhauer's *nihil negativum* (which is "not just about the limits of language... [but] about the horizon of thought as it confronts the unthought, the horizon of the human as it struggles to comprehend the unhuman," (47)), as evincing a "Cosmic Pessimism," which Thacker describes as "noumenal occultism" or, more plainly: "the difficult thought of the world as absolutely unhuman, and indifferent to the hopes, desires, and struggles of human individuals" (17). Thacker's analysis of black metal showcases the way one of its best examples "ultimately negates itself even in a kind of musical anti-form" as the "individual performer is dissolved into a meshwork of tones" (21). Therefore, like the philosophical thought horizons that Thacker describes, some elements of black metal music seem to exist only as modes of negation. (Thacker's own writing also depends on litotes and negations, his philosophy existing as much in the "what is not" as it does in the "what is.")

Of the demon, Thacker writes that it is "not really a supernatural creature, but an anthropological motif through which we humans project, externalize, and represent the darker side of the human to ourselves," and, thus, "the antagonism so central to the demon is also a non-human antagonism, an antagonism that is beyond human comprehension" (26). Thacker proposes in place of an ontology a *demontology*: "If ontology deals with the minimal relation being/non-being, then demontology would have to undertake the thought of nothingness (a negative definition), but a nothingness that is also not simply non-being (a privative definition)" (46). Here, too, Thacker is looking at the paradoxes of monsters, not just at their teeth, but at the interstices between them: this is a book about stark contradictions and negative presences.

Here is my favorite line of the whole book, so snide, so punk, so hipster: "And yet, it is precisely this domain—the anonymous "there is"—that has for so long remained a point of attraction for ontology" (112). In this short sentence, Thacker points out the way non-being has been excluded from ontology, as others have begun to recently think about non-life forms in a field called Object Oriented Ontology.

Just as a hipster would assert that what, at first glance, might be mistaken for a quaint trip down memory lane ("speculative mysticism," what is this, the 70s?) is anything but, so Thacker's invocations of "mysticism" and "theology" are not merely nostalgic. He makes use of occult philosophy's view of the hiddenness of the world "that is, exterior to the world-for-us" (96) as a kind of model for the unthinkable "world-in-itself." Similarly, though his handlebar mustache may not be a blistering critique of consumer culture, the hipster in his sock garters, like Eugene Thacker's wily, wiry volume, with all its reinvestigations of the ideas of bygone eras, from metaphysics to medieval scholastics, yearn not just for simpler times. Rather both serve as ironic icons of the fact that we can never go back. As such, they both help me to better understand my own relationship to the contemporary moment: though one be characterized by a tongue-in-cheek retreat into an irrecoverable past, the other considers not only (what can only be, in our contemporary crash course, hell-bent on the destruction of the planet) a grim future, but also, a present World that both is and is not.

PUZZLING IT OUT

Lance Weller. *Wilderness*. New York: Bloomsbury, 2013. Pp 304. $15.91 paperback.

Reviewed by Meredith McCarrol

Weller says, "Just queer is all. People interested in a thing like that. From that long ago. Says to me that nobody's got it puzzled out yet—just like I always thought" (215). Confederate veteran Abel Truman reflects thus on the American Civil War in 1899 to a white Oregon woman who is married to a black man and sees the war as "sad and useless" (213). Truman begins to explain the Civil War, but the more he talks and the more he remembers, the less sense it seems to make—not because of his confusion, but because of his understanding. This conversation between Abel Truman and Ellen Makers is metonymic in its resistance to clarity. If there is anything that can be said concisely about Lance Weller's first novel, *Wilderness*, it is that he skillfully takes the still-dichotomizing event of the Civil War as the setting for a tale that refuses to take sides.

He sets fragmented and woven stories in landscapes that tend toward extremes, but bows neither to the pressure to romanticize nor demonize. What remains, in part, is a beautiful mess of characters thrown together by circumstance that seems neither suitable nor ironic. As Weller lifts the veil of fate from the lives within these narratives, we are forced beyond an understanding of "what was meant to be" toward a reckoning with meaninglessness.

The characters that Weller imagines for us retread the well-worn area upon which so many stories—often passion plays with clear moral agendas—have been placed. The primary figures who revive and complicate this narrative are a blind Chinese-American Immigrant, a New York Confederate veteran, a biracial Oregon couple, a group of circumstantially nomadic indigenous men, and a pair of roaming criminals. From the indigenous Haida man who is crippled by cancer but can heal others to the blind woman who teaches her caretaker to see, Weller draws from but complicates familiar tropes. Weaving together disparate narratives, Weller refrains from arranging them in a harmonic relationship, and allows the dissonance to reverberate in a historically accurate way. Abel, a New Yorker who fought for the confederacy "for no other reason than that was where he happened to be," resists heroic revelation and awakening. When he happens to see Lincoln's death train pass, and is asked whether he is a "Lincum man," he says softly, "I always was," but admits to himself "all the while he wished, desperately, that it were true" (251). Reflecting years later about his own role in the war that had been too neatly split along geo-political boundaries, Abel explains, "Truth is, every one of us on both sides was fighting for the nigs and every one of us on both sides hated that fact. That's why it was so bad. Why it went on so long" (214). Another voice of the narrative, and Abel's audience in the aforementioned conversation, comes from Ellen Makers. Ellen and her husband Glenn seek retreat in their own wilderness on a "hardscrabble mountain" to escape the hauntings of her rape and the ever-present judgment of the small Oregon community. A lesser work would enlighten each character through their interactions, but Weller resists this move—linking the private and public wars at hand and reminding us that neither can be won.

Weller manages this resistance not only through the distinctive characters he imagines in minute detail, but also in his narrative methods. The majority of the novel is set in the Pacific Northwest, punctuated by chapters set in early May of 1864 surrounding the Battle of the Wilderness. Although the Civil War scenes may be familiar to some, their juxtaposition with a vastly different landscape and sentiment casts them in a new light. Even the most familiar moments are enlivened by the tangibility of descriptions, which are unwieldy at times but more often beautifully functional. Weller balances *specificity* (the color of the paint that Abel's wife drinks in her mad grief, the tablecloth *qua* shirt which is sewn with the silver hair of a deceased mother) with remnants of a fable (an old man named Abel Truman, for goodness sake, begins a journey to remember his past) to create a story—or set of stories—that vivifies rather than memorializes the complex nature of the American Civil War. Scanning the battlefield on May 5, 1864, a narrator describes the scene from multiple perspectives and multiple senses. Weller introduces an omniscient narrator whose description is italicized and unlike any other of the voices in the book. The retelling begins in second person, mid-sentence, "...*and had you been there to see it, to hear and taste and feel it, to smell it, it would have been something*" (132). In a postmodern and cinematic imagistic collage, Weller attempts to capture the chaos of the battlefield: "*There: A clean-shaven Union boy with arms too short for the man-sized sleeves of his frock coat is struck on the shoulder by a spent ball, is spun around and skewered on the readied bayonet of the old veteran behind. [...] And over there: A thin and ragged Confederate, hirsute and wild-looking, falls to hands and knees behind the works as though he means to pray there, then leans with slow, calm, resigned weariness against a bullet-chewed old pine. A neat red hole decorates the center of his forehead and it is not long before the hat, his name stitched with great care into the band by his sister back in Galveston, is stolen from his head"* (132-33). Early in the novel, in the narrative frame, Jane Dao-ming Poole speaks directly to her nurse, but indirectly to readers guiding both toward careful attention: "The details. They're important. The smallest things. They loom" (6). Indeed, it is the "smallest things" that make *Wilderness* more than a Civil War novel, while still being a very good Civil War novel.

Weller's cross-section of America functions both to create connections and illuminate tensions. Basic human needs connect characters across time and culture; desperation links a Chinese immigrant who eventually eats a beloved pet to the confederate soldier whose "cheeks caved and his Adam's apple bobbed" as he sucks the wasting milk of a slave whose infant has died. Just as a reader might begin to settle into an understanding of the connectedness across time and culture, though, Weller unsettles each and every perspective. The novel's premise is based upon the inability to find connections across constructed barriers, and he leaves these barriers functionally opaque. The use of wilderness as a referent to the battle but also to the uninhabited space that threatens death but offers shelter exemplifies Weller's recurrent move toward linking and differentiating, which effectively reflects the complexity of humanity. Wilderness functions throughout the novel as the battle did in the war—offering individual protection while exposing human vulnerability.

It is the overlapping of human experience, sometimes valid and other times misread, which transforms this novel from a Civil War story to a story of humanity for which the American Civil War becomes an apt setting. Moreover, *Wilderness* wrestles productively with the definitions of history and truth, enabling a contemporary writer and contemporary audiences to try to "puzzle out" the war that historian Shelby Foote calls "the crossroads of our being." The truths of the novel appear variously: in one moment a young student of the Civil War attempts to educate a veteran about a key battle that he experienced firsthand, valuing neither truth over the other. More personally, Abel Truman's remembrance of his infant child's death serves as a reminder that narrative itself creates truth. Weller allows moments like this one to tumble about in the minds of characters across 60 years so that what remains may have only a thread of fact, but has become truth. What Truman says to a young Indian boy about the battle of the Wilderness is as true of any memory he has carried, "It was only afterwards that it all turned into something more than what it was and that was only because by then we needed it to be" (113). *Wilderness* becomes, then, a novel about myth-making more than a novel about a particular myth. More like Kurt Vonnegut's *Slaughterhouse Five* than Stephen Crane's *Red Badge of Courage*, *Wilderness* poses questions about the function of the retelling of war more than the function of war. More than a novel of the Civil War, Weller has written a novel of human vulnerability, told from varied points of view—each in hyperfocus. Rather than a novel of defined and contradictory ideologies, *Wilderness* features the recurrent figure of the half-wolf/half-dog as a reminder of the productive tension of opposites, celebrating a mongrel conception of the past which may well be a way to move forward.

AMERICAN CIVIL WAR AND ART

Eleanor J Harvey. *The Civil War and American Art*. Smithsonian American Art Museum, Washington, DC, in association with Yale University Press. New Haven, Connecticut, 2012. xvii + 316 pp. $65.00, cloth.

Reviewed by: Andrea Feeser, Clemson University

Eleanor Jones Harvey, author of the book and curator of the exhibition *The Civil War and American Art*, has made a major contribution to the history of American art as well as the Civil War. Harvey's project focuses on work by Northern artists since economic hardship in the South thwarted art production in the Confederacy, although she is careful to include much extant Southern artwork of the period. Harvey's careful analysis of art created just before, during, and after the war focuses on painting as well as photography. She does not engage sculpture, noting that it has been ably studied by Kirk Savage, and examines prints less on their own terms and more in the context of painting. Public monuments and popular art are thus largely absent from her project, although she demonstrates that many of the paintings and photographs she considers were prominently exhibited and reviewed and thus an integral part of Civil War discourse. Harvey maintains that history painting, a pictorial form often used to represent war, added little to Americans' understanding of their plight. She argues that history painting concerned with Civil War subjects was too didactic and partisan, thereby failing to reflect something of "universal significance," (13) not only the genre's goal but also Harvey's criteria for great works of art. She contends that landscape painting, photography, and genre painting successfully captured key components of the human condition that colored the Civil War: fear, suffering, and hope. Her project focuses on symphonic landscape paintings of deeply symbolic locales, documentary photographs of shattered soldiers and sites, and meditative genre paintings with subtle, metaphoric resonance. The artwork in *The Civil War and American Art* is horrifying, sublime, or beautiful, and wonderfully reproduced in the book alongside engaging and persuasive prose.

Landscape painting produced by or in the tradition of the Hudson River School appears first in Harvey's book. Lush, sweeping vistas of places rendered idealistically and loaded with allusion characterize such work. Alongside American prose and poetry dedicated to nature, paintings by admired artists such as the Hudson River School's Fredrick Edwin Church rooted American identity, dreams, and ambitions in the land. Harvey demonstrates that Church, among other artists, symbolized varied attitudes and feelings about the Civil War through landscapes shaped by meteorological and geological phenomena. In 1860, comets, meteors, and the Aurora Borealis made rare appearances in the nighttime sky along the eastern seaboard and many Americans saw them as portents of coming war. Although Harvey doesn't directly link Church's *Meteor of 1860* to such hue and cry, she argues that the painting must be seen in this context given the popular media's focus on the meteor as a sign of approaching battle. Harvey is able to show specific connections between the Civil War and Church's famous 1861 *The Icebergs*. Although Church originally conceived the painting as a tribute to arctic exploration, when war erupted he tied the work to the Northern cause by changing the title to *"The North": Church's Picture of Icebergs* and by exhibiting the painting to raise funds for the Union Patriotic Fund. Church subsequently made even more explicit his patriotism in his 1861 *Our Banner in the Sky* in which a blue, star-filled patch of sky breaks through stripes of white cloud and red Aurora Borealis to form an American flag. With such examples, Harvey shows that, subtly and overtly, Church and other American landscape painters produced dramatic images of the natural world as emblems of both fear and hope.

Subtlety has nothing to do with the most powerful photographs that address the Civil War, which depict battle sites strewn with ravaged corpses and Southern cities virtually obliterated during General William Tecumseh Sherman's March to the Sea. Matthew B. Brady, who championed photography as an art form and exhibited photographs at his well-attended New York gallery, sent fellow photographers to the front to document the war. Photographs, such as Alexander Gardner's 1862 *Bloody Lane, Confederate Dead, Antietam* and Timothy H. O'Sullivan's 1863 *Harvest of Death, Gettysburg* drove home to contemporary audiences the war's tragic human loss. Although such works are largely documentary, Harvey notes that in one instance Gardner, O'Sullivan, and fellow photographer James F. Gibson moved and manipulated a Confederate soldier's body in order to highlight his isolation and render him emblematic of defeat. George N. Barnard produced photographs that literally captured the massive destruction of Southern cities in the wake of Sherman's campaign while also imbuing his work with symbolic import. Harvey shows that Barnard's 1865 *Ruins in Charleston, South Carolina* not only documents the city's demolition but also subtly references European neoclassical painting that meditates mournfully on the demise of the classical world. American landscape painting of the Civil War era was idealized while photography of the time was not; Harvey makes clear however, that both made use of real and imagined phenomena to image profound experience and feeling.

Less elevated than wartime landscape painting and less horrific than wartime photography, genre painting of the Civil War for Harvey is the unstated but clear triumph in art of the period. Harvey teases out complex and nuanced interpretations of works that portray the everyday life of Americans during the war, paying special attention to paintings of slaves by Eastman Johnson and paintings of soldiers by Winslow Homer. Building on Nona Martin's scholarship, Harvey interprets Johnson's 1859 *Negro Life of the South* as an astute allegory of race relations. Among other cues, she sees a stealthy white cat sneaking into slave quarters as a surrogate for a male slave holder in search of sexual prey. This allows Harvey to interpret a seemingly white young woman venturing into a backyard with variously-hued slaves as one of their family who passes for white in the master's home. Although contemporary viewers did not reflect on these specific allusions, Harvey shows that Eastman's piece and those by other artists were read as an indictment of slavery by pro-abolitionists. She is also able to demonstrate that less coded representations of human challenges appear in Homer's canvases that address the wartime and postwar life of soldiers. In perhaps her subtlest interpretation of an artwork, Harvey argues that Homer's 1865 *The Veteran in a New Field*, which shows a lone former combatant from behind threshing wheat, not only refers to the grim reaper of the battlefield but also to the isolating pain faced by men who endured the horrors of war.

In her conclusion Harvey points to directions that art took after the Civil War. She notes that genre painters did not sustain a "level of direct engagement with American politics beyond the Centennial" (234). She observes that many photographers turned their attention to depicting westward expansion and that notable landscape painters such as George Inness focused on softly diffused images that convey a sense of melancholy rather than suggesting a specific narrative. Although she does not claim to paint a comprehensive picture of post-Civil War art, she does leave out one important development in art after the war that deals with its strife. This is the panorama and cyclorama (huge and immersive paintings) phenomenon of the 1880s and beyond that often treated battle scenes in detail. The 1887 cyclorama now known as the *Battle of Atlanta* is a prime example of this movement in which art functioned as a popular form of education and entertainment. The work was commissioned by Civil War General John A. Logan and was meant to celebrate his victory in Atlanta as a means of promoting his bid for Vice President on the Republican ticket. Produced by the American Panorama Company in Milwaukee and painted by German artists who specialized in battlefield paintings, the accuracy of the huge work's visual detail was guaranteed by Theodore Davis, an artist based at *Harper's Weekly* during the war who witnessed the Battle of Atlanta firsthand. *The Battle of Atlanta* was exhibited both in the North and South, and was owned by several men until it was gifted to Atlanta in 1898 and put on permanent display just in time for a reunion of Confederate soldiers in the city. Initially a tribute to Northern victory it became a literal backdrop to honor Southern valor.

Harvey is clear that her project concerns itself solely with great works of art, which Civil War battle panoramas and cycloramas clearly are not. Nevertheless, such painted entertainments detail specific events of the war, and combine key effects Harvey locates in landscape and genre painting as well as photography, namely pathos as well as stark documentation. Well beyond the scope of her inquiry, and more aligned with the unsophisticated history painting that Harvey dismisses, *The Battle of Atlanta* nevertheless points to a clear project of historical memory that Harvey suggests in large part diffused. However, investigating the legacy of the Civil War in American art and popular culture is another project, and not Harvey's in her riveting and brilliant *The Civil War and American Art*. Written with elegance and finesse, and illustrated with breathtaking reproductions of important artworks, Harvey's book will inform and move readers for many years to come.

SACRED SECRETS AND THE MYSTERIOUSLY ORDINARY

Philip Gerard. *The Patron Saint of Dreams*. Spartanburg, SC: Hub City Press, 2012. Pp. 212. $14.03 paperback.

Reviewed by Lindsey Jones

Gerard's *The Patron Saint of Dreams* could serve as a primer for the student of creative nonfiction. That's because Philip Gerard is a teacher, and even when he isn't aiming to teach students how to write, insights about the nature and practice of the genre find their way into his essays. Creative nonfiction is a sweeping term, and its readers are often unsure what to expect. Gerard is acutely conscious of nonfiction's limitations and possibilities; he prods the boundaries with everything from exhaustive investigative journalism to concise lyric essays. In many places, *The Patron Saint of Dreams* is writing about writing, and as Gerard's readers we are not merely entertained but educated. What can this genre do? What can we learn from his characters? What can the act of writing teach us? In this collection, diverse essays converge with a shared sense of the mysterious and an emphasis on the value of wondering—and, ultimately, the redemption those things might afford us.

The book's core is its title essay, which Gerard confesses was difficult to write. It is an essay about his mother, about her death, and about writing. "The patron saint of dreams" is his mother, the person who encouraged adventure in him (19). Gerard bestows on her this appellation in return for his own surname, which comes from Saint Gerard, the Patron Saint of Mothers. It was to this saint his mother prayed after losing her first child, and she subsequently named all three of her sons after him (Gerard dropped his given surname). Gerard was a miracle child, yet there was nothing extraordinary about his mother to merit canonization in exchange—not, at least, "in most ways that matter to a biographer" (22). Nonetheless she is, Gerard explains, "the looming unseen presence, the invisible character" (21) in almost everything he has written.

Gerard's mother is a visible character in this essay, though she is on her deathbed when we are introduced to her. After a heart attack, she is kept alive for months with a ventilator, but Gerard is certain after the first day that "her spirit had left and was not coming back" (25). Without a trace of didacticism, Gerard questions the ethics of life support as his mother continues to suffer unnecessarily, complicating our thinking by blurring the lines between life and death. Does life equal a breathing body or is there something more? It's complex, he concedes, and yet it is simple, too: "You can argue the fine medical ethics of the thing. All I can add is this: I'd whip anybody who treated my dog so cruelly" (21). In the essay's key moment, a night nurse caring for Gerard's life-supported mother tells him he can pull the plug; she will look the other way. He feels too guilty to do it; later, he is guilty for having been unable to do it.

Guilt stays with Gerard long after his mother's death. The dynamic between them had changed when she could no longer talk, when others talked about her, when she could no longer write—and now it shifts again when he cannot write about her. Language has always played a central role in his interactions with his mother, and yet he is unable to use his most reliable tool to make sense of what has happened. For years, he is unable to write about his mother at all. Finally, in one sprinted effort, Gerard dashes off a short piece about his mother and is asked to read that piece on the radio. He feels guilty for penning so carelessly a topic so precious and wonders if it is wrong to profit from telling his mother's story. Yet he knows the abandon with which he composed the piece was the only way it would ever have been written, and he knows that he needed to write it.

When he asks, *Who are we to turn truths into stories?*, Gerard is questioning the validity of creative nonfiction as a genre. That is, after all, what we're doing when we shape and arrange, when we omit and include. Like most of the works in this collection, through occurrences both strange and ordinary, "The Patron Saint of Dreams" explores the craft of writing creative nonfiction. This essay is as much a reflection on the first piece he wrote about his mother as it is on his mother. As Gerard reminds us, he is not a biographer but something different; the things that matter in memoir aren't the same things that matter in biography. What does matter, then, in memoir? "Whatever else it has been for me," writes Gerard, "writing has always been a kind of deep meditation, clarifying the truth of difficult situations. And a way of saving important memories, freezing them in frame in all their complexity so as to re-experience and recreate the emotions, to recollect those emotions in serenity and so to comprehend their implications" (23-24). Writing then, is first a personal action and only incidentally a public one. A good writer may write with his audience in mind, but he must intend only to "min[e] his own passion for a truth he himself can use" (24). Universality is a byproduct, Gerard tells his reader. Ultimately the guilty son realizes the story he read on the radio was his mother's gift to him. All lives are stories and, in fact, all stories are gifts. More than that: they can, as Tim O'Brien has said, save us. They have a redemptive power. As if to pay it forward, "The Patron Saint of Dreams" is Gerard's gift to us.

Another much shorter essay entitled "Spelling" goes back in time to share Gerard's first encounters with his loves for learning and language. Like "The Patron Saint of Dreams," it reveals a deep appreciation for words, and like the title essay, it is imbued with the sacred. The nun in "Spelling" is "very ancient" and "float[s] above...saintly" (61). The setting is "Holy Angels School...a mysterious place" (61). Gerard wonders about the "secret things they did behind closed doors" (61).

One day he is permitted behind those doors to review his spelling words, and the experience is every bit as magical as he might have dreamed. Gerard writes, "'Parbuckle,' she would say. 'Portcullis. Premillenialism'" (62). For the first time, in a setting appropriately mystical, the author falls in love with words. "There was magic in the sounds," he remembers. "Each word was a little universe of possibility...The right combination of letters could capture it absolutely and forever" (62). This is a brief but beautiful lyric essay that reflects on the author's artistic origins. Gerard confesses, "Sister Stanislaus and her mysterious holy sisters, like all those incantatory spelling words, are still locked in my head somewhere, waiting only for the right letters, artfully assembled, to call them back" (63).

While these two essays seem to hint at holiness and hallowed language, both are leveled by the ordinary and profane in other essays. The celestial beings of Saint Gerard and Sister Stanislaus find their equivalent in "fucking Goofy" in the essay "Bear Country" (50). This piece is powerfully braided, alternating between Gerard's camping experience in the woods of Yellowstone Park and his nearly-fatal cardiac arrest. The latter, a real tragedy the author barely survived, is interwoven with an imagined one that he fears but that never transpires—that bears might attack him in the woods.

Alone and afraid in Yellowstone, Gerard imagines bears where there are none. At nineteen, he is the victim of his own paranoia. In the essay's second strand, Gerard literally dies and comes back to life at age forty-three, an experience that puts his earlier imagined fears into perspective. He discovers the lightness that comes from having literally died; after all, nothing is scarier than that. There is nothing in reserve that can happen to him now. And yet this profound insight comes absurdly. As he crashes and is cardioverted by an electric shock, Gerard's consciousness switches on and off as he feels intense, indescribable pain. He writes, "Each time the blackness turned into video images—scraps of old TV shows, snippets of movies, finally cartoons—as if one were flipping channels fast, continuously. The last image was of Goofy" (35). In the most serious moment of his life, the author sees a vision of the most absurd image his brain could conjure up. Gerard writes, "People always ask me…*Did you see a bright light at the end of a tunnel? Was it beautiful?…Were there angels?* No, I say. All I saw was Fucking Goofy" (36).

Another essay that combines the sacred and the ordinary is "Hardball." In this essay about the summer Gerard spent playing amateur baseball, he writes about the routines of the sport: "the crack of a line drive coming off the sweet spot of a wooden bat" (14) the blood on his jersey, "the thin crowd in the bleachers going nuts" (15). But then there are transcendent moments in the piece, in which the language is so beautiful it defies its subject: "We played under summer skies choked with thunderheads that scraped open their black bellies on the craggy rims of the mountains and doused us with hard rain, in golden afternoon light cooled by the deep verdure of swaying evergreen trees, into the sudden chilly twilight that carries voices for miles and years and calls children home to their suppers" (14). Baseball, he tells us, taught him everything he needed to learn about both heartbreak and glory.

Weaker essays in the collection are short reflections that seem undeveloped, such as "The Paranoid Nurse," "The Family Who Lived in the River," and "The Phantom Chess Man." These essays seem to reflect the author's personal preoccupations with secrets and conspiracies. They read like mini-mysteries, but the reader is left unwilling to share the author's enthusiasm for tales that seem potentially but not quite intriguing. In "More Things on Heaven and Earth," a triptych of several bizarre happenings, the three mysteries gain momentum and significance from one another, making this essay somewhat stronger than the pieces in which the scenes are left to fend for themselves. "Rebuilding Turtle Harbor," another brief piece, is a satisfying reflection but also lacks the depth Gerard demonstrates in other essays.

Two essays that make up a third of the collection, "The Thirteenth Hour" and "Imposter" are written in an entirely different style than the others, and the reader might have some difficulty shifting gears from the lyrical prose of the others to the investigative, journalistic style of these. The reader not too invested by this point in Gerard's more familiar style, however, may find these two long essays intriguing. "The Thirteenth Hour" is also a real-life mystery, but it is compelling in an entirely different way than "Bear Country" or "Maria." It tells the story of a man and three boys who drowned in the waters off the coast of South Carolina. Despite being meticulously researched, "The Thirteenth Hour" is a thrilling (if solemn) narrative. "Imposter" verges on being another of the author's personal preoccupations and may not captivate the general reader. For someone fascinated by historical legends, however, the essay will have more to offer.

Gerard is at his best when the writing is personal and lyrical and when the author allows for interplay between the holy and the irreverent, mystery and coincidence. In much of the collection, Gerard is able to intrigue readers with the most unexceptional occurrences and to make readers laugh irreverently at the most extraordinary events. Readers of *The Patron Saint of Dreams* are fortunate to sit for a while in the classroom of Philip Gerard and to come away with a greater understanding not only of how to write but also of how to think, observe, and be.

GOING TO THE STORY TELLERS

Jason Phillips (ed.). *Storytelling, History, and the Postmodern South*. Baton Rouge: Louisiana State University Press, 2013. 226 pp.

Reviewed by Bill Koon, Clemson University

In the introduction to this collection of essays, Jason Phillips tells the story of Ralph Ellison's 1968 speech to the Southern Historical Association in New Orleans. Ellison called the historians "respectable liars" in that they often select facts that distort history. As he put it "our written history has been as 'official' as any produced in any communist country—only in a democratic way: individuals write it instead of committees" (1). This has been, he says, especially true of southern history, which typically promotes a white patriarchy as it creates a "Master narrative." To get the truth, Ellison adds, we must go not to the historians, white or black, but to the story tellers. In effect, we should quit stripping away the stories to get to the history; instead, we should take history with the stories and story tellers together. And Phillips offers these essays to explore "the enduring dynamic between history, literature, and power in the American South" (3).

The first illustration of the point comes with Bertram Wyatt-Brown's essay on Will Percy and *Lanterns on the Levee*. The book is a series of stories out of Percy's life—an aristocratic childhood, Sewanee and *The Book of Common Prayer*, Harvard Law School and Boston, WWI and France, a stand-down of the Klan (which Walker Percy would use in *Lancelot*), a failure to prevent the stranding of black citizens during the great flood of 1927, a defense of share cropping, and some "darkie stories." We see Percy moving back and forth in his roles. As Wyatt-Brown says, "…he had to negotiate between the anti-intellectual proclivities and conventions of a rural, hierarchical, southern world and his own far more generous and accepting spirit and cosmopolitanism" (13—14). And he had to deal with his homosexuality. Now we begin to get the whole story—the history, the teller, and the tale.

Farrell O'Gorman follows with a treatment of gothic and religious elements in Faulkner, McCarthy, and Percy. The tactic freshens up old topics as O'Gorman argues that they have recognizable historical contexts which he traces out of British fiction. McCarthy, for example, moves from 1833 to 1861 in *Blood Meridian*, from the U. S. to Mexico, and has told us "a Gothic tale of the Americas at large…"(p. 63). We might note that McCarthy surely continued such in the border trilogy. Anne Marshall takes up *All the King's Men* and *The Burden of Southern History* to show how Warren and Woodward "employ similar mixtures of fact and fiction to approach the complexity of the South" and uncover the "brutal truths" in the region's master narratives (5). And Stephen Prince reads Thomas Nelson Page in a similar light. I would love to see one of these scholars treat Lewis Nordan's *Wolf Whistle*, the remarkable fiction about the murder of Emmett Till.

The second half of the collection—essays by Jewel Spangler, Orville Vernon Burton and Ian Binnington, Jim Downs, David Davis, and Robert Jackson—"examine how southern writers and scholars establish authority and address mastery" (6). They take up identifiers such as religion, Confederate Nationalism, race, white trash, and professional southerners. I did not recognize all of the writers discussed but was much pleased to read

Davis' piece on "white trash autobiography" which covers Dorothy Allison, Rick Bragg, Harry Crews, and Janisse Ray, all of them writers who deserve more attention. Davis goes straight into the contradictions of this genre. White trash, he says, "has been a common stereotype in southern literature, often portrayed as ignorant, lazy, and malicious. White trash autobiographies confront those characterizations, but, curiously, they do not exactly overturn them. These autobiographies humanize the often caricatured figures, but they bear out many of their stereotypical characteristics. [...] I understand that white trash people are often equally proud of and ashamed of their identity" (188).

Jim Downs' essay on racial categories works through the many ways racial identity has been marked; the "one drop" rule, of course, was part of this, but Downs documents a number of other methods. Interestingly, he becomes an illustration of his own case as he tells us the story of Rosina Downs, a light-skinned black girl who was his forebearer.

In the last essay, Robert Jackson traces "The Professional Southerner," from just after the Civil War to the present, showing how society responded to the type. He mentions such figures as Faulkner, Henry Grady, James Carville, Dizzy Dean, Tennessee Ernie Ford, Hank Williams, Jr., Col. Sanders (who was born in Indiana), George Wallace, Bill Clinton, and John Shelton Reed. It might be out of place, but it would be interesting to toss a little fiction into this. Flannery O'Connor's "A Late Encounter with the Enemy" depicts a southern family, which, eager for social credentials, flaunts a grandfather who is a Civil War veteran. The family steadily promotes the old man, once a foot soldier, until he becomes General Tennessee Flintrock Sash. At one hundred and four, the general dies in his wheel chair in front of a Coke machine.

I appreciated Jackson's good discussion of the Vanderbilt Agrarians who, in *I'll Take My Stand* (1930), called for an old South and of the more progressive Chapel Hill group, led by Howard Odum and taken up by Louis Rubin. This essay gets close to those of us southerners who teach southern literature and worry about exploiting our place. And the Chapel Hill/Vanderbilt competition reminded me of my days as a graduate student trying to decide which group to follow. The paths were that distinct.

Phillips' thesis that history can only improve with contributions from stories and storytellers makes room for a lot of good, fresh discussion. Not only does it help with the writers considered, but also it tempts us to follow the idea into considerations of many other writers, a few of them I have mentioned. The pieces are nicely written, and they hang together well especially as we note that they started out as conference papers.

"A LIFETIME OF BAD NEWS...ABOUT TO GET SOME MORE"

Jon Sealy. *The Whiskey Baron.* Hub City Press, 2014. Pp. 250. $21.28 harcover.

Reviewed by Mark Powell, Stetson University

The aging Sheriff Chambers warns a group of men: "Behave yourself gentlemen. I got a feeling something bad's about to happen" (236). But we don't need the warning: bad is all over the place in Jon Sealy's searing debut novel, *The Whiskey Baron.* Bad is one of the reasons, as a virtual who's who of southern writers has noted, *The*

Whiskey Baron is a high-octane thriller of the absolute first rank. That it is also a serious meditation on violence and place that should draw comparisons to the work of William Gay is a testament to Sealy's ability to write lyrically while never sacrificing the book's headlong momentum.

Set in 1932 in the mill hills of South Carolina, along the banks of the Broad River, and in the run-down streets of Charlotte, the novel centers on the whiskey empire of Larthan Tull. When a local veteran named Mary Jane Hopewell attempts to horn in on Tull's trade, a chase reminiscent of Cormac McCarthy's *No Country for Old Men* plays out in the pine forests and flophouses of the upstate. Meanwhile, two brothers find themselves drawn into Tull's violent orbit. The result is thrilling and heartbreaking; the ending as surprising as it is inevitable.

But more than that, the novel is a pitch perfect evocation of the Carolina countryside I grew up hearing about from my grandfather. While the plot tangles, rushing forward and then easing back only to rush forward again, a series of brilliantly drawn characters emerge from a world of menace and beauty. There is much of the hardscrabble here: an aging grandfather is "cut from an ancient mold, conceived right in a Confederate battlefield, the way men weren't made any longer" (87). Though only forty years old, the widow Abigail Coleman has lived "a lifetime of bad news and [is] about to get some more" (14). Perhaps most exquisitely drawn is Mary Jane, a man who "lived in a hovel by the dump and knew every lowlife who set foot in Castle County, though he himself was a nice boy" (13). A nice boy haunted by memories of the Great War, of the "mud, mud, and more mud, mixed together with blood" (25).

The novel is equally generous in its sensuous descriptions of nature, of the way, for Mary Jane, "the emerging stars lit his way through the kneehigh grass, crickets abuzz, brambles scraping his legs" (69). But even in the beauty of nature, menace—Sheriff's Chamber's "something bad"—is never far away. Evelyn Tull hurries "out of the woods because the choiring of the crickets was beginning to unnerve her" (212).

She has good reason to be unnerved. Her father chief among them. Larthan Tull is first seen as "sinewy, still calm. Like he knew what the future held and was just waiting idly for them to get on with it." The same might be said of Faulkner's Thomas Sutpen or the dictator of Garcia Marquez's *Autumn of the Patriarch*. Tull rules his kingdom with a severity that is as violent as it is personal. That Jon Sealy has found a way to capture this in a novel as gorgeous as it is thrilling is a tremendous accomplishment. There is badness all around in *The Whiskey Baron*, and that is very good news for readers.

CONTRIBUTORS

Derek H. Alderman is Professor and Head of the Department of Geography at the University of Tennessee in Knoxville. His research and teaching focus on the cultural and historical geographies of the American South, with special attention devoted to sense of place, media representation, public memory and commemoration, and heritage tourism. His work spans many aspects of the southern landscape, including Civil Rights memorials (especially streets named for Martin Luther King), slavery and plantation tourism sites, NASCAR, Graceland and Memphis, Mayberry and film tourism, and the invasive kudzu vine.

Brent Walter Cline is an associate professor of English at Spring Arbor University, in Spring Arbor, Michigan. His research focuses on mental disability and modern American literature.

Benjamin D'Harlingue received his PhD in Cultural Studies from UC Davis. He is currently a Lecturer in Communication at Saint Mary's College of California. He is working on a book about haunted tourism in the United States.

Glenn W Gentry is Adjunct Faulty in the Department of Geography at the State University of New York at Cortland. His research has focused with alternative geographic representations of culture and identity, with an emphasis on the American South. This includes dark tourism, dissonant history and tourist motivation and performance in ghost tourism in Savannah, Georgia, as well as, memory, memory work and representation through tattoos in following Hurricane Katrina in New Orleans, Louisiana.

Jesse Graves is an Associate Professor of English at East Tennessee State University. Graves's first poetry collection, *Tennessee Landscape with Blighted Pine*, was published by Texas Review Press in 2011 and won the 2012 Weatherford Award in Poetry from Berea College and the Book of the Year Award in Poetry from the Appalachian Writers' Association.

Kathleen Hellen's poetry collection *Umberto's Night* won the 2012 prize from the Washington Writer's Publishing House. Her chapbook *The Girl Who Loved Mothra* was published in 2010 by Finishing Line Press.

Sarah Hirsch has a Masters in Literature from the University of California, Santa Cruz and a Ph.D. in English from the University of California, Santa Barbara where she currently is a full-time Lecturer for the Writing Program. Her field is nineteenth-century and early twentieth-century American literature; yet her work follows an interdisciplinary model as her projects engage with maritime, transnational, and cultural studies. Her work on New Orleans and her interest in American southern literature stems from her work on seaports, their corresponding U.S. cities, and her field research done in New Orleans and Baton Rouge, Louisiana.

Sarah Juliet Lauro is the co-author of the article "A Zombie Manifesto: The Nonhuman Condition in the Era of Advanced Capitalism" (*boundary 2*, Spring 2008), and co-editor of the collection *Better Off Dead: The Evolution of the Zombie as Posthuman* (New York: Fordham UP 2011). Her first book, *The Transatlantic Zombie: Slavery, Rebellion, and Living Death*, comes out of the doctoral dissertation she completed at UC Davis (2011). It is in production at Rutgers University Press and will be out in print summer 2015.

James O. Luken is an ecologist at Coastal Carolina University in Conway, SC. He currently directs Graduate Studies at the university and also tracks the increasingly rare carnivorous plants of Horry County.

Kimberly Snyder Manganelli is an associate professor at Clemson University where she specializes in nineteenth-century British and American literature. Her book, *Transatlantic Spectacles of Race: The Tragic Mulatta and the Tragic Muse*, which was published by Rutgers

University Press in 2012, extends beyond literary, racial, and national boundaries to explore how representations of the mixed-race slave and Jewish actress were shaped by scientific and legal discourse, as well as such genres as the travel narrative, abolitionist narrative, and sensation novel. Her current work focuses on representations of slavery in contemporary culture.

Richard Michelson has won the Felix Pollack Prize in Poetry, the New Letters Literary Award and was a finalist for the Pablo Neruda Prize. His most recent collection of poetry, *Battles & Lullabies*, was selected by *ForeWord Magazine* as one of the twelve best books of poetry in 2006. Michelson is also known for his collaborations with artist Leonard Baskin on two books, *Masks* and *Semblant*. His experience with the former is the subject of his account in *The South Carolina Review* 40.2.

Tiya Miles is the Elsa Barkley Brown Collegiate Professor of African American Women's History at the University of Michigan and Professor of American Culture, History, Native American Studies and Women's Studies. She is the author of two prize-winning books: *Ties That Bind: The Story of an Afro-Cherokee Family in Slavery and Freedom*(2005) and *The House on Diamond Hill: A Cherokee Plantation Story*(2010). She is co-editor, with Sharon P. Holland, of *Crossing Waters, Crossing Worlds: The African Diaspora in Indian Country*(2006). Her forthcoming first novel, *The Cherokee Rose*, is set on a haunted plantation in the Cherokee territory of present-day Georgia.

Maxine Lavon Montgomery is the Frances Cushing Ervin Professor of English at Florida State University where she teaches courses in African Diaspora, American Multi-Ethnic, and Women's Literature. Her articles have appeared in scholarly journals such as *African American Review*; *College Language Association Journal*; *Obsidian, II*; *The Literary Griot*, *Mid-Atlantic Writers' Association Journal*, and *The Journal of Black Studies*. She is the author or editor of four books: *The Apocalypse in African-American Fiction*; *Conversations with Gloria Naylor*; *The Fiction of Gloria Naylor: Houses and Spaces of Resistance;* and *Contested Boundaries: New Critical Essays on the Fiction of Toni Morrison.*

Allen Stein teaches American Literature at North Carolina State University. His poems and stories have appeared in *Southern Poetry Review, Aethlon, Modern Age, SNReview, The MacGuffin,* and *The 5-2, Crime Poetry Weekly.*

Cameron E. Williams was born in Burlington, North Carolina, where she lived for three years before her family relocated to Florida. Despite her upbringing on Florida's east coast, Cameron was raised to appreciate all things Southern. In 2014, she received her Ph.D. in twentieth and twenty-first-century Southern literature from Florida State University. Her work has been published in the Cambridge volume *Constructing the Literary Self: Race and Gender in Twentieth-Century American Literature.* She is also a contributor at the *Southern Literary Review.* She currently lives in Atlanta and teaches at the University of North Georgia.

Lisa Woolfork is an associate professor in the English department at the University of Virginia, where she specializes in African American literature and culture. The University of Illinois Press published her book, *Embodying American Slavery in Contemporary Culture*, a study of slavery re-enactments and performance. Her recent work has concerned televisual representations, including her chapter "Looking for Lionel" in *Race-ing for Ratings: African Americans in Television*, edited by Lisa Guerrero and David Leonard. Professor Woolfork also teaches a popular course on George R. R. Martin book and HBO's television series *Game of Thrones.*